soul and spice

AFRICAN COOKING IN THE AMERICAS

HEIDI HAUGHY CUSICK
FOREWORD BY JESSICA B. HARRIS

CHRONICLE BOOKS
SAN FRANCISCO

Library of Congress Cataloging-in-Publication Data available.

Excerpts by permission with grateful acknowledgment from:

Franklin, John Hope, and Moss, Alfred A., Jr. *From Slavery to Freedom: A History of Negro Americans.*
New York: McGraw Hill, 1988.

Freyre, Gilberto. *The Masters and the Slaves: Study in the Development of Brazilian Civilization.*
Berkeley: University of California Press, 1986.

Genovese, Eugene D. *Roll, Jordan, Roll: The World the Slaves Made.*
New York: Vintage Books, Random House, 1976.

Simonson, Thordis. *You May Plow Here: The Narrative of Sara Brooks.*
New York & London: W. W. Norton & Co., 1986.

Wilson, Charles Reagan, and Ferris, William, eds. *Encyclopedia of Southern Culture.* Volume I.
North Carolina: University of North Carolina Press, 1989.

Printed in the United States of America.

ISBN 0-8118-0419-4

Book Design by Del Rae Roth

Distributed in Canada by Raincoast Books, 8680 Cambie Street, Vancouver, B.C. V6P 6M9

10 9 8 7 6 5 4 3 2

Chronicle Books
275 Fifth Street
San Francisco, CA 94103

Dedicated to the memory of my Texan mom whose southern cooking instilled a love of good food,
to everyone acknowledged at the end of this book,
and
to eating well in a changing world.

Table of Contents

Foreword
by Jessica B. Harris
8

Introduction
11

The Recipes
14

Caribbean
19

Bahia Brazilian
69

Soul Food
101

Louisiana Creole
163

Barbecue
203

Recent African Immigrants
243

Glossary
267

Resources
275

Bibliography
283

Recommended Reading
287

Acknowledgments
291

Index
295

Table of Equivalents
303

On a fall day in 1989, I was proud to see the publication of my second cookbook, a work entitled *Iron Pots and Wooden Spoons: Africa's Gifts to New World Cooking*. I took special pride in it as it had been a labor of love, one that I had to convince the publisher to take. It was a pet project because it was a formal look at what my tastebuds had been telling me for years as I journeyed from Africa to Brazil to the Caribbean to the southern United States—"Something is happening here. This food is connected. There is history in the pot." Time and distance have proved that I was correct. *Iron Pots and Wooden Spoons* was one of the first books to establish a culinary link between the food of West Africa and the cooking of the Americas and to detail the influences that one food has on the other. When the book was published, my pride was shared by my editor, my friends, and my family, but the book did not set the world on fire. Later, I would discover that it had indeed set some small flames in the culinary community. In fact, since the publication of that book, what was a personal epiphany has become a culinary given, one that is only beginning to be explored.

My formerly solitary odyssey now finds me with a companion on the road: Heidi Cusick. She is a companion who has also tasted *poulet yassa* and *thiebou dienn* in Senegal as she hitchhiked around that country and the Gambia in 1971. She, too, has savored *feijoada* in Rio and *vatapá* in Bahia, sampled curried goat in Jamaica, and dined on *colombo de porc* in Martinique. Heidi's culinary journeys have taken her around the corner, across the ocean, and across the South in search of the taste of African-inspired food. She's found caterers in Chicago and barbecue cooks in Berkeley and just plain old good cooks in Memphis, Mississippi, and just about everywhere that black hands stir pots. She's gone into the homes and kitchens of people of African descent in Brazil, the Caribbean, and the American South. The result of her research, *Soul and Spice: African Cooking in the Americas*, is a fascinating exploration of the culinary link between Africa and America.

Heidi Cusick's culinary voyage is doubly fascinating because she was not born into the heritage of African cooking in the hemisphere. She was not raised in a household where bevies of cooks humming spirituals prepared meals for all family occasions from baptisms to funerals. Raised in the East Bay area of Northern California, her love for the food of the African diaspora is one that transcends color and heritage and goes straight to the obvious fact that the food quite simply tastes fabulous.

Soul and Spice, therefore, begins a second phase of the exploration of the heritage of African cooking in the hemisphere, one that takes it from the hands of those who created it and transports it gently and with affection and respect to the tables of all those who love to eat well.

Heidi is one who understands full well the glories that lurk hidden in a steaming bowl of jambalaya. She, too, knows the history hidden in a pod of okra and the routes that lead from Nigeria's *efo* to the collard greens of the American South. She can sense the love and care that goes into the confections and the expertise that is necessary to make good "que" sing. In short, Heidi is one who knows the joy that comes from sitting down to a meal where the ingredients may be humble, but where the end product is sublime.

She is aided in her research by a wide circle of friends and acquaintances. In these pages, the food of Rousbert Pierre Jeanty from Port-au-Price, Haiti, meets up with that of Lee Bickford of Montego Bay, Jamaica. A hot sauce by Tania da Paixao of Bahia, Brazil, shares space with a stewed okra dish from Austin, Texas, and in the words of the spiritual, "The circle is unbroken."

Soul and Spice: African Cooking in the Americas is clearly the loving result of Heidi's self-proclaimed "infatuation with African culture." It opens the door on a cornucopia of cuisines for the future, cuisines that use a host of ingredients both familiar and exotic, that season the pot with love, and that place the accent on taste above all other elements.

Jessica B. Harris

Introduction

When we look at the African influence on cooking in the Americas, we are not just talking about food. Economics, history, religion, and family stand right alongside beans, grains, greens, seafood, and spices in Bahian, Caribbean, creole, soul food, barbecue, and recent African immigrant cooking styles.

Strong familial traditions established in ancestral African kingdoms persevere. Uprooting from the mother continent and the debasement of slavery did not extinguish the spirit of the family or the legacy of good eating. Nowhere are these ties more evident than at mealtime in African-American homes, restaurants, and churches, where food is family style and cooking is shared.

In addition to the strength of family ties, the most important trait to abide from African tribal beginnings is the ability to take whatever food is available and make it better. "From the beginning of time, grains, beans, and greens were our mainstays. But we learned to season what food we had and make it taste good. The reason so many people had black cooks is because they cooked so well," says Rip Wilson, owner of Soul Brothers Kitchen in Berkeley, California. "The truth is, the only way we could survive was by making our food taste good."

The culinary legacy inherited from Africa varies with each American location. It incorporates Portuguese, Spanish, French, Dutch, English, East Indian, African, and Native American ingredients and cooking methods. Traditional African dishes reappear wherever Africans have had a hand in the kitchen. American versions blend methods, ingredients, and seasonings from the New World and the Old.

Fiery African rice-based mélanges became Bahian *moquecas*, South Carolina pilaus, and creole jambalayas. Grain mashes called *fufu* in Sierra Leone are couche couche in Louisiana and *foutou* in Martinique. *Sawyer* in Cameroon and *michui* in Togo are translated to barbecue in the United States. Bean-paste fritters made of black-eyed peas are called *akara* in Togo, *acarajé* in Bahia, and fried pea fritters in the American South.

Jessica Harris's *Iron Pots and Wooden Spoons* was the first book published in the United States to define African culinary influences in the New World. Here, each of the six areas of influence, along with its own historical experience, evolution of dishes, and definitive spice, is further described and commemorated.

In the Caribbean, in the early 1500s, when the Spanish first cultivated the sugarcane that led to the slave trade, African cooks became the major influence in the development of the region's cuisine. On each of the islands, be it under Spanish, English, Dutch, or French rule, these cooks blended the European and Amerindian styles with their own. Typical African one-pot bean-and-vegetable combinations became rich with seafood, hot with chiles, and cooled with coconut, tomatoes, and tropical fruits.

As the Europeans expanded their horizons in the Western Hemisphere, they converged on the coasts of both continents, with the Portuguese settling in Brazil and the English, French, and Spanish concentrating on the Caribbean Islands and Central and North America.

By the late 1500s there were several hundred sugar plantations on the northeast coast of Brazil, where Bahia, like the Caribbean and West Africa, is in the tropical zone. Bahian cooking is known for its simmering pots of coconut- and chile-spiked fish, meat, and fowl and for *feijoada*, the slave's rice-and-bean bowl that has become Brazil's national dish. African *dendê* oil, American cassava flour, and the Portuguese fondness for frying contributed to Bahian cooking.

The first Africans arrived in North America in Virginia in 1619. Within a hundred years, acres of sugar, cotton, rice, and tobacco were being tended by thousands of black slaves along the southeastern coast of the United States. What we call soul food derives from family kitchens before slavery was abolished. Beans, rice, stewed greens, and boiled meat scraps bolstered with bread made from corn form the basis of what today is still an economical and healthful way to eat. Vegetables, herbs, and chiles or plenty of ground black pepper characteristically spice the otherwise bland flavors.

In Louisiana, which alternated between French and Spanish rule until 1803, when it was purchased by the United States, slavery took hold with the French colonists in the 1700s. The blend of African, Spanish, French, and Choctaw ingredients and techniques known as creole cooking was created by black cooks in Louisiana's plantation kitchens. Here, the one-pot specialties became gumbos and jambalayas featuring chiles from the Caribbean, okra from Africa, file from the native American sassafras, roux from France, and meat-and-seafood combinations from Spain.

Upon emancipation, daily life didn't change much for ex-slaves. Sharecropping, legislated segregation, and continual discrimination kept most African-Americans poor and struggling.

The most significant African postslavery contribution to American cooking is barbecue. Whether due to the chile-rich sauces or the social atmosphere, a barbecue place in Memphis, Kansas City, Oakland, Jackson, Charleston, or Austin feels firmly rooted in its African heritage. Informal surroundings often offering take-out food only mean the center of attention is the barbecue itself. The barbecue chapter explores the regional differences and the sauces and side dishes that accompany American barbecue. It also includes barbecue recipes from West Africa and from the Caribbean, where the famed jerked meats and fish have a uniquely African history.

Adding to the African culinary importance in the United States are recent immigrants. In the last chapter, the culinary influences of African immigrants are explored to show the connection between many New World dishes and their counterparts in the mother countries. These African grain, vegetable, and rice dishes from Senegal, Sierra Leone, Togo, Gambia, the Ivory

Coast, Nigeria, Mozambique, and Mauritania, as well as Ethiopia, Eritrea, and Kenya, are prepared with American ingredients, and sometimes imported seasonings.

One method that distinguishes African cooking throughout the various styles is the common practice of spicing food before it is cooked. Herbs, onions, peppers, and citrus juice or vinegar are rubbed and dredged on chicken to fry, fish to sauté, beef to stew, or pork to barbecue. This extra step not only enhances the depth of flavors but also helps tenderize economical cuts of meat.

Africa's contribution to the world larder uses inexpensive ingredients, is well spiced, and is made with that enigmatic term *soul*. Served on communal platters in the company of family and friends, the dishes in this book demonstrate the African philosophy of food and dining. In Eritrea in eastern Africa there is a saying that "The one who eats alone, dies alone."

The following chapters embark upon a culinary journey enriched with historical, anecdotal, and personal details. In addition to the recipes, notes on ingredients, places, and people that contribute to the African influences on cooking in Bahia, the Caribbean, and the United States are included. At the end of the book you will find a list of suggested books and resources for more information.

This book celebrates a part of the American heritage that has long been taken for granted. It offers only an introduction to the vast wealth of African cooking in the Americas: a sampling of family food, comfort food, easy food, food that satisfies the most jaded palate, food that has been prepared by black cooks in the Americas for over three hundred years.

Out of Africa

Uprooted by slave traders, Africans were transported to Brazil, the Caribbean, and the southern United States to labor in sugar, coffee, rice, and cacao plantations. They came from the Bantu, Kaffir, Coromantee, Nago, Ibo, Congolese, Angolan, Cachio, Bissao, Bongo, Babindas, and Mandingo tribes in what are now Angola, Congo, Gabon, Cameroon, Zaire, Nigeria, Benin, Togo, the Ivory Coast, Sierra Leone, Guinea, Sudan, Central African Republic, Senegal, Gambia, Mali, and Mauritania. Those that survived the wretched ocean journey and endured the debasement of slavery became instrumental in leaving a culinary legacy that continues.

With the slaves came roots, seeds, leaves, and tendrils from the mother country. African yams, greens, red palm, dried shrimp, okra, sesame seeds, black-eyed peas, watermelon, and coconut reappear in variations on similar preparations wherever black cooks are in the kitchen, be it in Dakar, Bahia, Kingston, Havana, Charleston, Savannah, Atlanta, or New Orleans.

The Africans combined American corn, cassava, peanuts, tomatoes, peppers, beans, papaya, pineapple, guava, cassava, potatoes, and chiles with Spanish pork, French thyme,

Chinese eggplant, Indian curry, and the Portuguese penchant for frying, and added their own ingredients and methods to create the cooking styles known as Bahian, Caribbean, Louisiana creole, soul food, barbecue.

The Recipes

African-style cooking is for anyone who loves to cook healthful family food. The recipes are based on grains, beans, vegetables, and limited meat. What makes this cooking unique is the use of seasonings. No matter how mundane the ingredients, cooks of African descent have always had the knack as well as the desire to make them taste good by adding a little pork, the right amount of herbs, a dose of black pepper, a few hot chiles.

Onions, peppers, celery, garlic, herbs, and spices are mixed and mingled with various kinds of vegetables, grains, meats, and fish in different ways for every preparation. Traditionally the food came straight from the garden, the land, and the sea. To maintain authenticity, freshness is still a prerequisite when gathering the ingredients for these recipes. Rice is a mainstay and long-grain rice is recommended. Beans come in a hundred varieties; experiment and find your favorites.

Except for the *dendê* oil and cassava flour of Brazil and a few Caribbean foods, the ingredients are known throughout the Americas and are readily available. Sources for hard-to-find ingredients are listed in Resources.

The recipes, culled from cooks in Brazil, the Caribbean, and the United States, are written with specific measurements, but should be taken, except where noted, as outlines. The cooks laughed when I asked how much of this or that went into a dish. The whole point of cooking in the African style is using what is available. The success comes from adding the right seasoning. The recipes have been grouped by cuisine, but can easily be mixed and matched depending upon what you have on hand.

One of the criticisms of the African style of cooking has been its association with high amounts of salt, sugar, and fat. When these New World cuisines developed, the Africans in the Americas were slaves. Most worked long, sweat-soaked days in plantation fields. Meals of corn bread, beans, and rice were made to taste good with whatever seasoning could be had. With little or no refrigeration, meats (usually from the prolific pig) were smoked or preserved in salt. Pork fat was plentiful. Sugarcane and sorghum were readily available, and easily transformed into sweet syrup for the table and for cooking.

Seasoning with salt, fat, and sugar works miracles on tastes when the diet is the same day after day. What we now think of as unhealthful ingredients if eaten in abundance were worked off in the fields. Today, since most people aren't laboring on farms, there has been a concurrent reduction of salt, sugar, and fat in the cooking. The respect for seasoning hasn't changed, however. In the beginning, salt, pepper, onions, and wild herbs flavored the daily beans, rice, and stews. Next came garlic, celery, ginger, nutmeg, allspice, and chiles. Now, an almost limitless variety of vegetables, spices, herbs, and seasoning blends is accessible.

Sometimes, to achieve a particular flavor in a dish, a recipe calls for a brand-name sauce, condiment, or seasoning. Do not feel you must be tied to that particular condiment or brand. This cooking style embraces flexibility and personalization. When recipe testers brought me samples, I never ceased to be amazed at how two or three results, made from the same recipe, could taste so different. Different oil brands, herbs, stove heat, measuring utensils, and attention to detail all helped to personalize the dishes.

When an ingredient or technique affects the outcome, original method and an updated version are given. Some dishes are best done the old way. Fritters and fried chicken come out crispier when cooked in vegetable shortening; the flavor is even more incredible in lard. Lard also enhances the flakiness of a pie crust. To many cooks, the flavor of pork in greens and beans is essential. Instead of cutting up a big block of salt pork, however, a slab of bacon can be kept in the freezer. When a recipe calls for salt pork or bacon, a heavy cleaver is used to slice off what is needed from the frozen block. The pork stays fresh in the freezer, and you don't have to use up a large piece quickly.

I've tried to maintain the original flavor of classic dishes like black-eyed peas. Hog jowls aren't easily obtainable, but ham hocks are. Desalting the hocks by soaking them in water while the beans soak doesn't affect their smoky pork flavor but does reduce the salt considerably.

A little sugar added to a skillet of vegetables or a pot of beans accents a natural sweetness. You don't have to use it. But don't be afraid to try it either. In recipes calling for salt, the amount is given only when it is necessary, such as in breads or pastries. Otherwise salt to taste. Pepper, on the other hand, is an important seasoning in these African-influenced cuisines. Freshly or commercially ground, the amounts given are suggestions. Feel free to use it liberally.

All African-inspired cooking isn't meat-based, and vegetarian versions of bean, rice, and other one-pot dishes are included.

As you go through the book, you'll find historical and other information on ingredients when they are used and more in the Glossary. Also in the Glossary are directions for preparing chiles, plantains, coconuts, and other ingredients that are used in all the cooking styles.

Wherever possible, the recipes have been written so that the ingredients called for are in amounts that can be used up at one time. Instead of half cups of chopped onions, a whole small onion is listed. For small amounts of tomato paste, buy tomato paste in tubes that will keep in the refrigerator for several months. Whole cans of tomatoes or coconut milk are used in a recipe. Canned vegetables and fruits are used, too. Unless you put them up yourself or have other access to some items, resorting to commercially canned peas, beans, corn, fruits, and Caribbean jackfruit and ackee will do.

Some of the Bahian, Caribbean, and African recipes may sound exotic or formidable to U.S. cooks it they haven't tasted them at the source. Ingredients not found on supermarket shelves are worth making a special effort to obtain. I haven't included many recipes that require special foods, however. In a pinch, even the dishes that call for *dendê* oil or dried shrimp can be prepared without them. They will just taste different.

Special equipment isn't needed for these recipes either. They can be cooked in any household pots and pans just as they have for generations, but there are some recommendations that will ensure similar results every time. To get that dark, crisp crust on corn bread, to brown pork chops evenly, and to add an authenticity steeped through the ages in the African heritage, a cast-iron skillet is indispensable.

A nonstick skillet is good for lessening the amount of fat used when sautéing vegetables like glazed yams and fried green tomatoes. A Chinese wok makes a great deep-fryer because the curved sides require less oil and the deep steel sides become very hot and cause little splatter. Six- and twelve-quart saucepans will accommodate barbecue sauces and stewed vegetables, and a heavy cast-iron or enameled eight-gallon stockpot is perfect for gumbos and other one-pot dishes. A pit, of course, is required for barbecuing; details are included in the Barbecue chapter.

A colander, sieve, and food mill are necessary for draining and mashing sweet potatoes for pies and pone. A good-quality chef's knife and a paring knife will take care of chopping and slicing the ubiquitous onions and peppers that start many dishes. A heavy cleaver is helpful for carving chicken and goat into Caribbean-sized pieces and can be used for cutting off slices from a frozen slab of bacon. Cheesecloth is handy for tying a bunch of herbs for easy retrieval from a finished sauce. Big platters for serving are ideal for family-style dining.

The recipes in this book aren't fancy. The fun here is in seeing how many ways onions, peppers, celery, garlic, beans, greens, and rice can be combined, and how many different ways they can taste.

While searching for a route to India in 1492, Columbus landed on one of the seven thousand islands that dot the Caribbean Sea between North and South America. He christened this lush tropical paradise, laden with pineapples and papayas, Hispaniola, and called the islands the West Indies.

Although East India and spices had been the goal, he, and the European sailors that followed, discovered a climate and terrain amenable to other money-making propositions. Many islands were found to be perfect for growing the coveted sugarcane, demanded by Europeans in insatiable quantities. Columbus brought the first sugarcane on his second voyage in 1494.

By 1518, this beautiful setting, which straddles the equator between the Tropics of Capricorn and Cancer, hosted a growing and ambitious sugar industry. Its success produced a demand for labor that triggered the subsequent bondage of millions of Africans, abducted from their homeland and enslaved in the fields.

The sixteenth, seventeenth, and eighteenth centuries brought a steady stream of European voyagers who cultivated opportunism, piracy, exploitation, and colonization along with slave-tended sugar, coffee, and tropical fruits and spices. Spain, Portugal, Holland, France, and England alternately and concurrently dominated the islands over the next three centuries.

When Columbus arrived in the West Indies in 1492, the islands were settled by Arawak and Carib Indians living on a simple diet of cassava, corn, fruit, and fish. Their cooking methods included pit cooking and "barbecuing" over a green wood grate known by the Caribs as a *brabacot*, a word translated by the Spanish to *barbacoa*.

The rapid colonization by Europeans made an immediate culinary impact on the islands. Spanish ships delivered pigs, cattle, wheat, oil, vinegar, cilantro, and sugar and the technique of frying. In exchange, the Amerindians sent corn, peanuts, tobacco, sweet potatoes, and chiles on the return journey.

With the French came such seasonings as chives, onion, thyme, and garlic to add to the indigenous basil, purslane, and watercress. They also brought the know-how for making sausages.

The English carried their spicy condiments and sweet preserves. To this day, mustards, ketchups, Worcestershire sauce, and marmalades are commonplace on the islands with English heritage and many are still imported from Great Britain. Their favorite herbs—chives and green onions—prominently season many dishes. The British also introduced breadfruit from Polynesia as a cheap source of food for the slaves. This fast-growing large fruit, which resembles a melon with a prickly skin, is cooked like a starchy vegetable.

With the Dutch, who were in search of salt for their fisheries and new avenues of trade, came a penchant for the curry spices—cumin, turmeric, coriander, and ginger—developed during their previous trade with India and the Spice Islands. Many of these spices adapted well

to cultivation, and curry blends were already being used when the East Indians, indentured to work the fields in the postslavery 1800s, arrived.

The Africans had already been introduced to the exotic Eastern spices by Arab traders and became the link that unified the Spanish, French, Dutch, and British cooking methods and ingredients. Between 1518 and 1865, fifteen million Africans were transported to the Caribbean. With them came okra, callaloo, ackee, and a dark-skinned white- or yellow-fleshed yam unrelated to the Caribbean sweet potato. They found indigenous foods like starchy sweet potatoes and cassava similar to their own yams and other root vegetables. And with the Arawaks they shared an appreciation for the spicy hotness of the indigenous capsicum chiles, misnamed peppers when Columbus thought he was close to Indonesia, land of black peppercorns.

Spices native to the Caribbean include allspice, known as pimento on Jamaica, and annatto, a tiny red seed from a flowering plant used whole to color and flavor oils and sauces, or ground and mixed into a spicy paste to season meats for stews or the grill.

The most prominent spice to come from the West Indies is the chile pepper. In their native habitat, chiles come tiny, long, round, slim, tapered, fat, curled, and lantern-shaped. Because of their heat and pungency, chiles serve practical purposes in tropical climates. One is to cause sweating, which helps cool the body. Another is to conceal possible rancidity in unrefrigerated meats. In the diets of African-Caribbeans, chiles spike the bland flavors of a diet based on roots and greens day after day.

Every island has its own hot sauce. It can be simply chopped chiles in vinegar to sprinkle on food, or a complicated tomato-chile *sofrito* that forms the base for many dishes on Spanish islands. In Jamaica the Scotch Bonnet flavors the island's famous jerk seasoning for meats and chicken.

Because the Africans traditionally ran the kitchens, their influence is evident in similar dishes found throughout the islands. Seafood is dominant and rice-and-bean combinations prevail. Indeed, the most common West Indian staple is a dish of pigeon peas, also known as Congo or goongoo peas, and other dried beans cooked and served with rice. In Cuba, a dish of black beans and white rice is called Moors and Christians. *Djon djon*, a specialty of Haiti, flavors the rice with a particular wild mushroom that is also known as *djon djon*.

Legume and grain mashes called *fufu* in West Africa are made with cassava, corn, yam, or plantains in the Caribbean and eaten in place of bread. They are made with okra and cornmeal and called *coo-coo* in Jamaica, Trinidad, and Tobago. *Funchi* are made of corn in Haiti. *Foutou* is a cassava or yam purée in Martinique. *Mofongo* are balls of mashed plantains in Dominica.

The use of the native cassava (a brown-skinned, white-fleshed tuber also known as manioc and yuca), which is the main starch of the Caribbean (and also of Brazil) was taught to

the new arrivals by the Amerindians. Little cassava cakes, first made by the Amerindians, are known as bammies in Jamaica.

Pepperpot, the fish-and-vegetable stew prepared throughout the West Indies, descends from a dish originated by the island natives, and is similar to West African one-pot potages. It can be made fresh, but traditionally it is kept simmering on the stove top for days, sometimes generations, with new things added all the time—the quintessential ongoing stockpot. In Trinidad it is flavored with cassareep, juice pressed from the cassava.

The ubiquitous green found wherever cooks of African descent live is called callaloo in the Caribbean. It is a deep green spinachlike leaf that reputedly stems from West Africa. Okra, which grows up to eight inches long in the tropics, also came from West Africa, and, with its thickening viscosity, is found in the pepperpot, is stewed alone, or is added to poultry or meat stews as is customary in its native land.

The African, Spanish, and Portuguese penchant for frying turns up throughout the Caribbean, often in small grain-and-vegetable-based balls known in Yoruba as *akkras*. They are called *acras* on the French islands, *calas* on the Dutch, *frituras* or *bolitas* on the Spanish, and dumplings or festivals on English islands. Fish fritters made with salt cod (*bacalao* in Spanish), a European and African staple, are called *bacalaitos* on Spanish islands, *acras de morue* on French islands, and poor man's fritters on English islands. On Jamaica they are called stamp and go.

Choice of cooking oil used to be a differentiating factor among the island kitchens. The prolific coconut has long been a convenient source of oil, and Jamaicans still use a lot of coconut oil. Cubans and other one-time Spanish subjects prefer olive oil. Haitians and cooks from Martinique and Guadeloupe commonly use butter and olive oil like the French. On some islands, the red annatto seed colors vegetable or palm oil, making it reminiscent of *dendê*, the red palm oil of West Africa. Increasingly, however, canola and other less saturated oils are used.

Other influences that came to be incorporated in the cooking styles of the islands arrived with the East Indians and Chinese in the 1800s. The East Indians brought their curries, known as *kerry* on Dutch islands and *colombo* on French, and such hearth-style breads as *puri* and *roti*. The Chinese brought bok choy, green peas, and rice. Their reliance on rice gave an additional boost to its already important dietary status.

The recipes in this chapter are typical of the dishes found in homes and cafes around the islands. If a recipe changes dramatically from one island to the next, the different names are given, along with a list of variations. In keeping with African tradition, Caribbean meals are served family-style on heaping platters with all the dishes set out at one time.

West Indian Hot Sauce

What ketchup is to some, hot sauces are to the Caribbean islanders. Every cook has either a treasured home recipe or a favorite brand purchased at the market. Here is a basic sauce with rich flavors in which the heat can be adjusted. This ubiquitous condiment goes under the name *sofrito* in Spanish and *sauce piquante* in French.

The amount of onions, peppers, tomatoes, garlic, and herbs can all be increased or decreased according to the cook's taste. Other spices that can be added include chopped fresh or ground ginger, ground cloves, or bay leaves. Raisins, capers, vinegar, and lemon juice are still other possible additions.

Makes about 1 1/2 cups

2 tablespoons vegetable oil
1 large yellow or white onion, finely chopped
6 green onions, including tops, chopped
1 green bell pepper, seeded and finely chopped
1–4 small fresh red or green chiles, minced (see Glossary)
4 garlic cloves, minced
2 pounds fresh tomatoes, peeled, seeded and chopped, or 1 can
     (28 ounces) tomatoes with their juice, seeded and chopped
1 tablespoon dried oregano or marjoram, crushed
1 teaspoon ground allspice
dash of ground cloves
1 teaspoon dried thyme leaves
1 teaspoon sugar
2 tablespoons red wine vinegar, cider vinegar, or cane syrup vinegar
Salt and ground black pepper

In a heavy saucepan over medium heat, warm the oil. Add the yellow and green onions, bell pepper, and chiles and sauté until very soft, about 10 minutes. Stir in the garlic and sauté another minute. Stir in all the remaining ingredients, including salt and pepper to taste. Bring the mixture to a boil, reduce the heat to low, and simmer uncovered, stirring occasionally, until thickened, about 45 minutes.

Remove from heat and taste for seasoning. Let cool and serve at room temperature. Store in a covered container in the refrigerator. The sauce will keep several weeks.

Papaya-Chayote Hot Sauce

This Jamaican hot sauce is based on two prolific native Caribbean ingredients, the papaya, or pawpaw, and the chayote, or cho-cho. If a papaya isn't available, a mango can be substituted. Acorn squash can be used in place of the chayote; its texture is similar although its flesh is golden rather than cream-colored. The sauce is wonderful with steamed or grilled fish or as a dip with Fried Plantains (page 29) or Shrimp-Potato Fritters (pages 46–47).

Makes about 2 cups

1 green papaya or mango, peeled, seeded and finely chopped
1 chayote, peeled, seeded and chopped
1 small white onion, chopped
3 green onions, including tops, finely chopped
1/2 cup fresh parsley leaves
1 inch fresh ginger, peeled and finely chopped
2 teaspoons fresh thyme leaves, or 1 teaspoon dried thyme, crushed
3–5 small fresh red or green chiles, seeded and chopped (see Glossary)
3 garlic cloves, chopped
2 tablespoons sugar
1 teaspoon salt
1 cup distilled white vinegar
1 cup water
ground red or habanero (Scotch Bonnet) or red chile powder

Put all of the ingredients except the vinegar, water, and chile powder in a food processor or blender. Purée until very finely chopped. Transfer to a saucepan and add the vinegar, water, and chile powder to taste. Bring to a boil and boil 5 minutes.

Pour into a jar and let cool. Cover and refrigerate for up to 2 weeks.

The papaya, which is native to the Caribbean, is used green as a vegetable and ripe as a fruit. When ripe, its sunset colors range from golden yellow to burnt orange. The flesh is yellow to orange and the center is filled with black seeds that resemble fish eggs. In Cuba the papaya is called fruta bomba ("hand grenade fruit"), and in Jamaica it is known as pawpaw. The leaves are used to wrap meats for cooking because papain, an enzyme in the leaf, aids tenderizing.

Mango Relish

Mangoes hang from trees all over the islands, ready for picking most of the year. As messy and difficult as it is to separate the fruits from the seeds (see note), mangoes are still eaten for breakfast, lunch, and dinner. This example of the cultural crossroads of the Caribbean presents a fiery hot, chutneylike relish. Serve it with Cassava Chips (page 33) or Shrimp-Potato Fritters (pages 46–47).

Makes about 1½ cups

1 large ripe mango, peeled and cut into small cubes
1 yellow onion, finely chopped
1 inch fresh ginger, peeled and minced (about 2 tablespoons)
½ teaspoon ground allspice
1 tablespoon Curry Blend (page 28), or favorite curry powder
1 tablespoon brown sugar
juice of 1 lime
1 fresh red or green chile, minced (see Glossary)
salt and ground black pepper

In a nonreactive pot, combine all of the ingredients, including salt and pepper to taste. Add water just to cover. Bring the mixture to a boil, reduce the heat, and cook uncovered over medium-low heat, stirring frequently, until thickened, about 25 minutes.

Remove from the heat and let cool. Serve at room temperature. Store in a covered container in the refrigerator for up to 3 weeks.

NOTE: Peeling a ripe mango is a sensory pleasure for those who don't mind the juice running down their wrists. The best way to proceed is to make long, wedge-shaped cuts with a sharp knife and then separate the wedges from one another by cutting them from the stubborn seed. Next, slip the knife between the flesh and skin and remove the skin. Cut each wedge into cubes.

The mango is a voluptuous and perfumy fruit native to Asia, where it has been cultivated longer than history has been recorded. It has been in Africa since the year 1000, and arrived in the Caribbean and Brazil in the 1700s. Skins are red, green, and golden and flesh is pale to brilliant orange.

All-Purpose Caribbean Spice Blend

Nowhere is the African penchant for seasoning more visible than in produce markets in the West Indies. Colorful packets of mixed powdered spices and herbs are labeled for barbecue, fish, chicken, or meat. There are jerk blends and curry blends. Shoppers find their favorite and buy just enough to use once or twice, thus keeping the seasonings fresh and the results consistent. After talking to vendors, reading labels, and sampling variations, only personal taste determines whether sweet, hot, ginger, salt, allspice, pepper, or another flavor dominates.

This is an all-purpose blend, with variations recommended to suit the cook's taste.

Makes about 1/4 cup; enough for 2–3 pounds meat, fish, or poultry

1 teaspoon ground ginger
1/4 teaspoon ground turmeric
1 teaspoon ground cumin, or 3/4 teaspoon whole cumin seeds
1/4 teaspoon ground allspice
1 tablespoon paprika
1/2 teaspoon salt
1/4 teaspoon ground white or black pepper
1/2 teaspoon dried thyme, crushed
1 teaspoon cayenne or other ground red chile pepper
optional additions: ground cinnamon, ground cloves, garlic powder,
    red pepper flakes, ground cardamom, freshly grated nutmeg,
    ground annatto seeds, ground coriander, ground mace

Combine all the ingredients in a bowl and mix well. Store in an airtight container at room temperature. When ready to use, rub the mixture into the meat, fish, or poultry and let stand 30 minutes or longer before cooking.

VARIATIONS: *Fresh ingredients such as chopped garlic, chopped green onions, minced and peeled fresh ginger, chopped bell peppers, and chopped onions can be combined with the spice mixture when ready to rub into the meat, fish, or poultry. Liquids such as coconut milk, rum, or lime, lemon, or orange juice are optional additions.*

The West Indies *encompass a sea area of 750,000 square miles, marked on the north by the Tropic of Cancer and on the south by the Tropic of Capricorn. Cuba, Puerto Rico, Trinidad, Tobago, and the Dominican Republic came under Spanish rule. Haiti, Guadeloupe, Martinique, half of St. Martin, and St. Barthelemy were French. Jamaica, Barbados, Antigua, Anguilla, Montserrat, Dominica, and Grenada had British stepparents and St. Maarten, Aruba, and Curaçao carry Dutch lineage. The mixed heritage of the Virgin Islands includes being a subject of Spain, Holland, France, Denmark, and now the United States.*

Bajan Fish Spice

Here is a typical spice blend from Barbados, where it is rubbed into fillets of flying fish before grilling, broiling, or steaming. Whole red snapper or other rockfish can be substituted.

Makes about 1/3 cup, enough for 3–4 pounds fish

1/2 yellow onion, chopped, or 6 green onions, including green tops, chopped
1 garlic clove, minced
2 teaspoons paprika
1/2 teaspoon cayenne or other ground red chile pepper
1/2 teaspoon ground dried thyme or dried thyme leaves
leaves from several fresh parsley sprigs, chopped
2–3 tablespoons fresh lime juice
2 tablespoons vegetable oil
salt and ground black pepper

Combine all the ingredients in a blender or food processor, including salt and pepper to taste. Purée until smooth. To use, cut diagonal slits along the sides of a whole cleaned fish and rub the seasoning mixture into the slits, or rub the mixture on fish fillets. Cover and refrigerate at least 30 minutes or up to several hours.

Curry Blend

This basic blend combines the most common curry spices in a pleasant balance of flavors. Cumin gives the characteristic flavor and turmeric the golden color. Commercial blends from the Caribbean, which are found in Latin American markets (see Resources), have their own distinctive flavor, one that seems more vibrant and lively than that of their East Indian counterparts.

I asked Caribbean cooks why the flavor of curry in the islands is different from the blends used in India. Answers ranged from the smaller amount of cumin used in most mixtures to the effect of the salty cross breezes of the Atlantic on the the cumin, oregano, ginger, coriander, and turmeric grown there. Experiment with different combinations and see what you like.

Makes about 1/2 cup; enough for 2–3 pounds meat, fish, or vegetables

1/2 teaspoon ground allspice
1/2 teaspoon ground mace
1 tablespoon ground turmeric
1 teaspoon ground ginger
1 tablespoon ground coriander
1 1/2 teaspoons ground cumin
1 teaspoon dried oregano, crushed
1/2–1 teaspoon cayenne or other ground red chile pepper
1/2 teaspoon garlic powder
1/2 teaspoon salt

Combine all the ingredients in a bowl and mix well. Store in an airtight container. When ready to use, always sauté the mixture to release its aromatic oils and thus brings up its full flavor potential.

Fried Plantains

Whether called *bananes pesées* on the French islands or *tostones* on the Spanish, fried plantains are as popular in the West Indies as they are in West Africa, where they are seasoned with ground ginger and cayenne. The mealy texture and bland starchiness of plantains, which came to the West Indies via Africa, make this side dish a refreshing counterpoint to spicy-hot Pepperpot (pages 40–41), Haitian Gumbo (pages 48-49), or Jerked Chicken Drumettes (page 230). They are frequently eaten for breakfast as well. Green bananas can be substituted.

Serves 6–8

2 plantains or 3 green bananas
1 tablespoon vegetable oil

Peel the plantains (see Glossary) and slice into ½-inch-thick rounds. In a nonstick skillet over medium-high heat, warm the oil until just beginning to sizzle. Add the plantain slices, and fry, turning once, until just browned, about 1 minute on each side. Serve warm or at room temperature.

Baked Plantains

Here's a way to use the dark-skinned ripe plantains. When the normally blotchy-yellow skin begins to turn black, the plantains are getting soft. At this point their maximum flavor potential is developed. The sweetness and creamy texture is perfect with Jerked Chicken Drumettes (page 230) or Spiced Chicken (page 52).

Serves 4

4 ripe plantains
butter for serving

Preheat an oven to 450 degrees F. Place the unpeeled plantains on a baking sheet. Bake, until soft and cooked through, 20–30 minutes.

Remove from the oven and, using a sharp knife, cut them in half lengthwise. Serve the halves hot with a little melted butter or scoop out the flesh and serve mashed, like potatoes.

Boiled Green Bananas

This side dish is always a surprise if you weren't raised on it. Given the prolificacy of bananas, which were introduced from West Africa to the islands in 1516, it's no wonder they are used in every imaginable way. When green, they taste quite starchy and are more vegetable than fruit. Here is how to cook those green bananas we are often faced with in the supermarket. In addition to serving them whole, they can be mashed and mixed with butter, milk, salt, and pepper and served like mashed potatoes.

Serves 4

4 green bananas
1 lime, cut in half
salt

Peel the bananas. (If they are difficult to peel, follow the directions for peeling plantains in the Glossary.) Rub the surfaces with lime and leave the bananas whole. Place in a saucepan with water just to cover. Add a little salt and bring to a boil. Reduce the heat to low and simmer uncovered until soft, 6–15 minutes, depending on how green they are.

Drain the bananas and serve whole as a side dish for breakfast or dinner.

Steamed African Yams

The white- and yellow-fleshed West African yams that arrived in the West Indies with the slaves continue to be important daily sustenance in African-Caribbean diets. Their delicious sweet, starchy flavor falls somewhere between that of an American sweet potato and a just-harvested new potato. They are perfect simply steamed, as described in this recipe, and used as a bread substitute for mopping up the drippings of Jamaican mackerel run down (page 39) or Codfish and Ackee (pages 42–43). They can also be boiled in a generous measure of water for about the same amount of time.

Serves 4

1 African yam, about 1 pound

Bring the water in a steamer pan to a boil. Meanwhile, using a vegetable peeler, peel off the dark fibrous skin from the yam. Cut the yam lengthwise into wedges or other uniform chunks. Place the yam pieces on the steamer rack, cover the steamer, and cook until tender when pierced with a bamboo skewer, 15–20 minutes.

Serve hot.

Breadfruit, the giant of the starchy fruits, was brought to the Caribbean from Polynesia as a cheap source of food for the slaves. It grows quickly in tropical climates and produces a versatile ingredient that is starchy, filling, and adapts to many seasonings. The Jamaican demand for this fruit unwittingly precipitated the famous mutiny on the Bounty.

When Captain William Bligh set sail from the South Pacific for the Caribbean, he hadn't provisioned enough water for both the crew and the breadfruit saplings he was commissioned to transport. By opting to keep the breadfruit alive, he found himself stranded alone in a rowboat. He survived, however, and in 1793, he completed the mission, sailing into Jamaica with a shipload of the fast-growing breadfruit saplings.

Baked Chayote

Known as christophene on the French islands, chocho on Jamaica, and mirliton in Louisiana, chayote is the Spanish name for a common squash in the Caribbean. Pale green and avocado-shaped, it has a sweet flavor and firm texture. Steamed alone or added to any stewed mélange, it adds a distinguishing fresh flavor and complementary texture to foods it accompanies. In this recipe from the island of St. Vincent, it is sliced and cooked like scalloped potatoes in stock with a bit of butter.

Serves 4–6

4 chayotes, peeled, seeded, and sliced crosswise into 1/4-inch-thick rounds
2 tablespoons butter, cut into bits
salt and ground black pepper
1/2 cup chicken stock (see Glossary) or water

Preheat an oven to 350 degrees F. Butter a 2-quart baking dish.

Arrange the squash slices in layers, dotting each layer with a few bits of butter and a sprinkling of salt and pepper. Pour the stock evenly over the top. Cover the dish with aluminum foil. Bake until tender and bubbly, 30–40 minutes.

If no oven is available, butter a cast-iron skillet and layer the squash and the rest of the ingredients as directed. Cover and cook over medium-low heat, shaking the pan occasionally to loosen the bottom, until the squash is tender, 25–30 minutes.

Cassava Chips

Fried cassava, plantain, and banana chips are common snacks throughout the Caribbean. On Cuba these chips are called *yuca frita,* and on Guadeloupe they are *frites de manioc.* The hard cassava root, which must be parboiled before it can be fried, can be cut into rounds or into spears for frying. The chips are similar to French-fried potatoes with a whiter appearance and fresh starchy flavor. Serve these chips with West Indian Hot Sauce (page 23) or Papaya Chayote Hot Sauce (page 24).

Serves 4

1 cassava, 8–10 inches long
vegetable oil for deep-frying
salt

Bring a large pot of water to boil. Meanwhile, using a vegetable peeler, peel off the tough dark skin of the cassava. Cut the white tuber into thirds, drop the pieces into the boiling water, and cook until tender when pierced with a bamboo skewer, 15–20 minutes. Drain well in a colander.

When cool enough to handle, cut the cassava pieces into ¼-inch-thick rounds or spears. In a deep-fryer or heavy pot, pour in vegetable oil to a depth of 3 inches. Place over high heat until it sizzles. Working in batches, carefully drop a few cassava pieces into the oil. Fry until browned, 3–4 minutes. Using a slotted spoon, remove the chips to a rack or paper towels to drain briefly. Sprinkle with salt and serve hot.

Callaloo

This is the Caribbean's pot of greens. Callaloo is the name of the dish as well as of the bundles of thick green leaves similar to spinach or collard greens sold in the open markets of Jamaica and Trinidad and increasingly available at West Indian markets in the United States. Typically the greens are cooked with salted and fresh fish and meats into a chile-spiked nutritious soup. The following recipe uses a little bacon and crab to retain the original flavors. Although the crab is optional, it gives the soup a full-bodied nature, especially if water instead of chicken stock is used.

Callaloo is often garnished with cornmeal dumplings called *funchi*, which are similar to the cornmeal dumplings found in the American South (see recipe on page 146).

Serves 4–6

2 ounces bacon, finely diced, or 2 tablespoons vegetable oil
1 yellow onion, finely chopped
1 or 2 cloves garlic, minced
2 tablespoons Papa Joe's brand Scotch Bonnet red or green hot-pepper
 sauce, or to taste
1/2 pound fresh callaloo, collard greens, or spinach leaves, or 1 can
 (15 ounces) callaloo, well drained
3 cups chicken stock (see Glossary)
salt and ground black pepper
1/2 cup coconut milk
2–4 ounces crab meat, picked over for shell fragments

If using the bacon, in a heavy soup pot over medium heat, fry it until crisp. If using the oil, simply heat the oil in the pot. Add the onion and sauté until browned, about 8 minutes. Stir in the garlic and cook 1 minute. Add the Scotch Bonnet sauce and the fresh callaloo, if using. Stir in the stock and simmer over medium heat to cook the callaloo, about 15 minutes.

If using canned greens, stir them in after the stock and seasonings have simmered for 15 minutes. Then add the coconut milk and crab. Heat to serving temperature and taste and adjust the seasonings. Serve at once.

NOTE: You can also use 1 can (3 ounces) crab meat for making this dish. Drain it well and pick over to remove any shell fragments or cartilage. Place in a bowl and add 1/2 cup milk; let soak for 1–2 minutes, then rinse in cold water and drain. Proceed as directed.

Taro, dasheen, eddo, malanga, yautia, cocoyam, and tannia are all names of tuberous white-fleshed starchy roots from the same family that grow well in tropical climates. They have varying elongated shapes, fibrous or hairy skins, white to yellow flesh, and are used like potatoes. Look for them in Latin American markets. Sample a few of the many varieties to discover their various flavors and textures. The leaves of these tubers are called callaloo.

Pigeon Peas and Rice

This Caribbean mainstay is found on all the islands in a variety of forms. Sometimes it is cooked with pork; other times it is prepared with water, onions, and salt. The peas can also be cooked with coconut milk, and garlic, tomatoes, and green onions can be added. Curry powder is another option. And the hot *habanero* (Scotch Bonnet) chile is optional.

Serves 6

2¹/₂ cups (1 pound) dried pigeon peas, rinsed and picked over
8 cups water, or 6¹/₂ cups water and 1¹/₂ cups coconut milk
¹/₂ pound ham hocks, cut into 2-inch pieces (see note), 1 whole smoked
    turkey neck, or 3–4 pig's tails
1 yellow onion, finely chopped
2 garlic cloves, minced
1 fresh or pickled habanero (Scotch Bonnet) chile, or 1¹/₂ teaspoons
    Papa Joe's brand Scotch Bonnet red hot-pepper sauce
1¹/₂ cups long-grain white rice, rinsed and drained
salt and ground black pepper

Soak the pigeon peas overnight in water to cover by several inches. Drain.
Combine the drained pigeon peas with the water (or water and coconut milk) in a large, heavy saucepan. Bring to a boil and add the ham hocks, onion, 1 clove of the garlic, and the chile. Cook uncovered over medium-high heat until the peas are tender, about 45 minutes.

Stir in the rice, reduce the heat to medium, cover, and cook until the rice is tender, another 20–30 minutes. About 5 minutes before the rice is ready, squeeze the last clove of garlic through a garlic press into the mixture.

Adjust the seasonings with salt and pepper and Papa Joe's sauce, if using, and serve.

NOTE: If you think the ham hocks may be too salty for your taste, parboil them in water to cover generously for 3 minutes, then drain.

Pigeon peas are native to Africa and resemble black-eyed peas. They are pale yellow and have a small "eye"; black-eyed peas can be substituted. In the West Indies, pigeon peas also go by goongoo, Congo, and gungo peas. The peas' earthy flavor is wonderful; when these legumes are combined with rice the resulting texture is a mouthful to behold.

In Cuba red beans and rice are called congri. A dish of black beans and rice on the island is called Moros y Cristianos, for Moors and Christians.

Haitian Red Beans and Rice

Rousbert Pierre Jeanty, from Port-au-Prince, Haiti, attended Piney Wood Country Life School outside of Jackson, Mississippi. He was president of the school's International Culinary Club when he shared this recipe, known as *riz et pois* in his native country. Serve it with Haitian Gumbo (page 48).

Serves 6–8

1¼ cups (½ pound) dried red beans, rinsed and picked over
5 cups water
5 tablespoons olive oil or palm oil
1 yellow onion, chopped
2 garlic cloves, minced
salt and ground black pepper
2½ cups long-grain white rice, rinsed and drained

Soak the beans overnight in water to cover by several inches. Drain.

In a large, heavy pot, combine the drained beans and water and bring to a boil. Reduce the heat to a simmer, cover, and cook, stirring occasionally, until the beans are tender, about 1 hour.

In a skillet over medium heat, warm the oil and sauté the onion and garlic until softened, about 5 minutes. Stir into the beans. Add salt and pepper to taste. Cook 5 minutes.

The beans should be quite soupy at this point, with at least 2 inches of water to cover. If they aren't, add more water. Bring to a rolling boil and stir in the rice. Reduce the heat to low, cover, and simmer at least 20 minutes without lifting the lid.

Check to see if rice is tender, stir, and serve hot.

Haitian Rice

In Haiti, where the mountainous terrain adds a cool dimension to the tropical climate, a wild mushroom called *djon djon* emerges when the weather conditions permit. It resembles the black chanterelle or trumpet, which is the poor man's truffle in southwestern France. Any dried mushrooms can be substituted, but porcini or shiitake (black) mushrooms are preferred. This rice dish, which is also known as *djon djon*, shows off the intense essence that dried mushrooms are known for. It may be made without the bacon, but it is only an ounce and the smokiness complements the earthy flavors very well.

Serves 6

2–3 tablespoons (1 ounce) dried mushrooms (see recipe introduction)
about 1 cup boiling water
1 ounce slab bacon, finely minced, or 2 tablespoons butter
3 green onions, including tops, chopped
1/2 green or red bell pepper, seeded and chopped
3 garlic cloves, minced
1/4 teaspoon dried thyme, crushed
1 1/2 cups long-grain white rice, rinsed and drained
2 cups water or chicken stock (see Glossary), heated
salt and ground black pepper

In a bowl, combine the mushrooms and boiling water to cover. Let stand 15 minutes until the caps have softened. Remove the mushrooms and strain and reserve the soaking liquid. Chop the mushrooms. (If using dried shiitake mushrooms, cut off and discard the tough stem before chopping.) Set the mushrooms and liquid aside.

In a 10- or 12-inch skillet over medium-high heat, fry the bacon until crisp (or melt the butter). Add the green onions and bell pepper and sauté until just soft to keep the color, about 1 minute. Stir in the garlic, thyme, and rice and cook to coat the rice, about 1 minute. Stir in the hot water. Add the mushrooms and strained liquid and bring to a boil. Season with salt and pepper, reduce the heat to medium-low, cover, and cook until the liquid is absorbed and the rice is tender, 15–18 minutes.

When the rice is cooked, uncover and, using a fork, fluff the rice to evenly distribute the ingredients. Serve immediately.

In 1804, Haiti became the world's first black republic as a result of a rebellion against the British and French led by former slave Toussaint L'Ouverture. Haiti is located on the western third of the island Columbus called Hispaniola. The Dominican Republic occupies the eastern part. Specialties of African-French-Haitian cooking include manba, a spicy peanut butter; griots, pork marinated in lime juice and fried and served with hot sauce; and tablette, a coconut candy.

Cornmeal with Okra

From Mali to Bahia, Trinidad to New Orleans, cornmeal mush has been a basic food in the diet of those of African descent. Before corn arrived in Africa, plantains, yams, beans, or rice formed the base of this breadlike staple, most popularly known as *fufu*. *Coo-coo*, also spelled *cou-cou*, is a staple on all the islands, where it is also known as *funchi*, which comes from a West African dialect, and as *couscous de mais* on the French islands. This delicious version, popular in Barbados, is like an okra polenta. It can be made with coarse or fine yellow cornmeal. I prefer using coarse stone-ground cornmeal because the flavor is so rich.

This is a sneaky way to introduce people to okra for the first time and is guaranteed to make them fans. Frozen sliced okra can be used in place of the fresh; add it after the water comes to a boil. The dish can be served straight from the stove top or it can be placed in a 350 degree F oven for 20 minutes to give the top a nice crust. It can also be chilled and reheated in a 350 degree F oven for 25 minutes.

Serves 6

2 tablespoons butter or oil
3 green onions, including tops, finely chopped
$^1/_2$ teaspoon cayenne pepper
$^1/_2$ pound okra, cut into $^1/_4$-inch-thick slices
1 teaspoon salt
1 cup coarse yellow cornmeal
4 cups water

In a large, heavy saucepan over medium heat, melt the butter. Add the green onions and sauté until just wilted, about 2 minutes. Stir in the cayenne pepper and cook 30 seconds. Stir in the okra, salt, and cornmeal. Slowly stir in the water and, stirring constantly, bring to a boil. Reduce the heat to low and cook, stirring frequently, until the cornmeal is tender and creamy, 20 minutes or so.

Lightly oil a pie dish or quiche dish. Pour the hot cornmeal mixture into the prepared pan and smooth the top with a spatula. Serve immediately.

The Arawak word for corn is mahiz *from which comes maize, the word used by Europeans. The Arawak dish* loblolly *was a mush that became a staple to the newly arrived Africans, who called it* coo-coo *or* couscous de mais *and adopted it in place of their own grain mushes.*

Having a garden became important to African slaves in the Caribbean for their own economic reasons, but ended up benefitting both master and slave. Because much of the food served in the plantation houses was imported, the owners encouraged their slaves to plant gardens, thereby reducing the amount of food they would need to provide. On islands like Antigua, slaves were given forty-square-foot plots. On other islands, plots were on hard-to-reach mountainsides and had to be tended at night and on Sunday when that day was given off. The slaves grew yams, callaloo, potatoes, pigeon peas, beans, peppers, sugarcane, bananas, coconut, mangoes, avocados, and squash. Having come from agrarian and mercantile societies, they ably transformed their excess produce into trade wherever it was permitted. Sunday markets throughout the West Indies, and also in South America and in South Carolina, became a ticket to freedom for many who sold their surplus crops.

Vegetable Run Down

Run down is the name of a popular dish made with coconut milk and mackerel that is served for breakfast in Jamaica. It is also a term that means to cook something in coconut milk until it thickens and the oil "runs down," according to Montego Bay cook Lee Bickford. Here is his version for cooking vegetables in the run down manner without the salted mackerel. This creamy mélange is satisfying as a main course and is typically served with bammies or bakes (see recipe for latter on page 59). It is also great as a side dish to accompany Spiced Chicken (page 52) or grilled fish with Bajan Fish Spice (page 27).

Serves 6–8

1 yellow onion, cut into wedges
2 garlic cloves, minced
1 green or red bell pepper, seeded and sliced lengthwise
1 carrot, peeled and sliced
1 russet potato, peeled and thinly sliced
1 African yellow yam or sweet potato, peeled and sliced
$1/_2$ pound callaloo or collard greens, sliced
$1/_2$ head cabbage, shredded
leaves from 3 fresh thyme sprigs, chopped, or 1 teaspoon dried thyme,
    crushed
$1^1/_2$ cups coconut milk
$1/_2$ cup water
salt and cayenne or other ground red chile pepper
4 green onions, including tops, chopped

In a heavy pot, combine all of the ingredients except the green onions and stir to mix. Bring to a boil and cook until all the vegetables are tender, about 20 minutes. Then, continue cooking until the coconut milk has reduced down, another 5–10 minutes. The yam or sweet potato will cook down to orange flecks and help the coconut milk thicken the stew.

Stir in the green onions, cook another minute or so, and serve.

Pepperpot

Most West Indian cooks prepare a version of this stew, which combines salted and fresh meats plus chicken and vegetables in the same way a creole gumbo, a Brazilian *cozido*, or a Senegalese *tiebe* does. Traditionally this pot simmers on the stove daily, with the end of the previous day's pepperpot forming the beginning the next day's stew. Some pepperpots have been simmering for generations.

On Trinidad, the pepperpot is typically flavored with cassareep, a thick brown essence of cassava juices made by boiling down the liquid until it becomes thick and dark. West Indians in the United States have found two commercial products, Kitchen Bouquet and Worcestershire sauce, suitable substitutes.

This recipe is based on one Icilda Pinnock of Mammee Bay, Jamaica, showed me how to make. She sent me with a list of ingredients to the market, where I received more advice on which vegetables should go into a pepperpot. We used chicken feet to ensure a rich stock and added callaloo, bok choy, carrots, chocho (chayote), ginger, yellow African yams, sweet potatoes, Irish (russet) potatoes, green beans, green onions, thyme, and a Scotch Bonnet (*habanero*) chile.

It can also be made with chicken parts as is done here or with chicken stock (see Glossary) only. In addition, bacon, salt pork, *carne seca* (dried beef), pig's feet, and pig's tails are commonly included to make an aromatic and comforting pepperpot. Serve it with Bakes (page 59) or with Skillet-Baked Corn Bread (page 194) from the Louisiana Creole chapter.

Serves 6–8

1 chicken, cut into serving pieces and skinned
salt and ground black pepper
1/2 pound callaloo, kale, collard greens, or spinach, ends trimmed but
    leaves left whole
1 head bok choy
2–4 ounces slab bacon, finely chopped, or 3–4 tablespoons vegetable oil
1 yellow onion, sliced
1 carrot, peeled and sliced
1 garlic clove, minced
1 tablespoon minced peeled fresh ginger

African-Caribbean one-pot dishes were typically combined in cast-iron calderos or round clay yabbas and cooked over coals. Today these pots are more often made of aluminum or stainless steel. At roadside stands, where the most authentic home-style cooking can be enjoyed by visitors to the Islands, the fire is often built inside old heavy tire rims removed from big American cars, a resourceful display of modern recycling.

1 fresh habanero (Scotch Bonnet) chile, or 1 pickled bird chile
    (see Glossary)
8 cups water
1 sweet potato or garnet yam, peeled and cut into cubes
1 small African yam or boniato (Cuban white sweet potato), peeled and
    cut into cubes
1 russet potato, peeled and cut into cubes
1/2 cassava, peeled and cut into cubes (optional)
2 fresh thyme sprigs, or 1 teaspoon dried thyme, crushed (see note)
salt and ground black pepper
1/4 pound green beans, cut into 11/2-inch lengths
1/4 pound okra, sliced (optional)
4 green onions, including tops, chopped
chopped fresh parsley

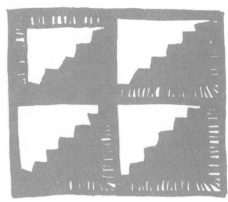

Sprinkle the chicken pieces with salt and pepper.

In a bowl combine the callaloo leaves and bok choy leaves and cover with water to soak for 10 minutes. Drain.

In a large, heavy pot over high heat, brown the bacon pieces to render their fat (or warm the oil). Add the chicken pieces and brown well on all sides. Remove from the pot. Stir in the yellow onion, carrot, garlic, ginger, and chile (if using *habanero*, leave it whole and be careful not to puncture it when stirring). Sauté until the onion is softened, about 3 minutes. Return the chicken to the pot and add the water. Stir, reduce the heat to medium, and simmer, uncovered, for 15 minutes. Stir in the callaloo and bok choy and cook the greens until tender, 6–8 minutes. Using a slotted spoon, retrieve the greens, place in a blender or food processor, and purée. Reserve them.

Now, stir the sweet potato, yam, russet potato, cassava (if using), thyme, and salt and pepper to taste into the simmering chicken and cook until everything is tender, 20–30 minutes. Stir in the green beans and okra and cook until tender, another 3 minutes. Stir in the puréed greens and the green onions. Heat to serving temperature and adjust the seasonings. Sprinkle with parsley and serve.

NOTE: If you don't want a strong thyme taste or the thyme leaves in the broth, you can do one of two things: Tie the fresh or dried thyme in a small piece of cheesecloth to add and then discard before serving. Or blanch the thyme in a little simmering water and strain the liquid into the pot, as Miss Icy does.

Codfish and Ackee

One of the national dishes of Jamaica, this recipe combines ackee, a red pear-shaped fruit native to Africa, with salt cod, a staple handed down by the Africans and Europeans. Ackee adapted well to the Islands, where it is found fresh. Elsewhere, the pale yellow flesh, which looks like scrambled eggs, is available in cans in Latin American stores (see Resources). Salt cod has traditionally been an important part of the diet where there is limited or no refrigeration. Salting and drying is an easy preservation method in hot climates, providing protein and calcium throughout the year. One of the drawbacks of salt cod is that it is too salty for some palates, even after the prescribed soaking. And if the salt is too fully leached out by soaking, the flavor of the fish is quite bland. Because the traditional recipe is still widely prepared, and cooks like Prince Neville, a Jamaican restaurateur in San Francisco, always prepare it this way, I'm giving both the classic recipe and an updated version using fresh cod, which is widely available. The dish will not have the same texture as it does when made with dried cod, but the flavor and ease of preparation make it equally appealing.

Serves 4–6

1/2 pound boneless salt cod, or 1 pound fresh cod fillets
2 ounces bacon, finely chopped
1 tablespoon vegetable oil
1 yellow onion, finely chopped
1/4 teaspoon dried thyme, crushed
1 can (19 ounces) ackee, drained
3 or 4 Roma tomatoes, seeded and cut into wedges
salt, if using fresh cod
ground black pepper

If using salt cod, place it in a bowl with cold water to cover for 10–12 hours. To maximize desalting, change the water every few hours. Drain and rinse the cod. Place the cod in a saucepan, add cold water to cover, and bring to a boil. Reduce the heat to medium and cook, uncovered, until the fish flakes easily, 20–30 minutes. Remove from the water and, when cool enough to handle, flake the fish, checking carefully for any errant bones. Set aside.

If using fresh cod, cut the fillets into 1/2-inch pieces. Place in a skillet and add water to a depth of about 1/4 inch. Cover and cook over medium heat until the fish flakes and is opaque throughout, about 5 minutes. Remove from the water and when cool enough to handle, chop it finely. Set aside.

Although the indigenous annatto is not found extensively in African-Caribbean cooking, the seed turns up occasionally to color dishes such as Stamp and Go (pages 44–45) and the meat for Jamaican Meat Patties (page 57).

The bright red seed grows on a short green bush. The Arawaks used it to make a paste for spreading on their bodies as an insect repellent. When the Europeans first saw the Amerindians with annatto on their skin, they called them redskins.

In a skillet over medium heat, fry the bacon until crisp. Using a slotted spoon, transfer the crisp bacon bits to a bowl and set aside. Drain off the fat.

In the same skillet, warm the oil over low heat. Add the onion and sauté until very soft, 5–6 minutes. Add the salt or fresh cod and the reserved bacon. Sprinkle with the thyme, and pour the ackee over the top. Stir in the tomatoes, and add salt to taste, if using fresh cod. Season with pepper, heat through, and serve.

Oven-Roasted Peanuts

In Jamaica, peanut shells have a rusty color when harvested because of the high concentration of bauxite in the soil. In all African-influenced cooking, peanuts play a vital high protein role as a snack and in sauces and stews. They must be cooked before being eaten, and this simple roasting prepares them for eating right away or for using in a dish such as Lamb or Chicken Peanut Stew (pages 262–263) in the Recent African Immigrants chapter.

Serves 4–6

2 pounds raw peanuts in the shell

Preheat an oven to 350 degrees F.

Spread the peanuts on a baking sheet in a single layer. Roast until the shells are crisp and the peanuts are cooked through, about 20 minutes. Check by opening one and tasting. Let cool and serve.

Peanuts traveled from the American mainland to the Caribbean, and also to Africa, where they were quickly embraced as a major crop. Next to garbanzos (chick-peas), peanuts yield the highest percentage of protein per acre. Although the peanut itself grows underground, it is actually attached to a tendril that flowers from the plant and then shoots into the earth.

Stamp and Go

Although salt cod cakes are common on all the islands, their Jamaican name, stamp and go, is the most celebrated. Diane McIntyre-Pike, director of Countrystyle Limited, a community-oriented tourism program, and proprietor of Astra Country Inn in Mandeville, Jamaica, explains that the name comes from the motion of "stamping out the cake between your hands so you can quickly fry it and go." Another explanation suggests that the name refers to a British naval order for directing sailors to disembark.

Here, as in the recipe for Codfish and Ackee on pages 42–43, directions for using salt cod or fresh cod are given. The annatto oil for sautéing the ingredients gives the cakes their characteristic orange color. These are typically eaten for breakfast with Boiled Green Bananas (page 30), Steamed African Yams (page 31), and Bakes (page 59). Or serve them for dinner with one of the West Indian hot sauces.

Makes six 3-inch cakes; serves 3–6

3/4 pound boneless salt cod, or 1 pound fresh cod fillets
2 tablespoons annatto oil (see Glossary) or vegetable oil
6 green onions, including tops, finely chopped
1 small fresh green or red chile, seeded and minced (see Glossary)
2 large garlic cloves, minced
1/2 teaspoon chopped fresh thyme
1 egg, lightly beaten
1 cup all-purpose flour
1 teaspoon baking powder
1/2 cup milk or coconut milk
salt
minced fresh parsley
2–4 tablespoons vegetable oil

If using salt cod, place it in a bowl with cold water to cover 10–12 hours. To maximize desalting, change the water every few hours. Drain and rinse the cod. Place the cod in a saucepan, add cold water to cover, and bring to a boil. Reduce the heat to medium and cook, uncovered, until the fish flakes easily, 20–30 minutes. Remove from the water and, when cool enough to handle, flake the fish, checking carefully for any errant bones. Place in a bowl.

If using fresh cod, check the fillet carefully and discard any errant bones, then finely chop the cod and place in a bowl.

In a heavy skillet over medium heat, warm the annatto oil. Add the green onions and chile and sauté until softened, about 3 minutes. Stir in the garlic and sauté 30 seconds longer. Add the onion mixture to the cod and then stir in the thyme, egg, flour, baking powder, and milk. Add salt to taste and mix well.

In a large, nonstick skillet over medium-high heat, warm 2 tablespoons of the vegetable oil. Spoon the cod mixture into the skillet to form 3-inch patties. Fry the cakes, turning once, until browned on both sides, about 3 minutes on each side. Transfer to paper towels to drain. Serve hot or at room temperature.

Shrimp-Potato Fritters

You can deep-fry these popular fritters or, to reduce the fat, you can form the mixture into patties and cook them in a small amount of oil in a nonstick skillet. They will come out equally colorful and delicious. Serve with West Indian Hot Sauce (page 23) or Mango Relish (page 25).

Makes about thirty 1½-inch fritters, or 6 patties

1 pound potatoes, peeled and cut into 2-inch chunks (or 2 cups mashed
    potatoes)
3 tablespoons butter
¾ pound medium shrimp, peeled and deveined
4 green onions, including tops, finely chopped
1 red or green bell pepper (or one-half of each), seeded and finely
    chopped
1 small fresh red or green chile, seeded and finely chopped (see Glossary)
2 eggs, beaten
salt and ground white pepper
½–1 cup fine dried bread crumbs, or more as needed
peanut oil or vegetable oil for deep-frying

Place the potatoes in a saucepan with water to cover generously and bring to a boil. Boil until tender, about 10 minutes. Drain and either place in a bowl and mash with a potato masher or fork, or pass through a food mill set over a bowl. (If using mashed potatoes, skip this step.)

In a skillet over medium heat, melt the butter. Add the shrimp and sauté until pink, 2–3 minutes, depending upon size. Using a slotted spoon, remove from the skillet and chop into small pieces. Set aside.

To the butter remaining in the skillet, add the green onions, bell pepper, and chile. Sauté over medium heat until softened but the color is still bright, about 3 minutes. Add to the potatoes and mix well. Stir in the shrimp and the eggs. Season to taste with salt and pepper. Stir in some of the bread crumbs if needed to make dough stiff enough to form into balls.

Shape the mixture into 2-inch balls. Put the bread crumbs in a saucer. Roll the potato balls in the crumbs. Cover and chill at least 30 minutes or up to 4 hours.

In a deep-fryer or deep heavy pot, pour in oil to a depth of 3 inches. Heat until very hot (375 degrees F). To check the temperature, dip a corner of a potato ball or a piece of bread into the oil. If it immediately sizzles and tiny

Cuba takes its name from the Amerindian word Cubanacan. The island is the largest and most western of the West Indies. Its turbulent history under Spanish rule until 1898 was exacerbated by a nearly permanent state of revolution by both slaves and colonists. Cuban slavery wasn't abolished until 1880. Sugar is still the largest cash crop. Tobacco, citrus fruits, pineapple, coconuts, and coffee follow.

bubbles form around it, it is ready. Fry the balls, 3 or 4 at a time, until very brown and crisp, about 4 minutes. Using a slotted spoon, retrieve the balls and drain on a rack or on paper towels.

Serve immediately.

Steamed Whole Fish with Aromatic Spices

Steaming is a favored method of cooking fish in the Caribbean. Whether wrapped in banana leaves and steamed in their own juices over charcoal or placed in a steamer over simmering water on the stove, whole fish retain their shape and texture. In Haiti *poisson grossel* marries the fish with onions, shallots, and garlic. Here, in a dish known as *poisson aux aromates*, a whole fish is rubbed with Bajan-style fish paste before steaming. Try keeping the fish upright when cooking and serving, as it makes a particularly nice presentation. Serve with Pigeon Peas and Rice (page 35) and Baked Chayote (page 32). Save the fish bones to make a spicy stock (see Glossary).

Serves 4–6

1 whole snapper or other firm-fleshed fish, 4–6 pounds, cleaned
1½ recipes Bajan Fish Spice (page 27) or All-Purpose Caribbean Spice
  Blend (page 26)
½ yellow onion, sliced

Cut diagonal slashes along both sides of the fish. Rub the spice blend into the slashes, over the entire fish, and inside the cavity. Place the onion slices inside the cavity. Let stand 15 minutes or so.

In a pan with a steamer rack big enough to hold the fish, pour water to reach just under the rack. Bring the water to a boil and place the fish upright, cavity down, on the rack. Reduce heat to medium, place a lid on the pan, and cook until the fish is firm to the touch and cooked through when tested with a fork, 20–30 minutes.

Remove the rack with the fish on it from the pan and gently slide the fish onto a serving platter without knocking it over. Serve hot.

VARIATION: A whole fish seasoned this way can also be grilled over hot coals or baked in the oven. If grilling, cook on each side about 15 minutes. For baking, place on a baking sheet in a 375 degree F oven for 30–40 minutes.

Avocados, native to Central and South America, grow to the size of footballs on the English islands, where they are known as alligator pears. Mounds of the pale green-fleshed fruits fill the markets year-round. They are eaten sliced and sprinkled with a simple squeeze of lime juice to cool chile-spiked dishes, or combined in guacamolelike sauces such as feroce d'avocats, *popular in the French West Indies.*

Haitian Gumbo

Inspired by the gumbo made by Gerard Noel at La Belle Creole, his restaurant in Emeryville, California, this delicately balanced stew exhibits both French and African heritages. The allspice-scented broth is thickened with a little flour and file. I like eating the fish, meat, and vegetables first, and then dumping the rice and beans into the sauce to sop up every drop. At the restaurant, garlic French bread and Fried Plantains (page 29) or bananas are served on the side.

The amount and kinds of seafood and meat depends on how fancy or homey you want the gumbo to be. It can include blue crabs, Dungeness crab legs, oysters, mussels, chicken breasts or thighs, and any favorite sausage. Or it can be all chicken, all seafood, or perhaps sausage only. Even the vegetables can be varied. Simply put, you can personalize gumbo according to taste and pocketbook. Serve it with Haitian Red Beans and Rice (page 36).

Serves 6–8

2 tablespoons olive oil or vegetable oil

1 yellow onion, finely chopped
4 green onions, including tops, chopped
2 celery stalks, finely chopped
1 green bell pepper, seeded and finely chopped
1 or 2 small fresh red or green chiles, seeded and finely chopped
    (see Glossary)
3 garlic cloves, minced
2 teaspoons ground allspice
1 teaspoon ground black pepper
1 tablespoon dried sage, crushed
2 tablespoons all-purpose flour
8 cups chicken stock (see Glossary) or water
1^1/$_2$ teaspoons ground thyme
^{1}/$_4$ cup tomato paste
salt
6 chicken thighs or breasts, boned, skinned, and cut into 2-inch pieces
8–10 ounces creole or other spicy sausage links, sliced into
    ^{1}/$_2$-inch-thick rounds
^{1}/$_2$ pound okra, sliced or whole
1 cup corn kernels (from 2 ears)
^{1}/$_4$–^{1}/$_2$ pound medium shrimp in the shell

Conch comes from the large, pink ruffled shell we hold to an ear to hear the ocean. In the nineteenth century, the shells were shipped to England and used to make cameos. The snaillike flesh, commonly referred to as lambi in the Caribbean, is very tough and has to be pounded like abalone. It is usually cut up and fried or sautéed, marinated, and served in salads.

¹/₂–2 pounds assorted shellfish such as whole blue crabs, crab legs,
mussels, oysters, clams, crawfish, conch, and lobster tails in their
shells, in any combination (optional)
1 tablespoon file powder

In large, heavy pot over medium-high heat, warm the olive oil. Add the
yellow and green onions, celery, bell pepper, and chiles and sauté until softened,
about 5 minutes. Stir in the garlic and cook 1 minute. Stir in the allspice, black
pepper, sage, and flour and cook 1 minute, stirring all the while. Slowly stir in
the stock, then add the ground thyme, tomato paste, and salt to taste. Raise the
heat and bring just to a boil. Reduce the heat to medium and simmer 15 minutes
to blend the flavors.

Add the chicken pieces to the broth and continue to simmer until just
done, about 10-15 minutes. Using a slotted spoon, remove the chicken pieces
to a plate.

Add the sausage to the broth and simmer until cooked, 5–10 minutes.
Add the okra and corn and continue to simmer 5 minutes. Return the chicken to
the pot. Stir in the shrimp and other shellfish, if using, and simmer until done,
5–10 minutes longer.

In a small bowl, stir together a little of the hot broth and the file and
then stir the mixture into the pot. Taste and adjust the seasonings. Serve hot.

Pickled Fish

Pickled fish is found on all the islands and goes by a variety of names, including *escabeche* and *escovitch*. The various methods have come from the Africans, the Spanish, and the Portuguese, all of whom used pickling as a method to preserve a big catch. In this Caribbean adaptation, a jerk seasoning is combined with extra allspice and a hit of Scotch Bonnet red hot-pepper sauce to sock a powerful spike to the vinegar sauce.

Serves 6

1 tablespoon Jerk Seasoning (page 211, dry mixture only), or
    1 teaspoon cayenne pepper
$^1/_2$ teaspoon salt
ground black pepper
6 red snapper or other firm, boneless, white fish fillets
2 tablespoons vegetable oil
2 yellow onions, thinly sliced
1 green bell pepper, seeded and thinly sliced
1 red bell pepper, seeded and thinly sliced
2 teaspoons whole allspice
$^3/_4$ cup white wine vinegar or cider vinegar
$^1/_4$ cup water
1 bay leaf
1–2 teaspoons Trinidad or Papa Joe's brand Scotch Bonnet
    red hot-pepper sauce or Tabasco sauce

Sprinkle the Jerk Seasoning, salt and the black pepper evenly on both sides of the fish fillets.

In a large skillet, heat the oil until very hot. Add the fish fillets and sear quickly to brown each side. Transfer the fish to a shallow dish, arranging it in a single layer.

Pour off the oil from the pan. Add all the remaining ingredients to the pan and bring to a boil. Reduce the heat to medium-low and simmer, uncovered, 10 minutes.

Pour the vinegar mixture over the fish. Let cool, cover, and refrigerate overnight. Serve the next day. This will keep refrigerated for 3 days but the fish flavor will change noticeably the longer it is kept.

Curaçao, Aruba, Bonaire, St. Eustatius, Saba, and the southern part of St. Maarten are known as the Netherlands or Dutch Antilles and share an African-Dutch-Caribbean culture. The Dutch fondness for the Indonesian rijsttafel, or "rice table," is found on these islands, but here the various dishes are made with Caribbean roots and fruits and spiked with African hot sauces.

Caribbean Fried Chicken

Here is a version of fried chicken that is much like the one served at Cheap Charlie's, a roadside stand about fifteen miles inland from Montego Bay, Jamaica. Before frying, the chicken parts are marinated overnight in seasoning that includes a cupful or so of stock drawn from the pot bubbling away over a hot charcoal fire. After the parts are fried they are hacked into two-inch pieces with a cleaver or other heavy knife. For this adaptation, the chicken is cut into small pieces before cooking.

Serve the chicken with Pigeon Peas and Rice (page 35) or Cornmeal with Okra (page 38).

Serves 4

2¹/₂ pounds favorite chicken parts
3 green onions, including tops, chopped
¹/₂ yellow onion, sliced
1 inch fresh ginger, peeled and chopped
leaves from 3 fresh thyme sprigs, chopped, or 2 teaspoons dried thyme, crushed
1 whole Scotch Bonnet (habanero) or other fresh chile, or 1 teaspoon Papa Joe's brand Scotch Bonnet red hot-pepper sauce
1 cup chicken stock (see Glossary)
1 cup all-purpose flour mixed with 1 tablespoon paprika, 1 tablespoon garlic powder, ¹/₂ teaspoon cayenne or other ground red chile powder, 1 teaspoon salt, and ¹/₂ teaspoon ground white pepper
peanut oil for deep-frying

Using a cleaver or other heavy knife, cut chicken legs, thighs, and breasts in half. Remove the skin. In a large bowl or covered plastic container, combine the chicken parts, the green and yellow onions, ginger, thyme, chile, and chicken stock. Toss to coat chicken well, cover, and marinate in the refrigerator overnight, turning the chicken pieces occasionally.

When ready to fry, remove the chicken from the marinade. Place the flour mixture on a plate or in a paper bag. Dredge or shake the chicken pieces in the flour and set on a plate.

In a deep-fryer or other heavy pot, pour in oil to a depth of 3 inches and heat until almost smoking, about 375 degrees F. Add the chicken, a few pieces at a time, and fry until brown, crispy, and cooked through, about 15 minutes. With a pair of tongs, retrieve the chicken pieces and drain on a rack or on paper towels. Serve at once.

The cutlass, or cutlash as it is called in Jamaica, is an indispensable tool on all of the islands. This curved, sturdy swordlike knife was originally used on ships by sailors, who brought them ashore where they were adopted by the islanders. In rural areas, many people walk along the roads carrying a cutlass. It is handy for opening coconuts, cutting a stalk of sugarcane, and harvesting pineapples, mangoes, and breadfruit. In the markets it is used for butchering meat and poultry. And in restaurants and roadside cafes, the cook uses a cutlass to hack cooked chicken or goat into serving pieces.

Spiced Chicken

An everyday dish that combines the distinctive spices of African-Caribbean cooking, chicken like this is sold at roadside stands like the Cook House next to the Craft Market in downtown Montego Bay. Serve it with Haitian Red Beans and Rice (page 36) or with plain steamed rice.

Serves 4

2–3 pounds favorite chicken parts (see Glossary)
1 yellow onion, coarsely chopped
$^1/_2$ inch fresh ginger, peeled and chopped
3 garlic cloves, minced
1 tablespoon paprika
1 teaspoon ground turmeric
2 teaspoons whole cumin seeds, or $1^1/_2$ teaspoons ground cumin
$^1/_2$ teaspoon ground cinnamon
1 whole clove
1 teaspoon salt
$^1/_2$ teaspoon ground black pepper
2 tablespoons vegetable oil
6 large tomatoes, peeled and chopped, or 1 can (16 ounces) tomatoes
    with their juice, chopped
$^1/_2$–1 cup water

Skin and defat chicken parts. (To prepare in the traditional manner, cut the chicken through the bones into 2-inch pieces, or as directed in the Glossary.)

In a blender or food processor, combine the onion, ginger, garlic, paprika, turmeric, cumin, cinnamon, clove, salt, and pepper. Purée to a thick consistency. Using your hands, rub the mixture evenly all over the chicken parts.

In a heavy skillet or dutch oven, heat the oil over high heat until almost smoking. Add the chicken, a few pieces at a time, and brown well on all sides. Using tongs, remove the chicken to a platter.

When all the chicken is browned, add the tomatoes and $^1/_2$ cup water to the pan and bring to a boil, stirring well to scrape up browned bits on the bottom of the pan. Return the chicken to the pan. Cook over medium heat, turning occasionally, until chicken is thoroughly cooked, 25–35 minutes. Add additional water if needed to keep the mixture saucy.

Serve hot.

Barbados, a British possession for 350 years until 1966, got its name from a Portuguese sailor. He named it "the bearded ones," after the banyan trees with their shaggy exposed roots that dip into the sea along the shoreline. It is bounded on the east by the rough Atlantic Ocean and on the west by the placid Caribbean Sea. The thin, silvery flying fish is the national food and is prepared broiled, baked, fried, or in stews. To catch it, fishermen interweave palm fronds and lay them on the water's surface. The fish, seeing it as land and a place to lay their eggs, fly up and into it and are trapped.

Caramel flavoring is found in all the New World African-inspired cooking because sugar was a ready commodity. When the sugar is cooked slowly until caramelized, its sweetness is replaced by a rich earthy flavor and dark color that add depth to gravies and stews. In the Caribbean the mixture is called "browning." To make a caramel flavoring for adding to gravies and other preparations, heat 2 cups sugar in a heavy saucepan over medium-low heat. Stir continuously until the sugar melts and turns brown and syrupy. Add 1 cup boiling water to the caramelized sugar and heat until combined. Cool and store in a dark, cool cupboard or in the refrigerator.

Curried Goat

A love of curry came to the West Indies first with the Dutch colonists and later with thousands of indentured East Indians. Because Arab traders had brought seasonings to West Africa, these flavors were not strange to the African-Caribbeans, who stewed goat, chicken, and fish in spicy yellow sauces. In the French-speaking islands, curry is called *colombo*.

Whenever you add a curry blend or a similar spice mixture to a dish, it is important to sauté it before the liquid is added. Sautéing releases the oils and brings out the flavors of the spices.

Typically the goat is cut into pieces on the bone and is cooked that way. If you can't find goat cut like this, use boneless goat or use lamb shoulder, which will take about half as long to cook. Serve with rice.

Serves 6

> 3–4 pounds goat meat on the bone, cut into 1-inch pieces, or 2¹/₂ pounds
>   boneless goat leg or lamb shoulder, cut into 1-inch cubes
> 4 tablespoons vegetable oil
> 2 yellow onions, chopped
> 3 garlic cloves, minced
> 1 teaspoon ground allspice
> 1 small fresh red or green chile, minced (see Glossary)
> 3 tablespoons Curry Blend (page 28) or favorite Caribbean curry powder
> 1 teaspoon salt
> ground black pepper
> 2 cups water

In a bowl, combine the goat, 2 tablespoons of the oil, onions, garlic, allspice, chile, curry powder, salt, and black pepper to taste. Toss to coat meat well, cover, and refrigerate 2 hours or overnight.

In a large, heavy skillet over high heat, warm the remaining 2 table-spoons oil. Remove the meat from the marinade, reserving the marinade. Add the meat to the skillet, a few pieces at a time, and brown until well colored on all sides. Using tongs, remove to a plate. When all of the meat is browned, return it to the pan along with the marinade and sauté over high heat 30 seconds to bring out the flavor of the spices. Slowly add the water, scraping the bottom of the pan to dislodge any browned bits. Cover and simmer over medium-low heat, stirring occasionally, until very tender, about 2 hours (1 hour if using lamb).

Serve the curry hot.

CURRIED CHICKEN VARIATION: Cut up a whole chicken into 2-inch pieces (see Glossary). Proceed as directed, but reduce the cooking time to 40–50 minutes.

CURRIED FISH VARIATION: Cut 2 pounds firm fish fillets into 2-inch chunks and mix with marinade ingredients as directed, but marinate only 30–60 minutes. Proceed as directed, but reduce the cooking time to 15–20 minutes.

Goat, an easily raised animal because of its scavenger eating habits, has long been cooked by Africans for both everyday fare and in ceremonial dishes. In Montserrat and Antigua, stew is commonly referred to as "goat water."

A jar of bird chiles is a convenient way to ensure red chiles are always on hand. They are packed in vinegar, but the color and pungency of the chiles overwhelms the vinegar, so they can be used in any recipe calling for red chiles.

Curried Pork and Vegetables

Colombo de cochon is the name for curried pork in Martinique. It is also a popular dish in Jamaica. Curry complements strong-flavored meats, which is why it is traditionally paired with goat. But pork and curry are also a good match, as this scintillating vegetable-rich yellow sauce with strips of spinach and flecks of red chiles illustrates. Serve it with Haitian Rice (page 37).

Serves 6–8

3–4 pounds boneless pork shoulder, trimmed and cut into 1-inch cubes
1½ tablespoons Curry Blend (page 28) or favorite Caribbean curry powder
3 tablespoons olive oil or vegetable oil
salt and ground black pepper
2 yellow onions, chopped
4 garlic cloves, minced
1 or 2 fresh red or green chiles, seeded and minced (see Glossary)
6 cups water
1 small Japanese eggplant, cut into small cubes
1 chayote, peeled, seeded, and cut into small cubes
½ pound callaloo, chard, collard greens, or spinach leaves, shredded
2 limes, quartered

In a bowl, combine the pork cubes and curry powder and mix well. Cover and refrigerate at least 1 hour or overnight.

In a large heavy pot over high heat, warm the oil. Add the meat, a few pieces at a time, and brown until well colored on all sides. Using tongs, remove to a plate. Season with salt and pepper.

Add the onions and garlic to the pan and sauté until browned, about 5 minutes. Add the chiles and return the meat to the pan. Pour in the water and stir well. Cook over medium-low heat until the meat is tender, 30–40 minutes.

When the meat is tender, add the eggplant and chayote. Cook until tender, about 8 minutes. Stir in the callaloo and cook until wilted but still bright green, about 5 minutes.

Taste and adjust the seasonings. Serve with lime wedges.

In the Caribbean, as in all African cooking in America, pork is the favored meat. For holidays such as Maroon Independence Day, celebrated on January 6, a whole pig is spit-roasted over a pit in the same way it has been done since the first Maroons escaped the slave ships upon arrival in Jamaica three hundred years ago. Melville Currie, who has lived all of his sixty-plus years in the autonomous Maroon village of Accompong, told about stuffing the pig with "yams, bananas, bread, callaloo, scallions, thyme, pimento [allspice], peppers, cabbage, ginger, and bammies [cassava bread]." The cooked pork is served with roasted or boiled yams and plantains. Everything is prepared Rastafarian style with "no salt."

Ham is the centerpiece at Christmas. Traditionally it was sealed in tar and boiled for hours over a wood fire. Once cracked open, the skin was saved for beans or greens and the meat sliced and served with boiled yams and pigeon peas and rice.

Caribbean Meatballs

Spanish influence is found in this Caribbean adaptation of *albóndigas*. Here, the meatballs are seasoned with jerk spices and hints of allspice and cinnamon. This memorable combination is an excellent party dish, good for carrying along to a potluck buffet. Serve with Pigeon Peas and Rice (page 35), Haitian Rice (page 37), or Cornmeal with Okra (page 38).

Makes about sixty 1½-inch meatballs

2½ pounds ground beef
1 pound bulk pork sausage
3 ounces cooked ham, finely chopped
1 yellow onion, finely chopped
4 green onions, including tops, chopped
1 tablespoon ground allspice
1½ teaspoons ground cinnamon
¼–½ cups Jerk Seasoning (page 211, dry mixture only)
2 eggs
¾–1½ cups fine dried bread crumbs
salt and ground black pepper to taste
3 tablespoons vegetable oil
3 cups coconut milk

In a bowl, combine all of the ingredients, except the oil and coconut milk. Use as much of the bread crumbs as needed to form a good consistency for shaping into small balls. Form the mixture into small balls about 1¼ inches in diameter.

In a heavy 10-inch skillet over high heat, warm the oil. Brown the meatballs in about 4 batches. They should be well browned and cooked until almost done; this will take about 10 minutes per batch. (To speed up the process use two 12-inch skillets.) To test for doneness, push against a meatball with your fingertip. It should feel slightly firm with only a little resistance. Using tongs, remove to a plate.

When all the meatballs are browned, pour the coconut milk into the pan and deglaze over high heat, stirring to scrape up any browned bits.

Return the meatballs to the pan with the coconut milk. Heat through and serve.

The Dominican Republic, independent since 1844, was under Spanish, French, and Haitian rule at various intervals from the time of its discovery by Columbus in 1492. Its national dish, sancocho, *is a meat-and-vegetable stew that combines from seven to over eighteen ingredients, depending upon what's on hand and how many will be sharing it.*

Although coconuts originated somewhere in the Pacific tropics (they float and take up root wherever they land), they have been a mainstay in the Atlantic tropical world for five hundred years. They are used young for their refreshing liquid and sweet jellylike flesh and mature for their flesh, oil, and cream. Coconuts also have many nonculinary uses. Coconut fat is used for hair and body creams. The end of the stem is used to chew on for keeping teeth clean. The rough hairy inside of the shell makes a terrific scrub brush. And the palms and trunks have been used to build shelters.

Jamaican Meat Pastries

Fried meat-filled pastries, known as meat patties in Jamaica and *empanadas* on the Spanish islands, are popular snacks. The pastry can be fried in the traditional manner or, to cut down on the amount of fat, baked with equally good results. These half-moon pies can also be filled with Cuban Picadillo (pages 58–59.)

Makes about twelve 4-inch-wide pies

For the pastry:
3 cups all-purpose flour
1/2 teaspoon salt
1/2 teaspoon baking powder
1/2 teaspoon ground turmeric (optional)
2/3 cup shortening or lard
2/3 cup cold water

1 recipe Jamaican Meat Patty Filling (page 57) or
Picadillo (pages 58–59)
peanut oil for deep-frying

To make the pastry, in a mixing bowl, combine the flour, salt, baking powder, and turmeric. Using a pastry blender or fork, cut in the shortening until the mixture resembles coarse meal. Stir in the water and, using a fork or fingers, mix to form a ball.

Take walnut-sized pieces of dough and roll them out on a lightly floured board to make 4-inch circles. Place a couple of tablespoons of the filling in the center of each circle. Fold the pastry in half and pinch to seal the edges with the tines of a fork.

If frying the pastries, in a deep-fryer or heavy deep pot, pour in the oil to a depth of 2½ inches. Heat until almost smoking, about 375 degrees F. When the oil is hot enough to make a corner of the dough sizzle, carefully drop in 1 or 2 of the pastries. Fry, turning once, until golden brown, about 5 minutes. Using a slotted spoon, remove to a rack or paper towels to drain. Repeat with the remaining pastries.

If baking the pastries, preheat an oven to 400 degrees F. Place the pastries on an ungreased baking sheet and bake until golden brown, 25–35 minutes. If they don't brown on the tops, turn on the broiler for a few minutes at the end of cooking to give them a nice brown finish. Serve the pastries hot or at room temperature.

In Trinidad, baked cornmeal pastries filled with spicy meat mixtures are called pasteles; when fried, they are called arepas.

In the 1600s, on Montserrat, a British protectorate, a large group of Irish colonists arrived, bought slaves, and attempted to develop a major export agriculture based on vegetable farms and sugar and lime plantations. The terrain proved too rugged for success, however, and the tiny island remained isolated for centuries. The most popular dish is "goat water," a stew of goat meat mixed with vegetables grown in gardens that continue to produce well for the local population.

The Dutch St. Maarten and the French St. Martin are on the smallest parcel of land shared by two different nations anywhere in the world. Home cooking, which includes cod fritters, corn mush, rice and beans, steamed yams, and fish stews, is similar to that served on all of the islands. Restaurants on either side of the island stress regional differences. On the Dutch side the adopted Indonesian rijsttafel or "rice table" is served at Wajang Doll in Philipsburg. On the French side, La Rhumerie, near Colombier, serves French escargots and canard à l'orange next to West Indian colombos, conch, and spicy vegetables.

Jamaican Meat Patty Filling

The heritage of Jamaica's popular snack stems from the Cornish pasties of Britain, but the chile-laced filling is pure African-Caribbean. This filling can also be served as an entrée with Pigeon Peas and Rice (page 35) or Haitian Red Beans and Rice (page 36).

Makes enough to fill 12 pastries; serves 4–6

1 1/2 pounds ground pork, beef, chicken, or turkey
2 tablespoons annatto oil (see Glossary) or vegetable oil
4 green onions, including tops, finely chopped
1 yellow onion, chopped
1 fresh green or red chile, minced (see Glossary)
2 garlic cloves, minced
1 teaspoon paprika
2 teaspoons chopped fresh thyme, or 1/2 teaspoon dried thyme, crushed
1/4 teaspoon ground allspice
dash of ground cloves
1 cup canned tomato sauce
2–4 tablespoons fine dried bread crumbs
salt and ground black pepper

In a nonstick skillet over high heat, brown the meat until crumbly, about 8 minutes for pork or beef and 5 minutes for chicken or turkey. Using a slotted spoon, remove the meat to paper towels to drain. Discard any fat remaining in the skillet.

In the same skillet over medium heat, warm the oil. Add the green and yellow onions and chile and sauté until the chile is softened, about 4 minutes. Stir in the garlic, paprika, thyme, allspice, and cloves and sauté for 30 seconds. Stir in the tomato sauce, return the meat to the skillet, and reduce the heat to low. Stir in 2 tablespoons of the bread crumbs (add more bread crumbs later if needed to thicken the mixture enough to stand by itself on the pastry) and season to taste with salt and pepper. Continue cooking over low heat, stirring occasionally, for 20 minutes to blend the flavors. Serve immediately as an entrée or let cool to room temperature and use for filling pastries.

Grenada has been held by the French and by the English, from whom it gained independence in 1974. A microcosm of all the Caribbean Islands, it is blessed with exceptionally lush greenery, pristine beaches, imposing volcanic mountains, and a sublime climate. Its chief export is nutmeg, which was brought from the East Indies and planted by an English sailor in 1843. Mace, the lacy red outer covering of the nutmeg, is also ground and sold as a spice all over the world. Grenada produces about 40 percent of the world's nutmeg.

Martinique, known as the France of the Caribbean, is an autonomous French department with representation in the French parliament. Although France outlawed slavery at home in the late 1700s, it wasn't abolished in Martinique until the late 1800s. This is because Napoleon's empress, Josephine, who was from Martinique, asked him to reinstate it to help her family's plantation.

Cuban Picadillo

Picadillo is the Spanish word for "hash." This spicy beef dish from Cuba, which is also found on the other Spanish islands, exemplifies the island nation's mixed heritage. Beef was introduced to the New World by the Spaniards, who also contributed the vinegar, olives, and raisins to this recipe. The dish is seasoned with chiles and achiote, two ingredients from the Caribbean. The result is a mixture with a pungency that recalls African one-pot stews. When *picadillo* is used for filling *empanadas* (see page 56), the savory pastries are reminiscent of African and Portuguese fritters. It can also be served as a stew with Steamed African Yams (page 31), Cornmeal with Okra (page 38), or with Pigeon Peas and Rice (page 35).

Makes enough filling for 12 pastries; serves 4–6

2 pounds beef chuck, trimmed of fat and cut into 1/2-inch cubes
11/2 tablespoons achiote paste (see annatto in Glossary), or a mixture of
    11/2 tablespoons paprika, 1/2 teaspoon ground oregano, 1/2 teaspoon
    ground sage, 1 teaspoon garlic powder, 1/2 teaspoon ground ginger,
    dash of sugar, and 1/2 teaspoon salt
2 tablespoons vegetable oil
1 yellow onion, finely chopped
3 garlic cloves, minced
1 green bell pepper, seeded and finely chopped
1 or 2 red or green chiles, minced (see Glossary)
6 large tomatoes, peeled, seeded, and chopped, or 1 can (16 ounces)
    tomatoes, with their juices, seeded and chopped
3 tablespoons red wine vinegar
1 cup water
1/4 cup raisins, chopped
1/3 cup pitted green olives, chopped
salt and cayenne pepper

In a bowl, combine the beef and achiote paste (or seasonings) and, using your hands, toss well to coat meat on all sides.

In a cast-iron or other heavy skillet over high heat, warm the oil. Add the beef, one-third at a time, and brown until dark and crisp on all sides, about 6 minutes for each batch. Reserve the meat on a plate.

When all the meat has been browned, reduce the heat to medium and add the onion, garlic, bell pepper, and chile and sauté until softened, about

The melding of French and African reverence for good eating is exemplified in the cooking of the French West Indies, where the same food is served in homes and restaurants alike. African know-how combined with French refinements and Caribbean seasoning has resulted in the creation of one of the world's premier cooking styles. Examples of African-French creole dishes include *accras*, the African bean fritters that are called *accras pois* in Martinique and are also made with pumpkin (*accras de giraumon*) and eggplant (*accras aubergine*). Another is *blaff*, a citrus-based fish dish similar to Senegalese *yassa* that is flavored with French thyme and Caribbean limes. *Crabes farçis* are land crabs (originally from Africa), stuffed *à la française* with bread crumbs and spiked with indigenous chiles.

5 minutes. Return the meat and any juices to the pan. Stir in the tomatoes, vinegar, water, raisins, and olives. Cover and simmer, stirring occasionally, until the meat is very tender, 30–45 minutes.

Serve hot as an entrée or let cool to room temperature if using to fill pastries.

Bakes

In Trinidad and Tobago, these fried flattened rolls are sold on street corners and eaten all day long. In Jamaica a similar dough is made into round dumplings, fried, and served for breakfast with a little butter and guava jelly. Although they are fried, bakes take their name from the days when they were baked on hot stones on the hearth. The dough for these is reminiscent of Benny's Hoecake (page 141) in the Soul Food chapter, and like the hoecakes, these could be "baked" on a cast-iron skillet or griddle instead of fried.

Makes about 16

2 cups all-purpose flour
1/2 teaspoon salt
2 teaspoons baking powder
3 tablespoons shortening
2 teaspoons sugar
3–4 tablespoons water
peanut oil or vegetable oil for deep-frying

In a bowl, combine the flour, salt, and baking powder and mix well. With a pastry blender, a fork, or your fingers, cut in the shortening until the dough resembles coarse meal. Dissolve the sugar in 3 tablespoons of the water and pour into the dough. Mix with your fingers to form a ball, adding the last tablespoon of water if the dough is too dry. Knead lightly.

Pinch off walnut-sized pieces of the dough and roll them into perfect balls between your palms. Flatten into rounds about 1/4 inch thick.

In a deep-fryer or heavy, deep pot, pour in oil to a depth of 3 inches and heat to 375 degrees F. Using a slotted spoon, carefully slip the rounds into the hot oil, a few at a time, and cook, turning frequently, until browned, about 2 minutes. Using the slotted spoon, retrieve the breads and set on a rack or paper towels to drain. Repeat with the remaining dough rounds. Serve hot.

Bammie, the popular Jamaican cassava cake, comes from the West African word bambula, which means both a cake and a type of dance. The process for making these indispensable breads was shared by the Arawaks, who used the indigenous cassava root as a starch and as a vegetable, as well as for making breads. Keith Riley, a bartender at the Mandeville Hotel in Mandeville, Jamaica, explained that these cakes are made from the bitter cassava, which is grated and squeezed to remove the toxic liquid. The liquid is used to make starch for clothes, and the pulp of the cassava is dried and made into bread by pressing it into rings on a hot griddle and cooking until browned.

Banana Coconut Bread

Versions of this Jamaican sweet bread are found on all the islands. On Guadeloupe it is called *pain aux coco et banane*. Use very ripe bananas, as they give the bread the best flavor. Look for unsweetened dried coconut, available in natural-food stores. I store grated coconut in the freezer so it's on hand when those bananas turn black. If sweetened coconut is used, reduce the sugar to 1/2 or 1/3 cup. This a great breakfast bread, snack for kids, or teatime sweet.

Makes 1 loaf; 10–12 servings

3 very ripe bananas
1/2 cup shortening or butter
3/4 cup sugar
2 eggs
1/2 teaspoon vanilla extract
1 cup all-purpose flour
1 cup whole-wheat flour
1/2 teaspoon salt
1 tablespoon baking powder
1/4 teaspoon freshly grated nutmeg or ground cinnamon
1/3 cup hot water
1 cup unsweetened medium-thread dried coconut

Preheat an oven to 325 degrees F. Grease and flour a 9-by-5-inch loaf pan.

Peel the bananas and place in a small bowl. Using a fork, mash until smooth. You should have 1½ cups.

In another bowl, combine the shortening and sugar and beat with an electric mixer until fluffy. Add the eggs and beat well, then beat in the bananas and vanilla.

In yet another bowl, stir together the flours, salt, baking powder, and nutmeg. Beat the flour mixture into the banana mixture alternately with the hot water, beginning and ending with the flour mixture. When fully incorporated, stir in the coconut. Pour into the prepared loaf pan.

Bake until a thin skewer inserted in the center comes out clean or the top bounces back when lightly touched, about 1 hour and 10 minutes. Remove from the oven and transfer to a rack. Let cool at least 15 minutes, then turn out of the pan and slice to serve. Store wrapped in plastic wrap in the refrigerator up to 5 days.

Tropical Fruit Compote

The plethora of fruit available year-round for the picking contributes to its popularity as dessert all over the Caribbean. Here is a recipe that combines tropical fruits with a syrupy glaze of rum-flavored guava jelly. It is inspired by one that appeared in an old recipe collection from the island of St. Vincent. For a special occasion, serve the compote over Banana Coconut Bread (page 60) and top it with a little whipped cream.

Serves 10–12

2 tablespoons sugar
1/2 cup guava jelly
grated zest of 1 orange
1/2 cup water
2 tablespoons rum
8 cups cubed fruits such as pineapple, mango, orange, banana, papaya,
    lychee, watermelon, melons
shredded dried coconut

In a small saucepan, combine the sugar, guava jelly, orange zest, and water. Bring to a boil and boil 1–2 minutes. Strain and cool, then stir in the rum.

Place the cubed fruits in a serving bowl. Pour the cooled guava mixture over the fruit and, using a wooden spoon, gently toss to mix.

Chill and serve sprinkled with dried coconut.

Coconut Candy

Known as tablette in the Caribbean and *cocada* in Bahia, this confection combines the Spanish and Portuguese penchant for sweets with the African resourcefulness for using available ingredients: sugar from the cane fields and the abundant adopted coconut. Easy to make, these candies have been satisfying sweet tooths in the Caribbean for two centuries.

Makes six 3-inch rounds

2 cups sugar
1/2 cup water
2 cups finely grated fresh or dried unsweetened coconut

Line a baking sheet with parchment paper or waxed paper. Lightly oil it.

In a heavy saucepan over high heat, combine the sugar and water and bring to a boil, stirring occasionally to dissolve the sugar. Cook until it forms a syrup, about 10 minutes. Stir in the coconut and continue cooking, stirring constantly, until it registers 234 degrees F (soft-ball stage) on a candy thermometer, or until a small bit dropped into a glass of ice water holds together and is quite soft when pressed between your fingertips. Remove from the heat.

Drop by spoonfuls onto the prepared baking sheet and flatten to make 3-inch rounds. When cool and firm, wrap individually in plastic wrap. Store in an airtight container up to a week.

Sugarcane came to the Caribbean with Columbus on his second voyage in 1494, when he established the first European settlement in the West Indies on Hispaniola. Unrefined brown sugar was most commonly used in households. It came in foots, hard cylinders that were grated for use.

Fried Bananas

Bananas arrived with the slaves from their native Africa. In the West Indies a comparable climate contributed to their successful propagation. A popular and prolific staple, bananas are eaten green and boiled for breakfast, ripe for snacks all day long, mashed into condiments and sauces, and cooked for dessert. Imported bananas only hint at the potential flavor a freshly picked fruit delivers. There are dozens of banana varieties growing on the islands. I like to use the little sweet yellow- or red-skinned bananas for cooking. Their texture is firmer and the aroma more intense.

Instead of being deep-fried, as are the popular fritters, *beignets*, or *frituras* on English, French, and Spanish islands, these egg-and-coconut-coated bananas are sautéed in a nonstick skillet to minimize the amount of fat.

Serves 4

4 ripe bananas
1 egg, beaten
1 cup unsweetened finely shredded dried coconut
¹/₄ cup butter or canola oil

Peel the bananas and slice them in half lengthwise. Immediately dip the halves into the beaten egg and then roll them in the coconut. Set them in a single layer on a plate and let stand 15 minutes. (They may be refrigerated for up to 6 hours at this point.)

In a nonstick skillet over medium heat, melt the butter until sizzling. Add the bananas, a few halves at a time, and sauté, turning once, until golden on both sides, about 4 minutes' total cooking time. Remove from the pan and keep warm. Repeat with the remaining bananas. Serve hot.

Guadeloupe's Carib name was Karukera, which meant Island of the Beautiful Waters. But Columbus called it Santa Maria de Guadalupe de Estremadura because of a promise he had made to monks at a Spanish monastery of the same name. It and Martinique came under French rule in 1635, and became departments of France in 1946. The fiery creole blend of French and African cooking on Guadeloupe is highlighted at the annual Fêtes des Cuisinières, a festival honoring women chefs held in August. It is celebrated with a parade, and the chefs prepare their specialties to serve at a five-hour feast accompanied with music and dancing.

Lime Meringue Pie

Here is a company dessert from Icilda Pinnock, who lives in Mammee Bay in Jamaica. The egg yolk–rich custard topped with beaten egg whites has its roots in French meringues and in Spanish flans.

Serves 6–8

Pie Crust (page 152)

For the filling:
2 heaping tablespoons cornstarch
1/2 cup sugar
2 cups fresh lime juice (15–20 limes)
4 egg yolks

For the meringue:
2 tablespoons sugar
4 egg whites
juice of 1 lime

Preheat an oven to 350 degrees F.

Prepare the crust according to the directions and remove from the freezer or refrigerator. Using a fork, poke the bottom of the crust in several places. Bake until browned, about 25 minutes. Remove from the oven and set aside to cool. Increase the oven temperature to 375 degrees F.

To make the filling, combine the cornstarch and sugar in a nonreactive saucepan. Strain the lime juice into the pan, stirring to dissolve the cornstarch and sugar. Taste for sweetness. In a small bowl, beat the egg yolks until thickened.

Heat the lime mixture over medium heat until little bubbles begin to form around the edge of the pan, about 5 minutes. Whisk about 1/4 cup of the lime mixture into the egg yolks, and then add the egg yolks to the saucepan. Cook over medium heat, stirring constantly, until thickened, 4–5 minutes. Pour the hot mixture into the baked pie shell.

To make the meringue, place the egg whites in a bowl and beat until soft peaks begin to form, about 3 minutes. Slowly beat in the sugar and lime juice. Continue beating until the sugar dissolves and the egg whites are stiff and glossy, another couple of minutes or so. Spoon the meringue over the pie filling, making sure it covers the filling completely. Using the back of a spoon, fluff up the egg whites to make soft peaks. Bake until the meringue is set and begins to turn golden, 5-8 minutes. Remove from the oven and let cool completely on a wire rack before serving.

In tropical America, cassava and corn continued to be staple starches even after the wheat-loving Europeans arrived. This was true for two reasons. Wheat needs a cooler climate to grow successfully and flour sent from Europe was often infested with weevils by the time the ship sailed into port.

Sweet Potato Pone

The usual yam or sweet potato desserts found in all African-influenced cooking call for the potatoes to be cooked before seasoning and baking. Unlike the *gâteau patate* in Martinique and the *boniatillo* (made from a white sweet potato, the *boniato*) in Cuba, this recipe, adapted from one found on the island of St. Vincent, calls for grating raw sweet potatoes and then seasoning and baking them. This results in a more defined texture that is quite delicious. The pone is sweetened with West Indian molasses and candied ginger. Local production of the latter was initiated by Asian immigrants brought in by the sugar industry after slavery was abolished.

Served 6–8

2 eggs
1/2 cup molasses, preferably from the West Indies
1/2 cup firmly packed brown sugar
1/2 cup butter, melted and cooled
2 or 3 sweet potatoes or garnet yams (1 1/2 pounds), peeled and grated to make 4 cups
2–4 tablespoons candied ginger, finely chopped
grated zest of 1 large orange
juice of 1 orange
dash of salt
3 tablespoons all-purpose flour
ground cinnamon, cloves, and mace

Butter a shallow 2-quart baking dish. Preheat an oven to 375 degrees F.

In a bowl, using an electric mixer or wooden spoon, beat together the eggs, molasses, brown sugar, and butter until smooth. Stir in the sweet potatoes, ginger, orange zest and juice, salt, and flour, mixing well. Season to taste with cinnamon, cloves, and mace.

Pour into the prepared baking dish, cover with aluminum foil, and bake 20 minutes. Remove the foil and bake an additional 10 minutes to crisp the top. Serve hot or at room temperature.

Many of the spices Columbus sought when he came to the West Indies are now grown on the Caribbean Islands with much success. Allspice, which is native to the islands, has been joined by cinnamon, tamarind, and nutmeg.

Black Cake

Versions of figgy pudding, yam pudding, or fruitcake, known as dark or black cake in Jamaica, have been adopted in African kitchens on the English islands, where pots of rum- and wine-soaked fruits marinate all year before being steamed into the traditional Christmas treat. The cake is also finding increasing popularity at African-American weddings. The quantities below are for this recipe, but marinate as much fruit as you want and add other fruits as they come into season, and then use them throughout the year for ice cream or cake toppings.

This yam-based fruitcake calls for African yellow yams, which are available in Latin American markets, but garnet yams can be substituted. It may be steamed in the traditional British manner, which produces a moist, chewy texture, or baked to produce a denser cakelike crumb. The long, slow cooking is what makes the cake turn very dark or black.

Serves 10–12

1 cup port or sweet wine, or as needed
1 cup rum, or as needed
3 cups (1½ pounds) mixed fruits such as prunes, dates, raisins, currants
1 cup butter
1½ cups firmly packed dark brown sugar
3 eggs
dash of salt
1½ pounds African yellow yams or garnet yams, peeled and grated
1 cup all-purpose flour
dash of salt
1 tablespoon baking powder
1 teaspoon ground cinnamon
1 teaspoon ground ginger
½ teaspoon freshly grated nutmeg
½ teaspoon ground mace
½ teaspoon ground allspice
boiling water, as needed

At least 1 month before cooking, place the fruits in a bowl or wide-mouthed jar and pour in the wine and rum to cover the fruits. Cover and store on the kitchen counter or in the pantry. Stir occasionally and add more port and rum as needed to keep the fruits completely covered.

On the day to be served or as much as a week in advance, generously butter and flour a 4-quart pudding mold or a bundt or tube pan. If baking the fruitcake, preheat an oven to 300 degrees F.

In a bowl, using an electric mixer or a wooden spoon, beat together the butter and sugar until light and fluffy. Beat in the eggs, one at a time. Add the yams and mix well. In another bowl, stir together the flour, salt, baking powder, cinnamon, ginger, nutmeg, and mace. Stir into the yam-egg mixture. Using a slotted spoon, measure out 3 cups of the marinated fruits, draining well, and place in a food processor or blender. Process to chop into a coarse purée. Stir the fruits into the batter. Then measure out 1/2 cup of the marinating liquid and stir into the batter. Pour the batter into the prepared mold.

If steaming the cake, cover the mold tightly with its own cover or with aluminum foil. Place a rack or folded dish towel inside a deep, heavy pot, and set the mold on it. Pour in boiling water to reach within 2 inches of the top of the mold. Cover the pot. Place over medium-low heat and bring to a simmer. Continue to simmer until the pudding sets and is firm, 2 1/2–3 hours. Check to see if a shiny, firm top has formed. If so, remove the mold from the water and let the pudding cool in the mold until lukewarm, about 1 hour. Loosen the sides of the cake with a thin knife, place a serving plate over the top of the mold, and invert. Lift off the mold.

If baking the cake, cover the mold tightly with foil and bake until risen and set, about 2 hours. Remove from the oven, uncover, and let cool until lukewarm, an hour or so. Loosen the sides of the cake with a thin knife, place a serving plate over the top of the mold, and invert. Lift off the mold.

Serve the cake warm or at room temperature. If serving another day, store it, covered, in the refrigerator for up to a week. Pour a little rum over the cake, if desired, to keep it moist.

Cocoa Tea. In the countryside, rural dwellers grow their own coffee beans and cocoa plants. The beans for both are harvested and dried in the sun. The cocoa beans are then roasted, cracked open, and ground into a powder, which is pressed into little cakes. To make cocoa tea, the cake is grated into a small saucepot with water and sugar until the desired strength is reached. It is then brought to a boil and drunk like tea. Condensed milk is sometimes added to suit personal taste.

bahia brazilian

On the streets of Salvador, the capital city of the state of Bahia, sidewalk vendors under grass-roofed cabanas sell spicy snacks with lyrical names like *vatapá*, *caruru*, and *acarajé*. Long white beaches are colored with sun-faded red, blue, and green rowboats ready to be launched in search of tiny crabs, clawless lobsters, fat shrimp, and silver surf fish.

Next to the beach, a farmer's market sells okra, dried shrimp, watermelons, yams, coconuts, plantains, mangoes, and bottles of *dendê* oil—foods transplanted here three centuries ago. These ingredients continue to embellish the basic rice and bean fare familiar throughout this tropical coastal Brazilian state, where the African heritage is firmly integrated into architecture, religion, dance, music, and food.

Bahia, located fifteen hundred miles north of Rio and a thousand miles from the equator, is where the first Portuguese landed in 1500, and where the first African slaves were brought to Brazil to work sugar, and later cacao and coffee plantations. Some 80 percent of the population is still of African descent.

The Bahian experience, with its strong African imprint, differs from what happened in the rest of the Americas. Three factors contributed to this difference: colonization by Portugal, the Catholic-African tribal religious connection, and the physical elements of geography and climate.

The colonization by Portugal is noteworthy because of the country's long ongoing relationship with Africans. In southern Portugal the people had been subjected to rule by the Moors on and off for two hundred years until the end of the fourteenth century. Subsequently, the Portuguese became involved in trade with West Africa, where it controlled the coastal area between the Niger and Congo rivers until the mid 1600s. It is thought that this previous association with African peoples helped the Portuguese to be more tolerant and adaptive of other cultures. According to Gilberto Freyre, in his book *The Masters and the Slaves*, "slavery was a milder form of bondage [under the Portuguese in Brazil] than under Anglo Saxons or Spaniards."

Religion contributed to the strong African-Bahian culture two ways, both inadvert. For the slaves who were converted to Catholicism, their new "souls" gave them some rights, such as baptism and marriage. However Catholic on the surface, African-Brazilians maintained secret parallel religions, of which the *candomblé* rituals are the best known and most widely practiced today. That this mixture of Christian and ancestral religious worship could develop, however clandestinely in the beginning, was helped by the fact that Catholic saints had parallel African deities. For example, the Catholic Saint Barbara is also Iansa, and the Virgin Mary assumes the form of Iemanja, goddess of the sea. Today the two religions are practiced simultaneously by many African-Brazilians who wear Christian and *candomblé* symbols at the same time. Ritual *candomblé* offerings of dead chickens, rice, and beans on a plate are still spotted on sidewalk corners under the shadow of a Catholic church.

The endurance of the African sects helped keep the culture of the mother continent strong. Through the practice of oral history, a legacy inherited from tribal storytellers, priestesses and other spiritual leaders memorize and pass on the genealogy of their constituents. Because of this tradition, many black Brazilians have a record of their ancestry and thus conserve their African heritage.

Another reason Bahia was able to keep an African identity didn't require ethnological, historical, or religious help—Bahia and Portuguese Angola, the part of West Africa from which many of the slaves were abducted, are on the same latitude. The similarity of climate and geography made the cultivation of familiar ingredients possible. The red palm tree that produces the fragrant orange oil used for flavoring and coloring West African meat, fish, poultry, and vegetable dishes took root in Bahia. So did okra, yams, bananas, mangoes, coconut, black-eyed peas, and plantains.

Eating familiar foods and living in a parallel climate aided in the Africans' adjustment to and influence in Bahia. Today that influence is still evident in the most common dishes. The popular street snack known as *acarajé* is a black-eyed pea fritter known as *akara* in Togo and other West African nations. A fish-and-okra stew in Ghana or Cameroon became *caruru* in Bahia. Stews popular along the coast of West Africa that mix fish, nuts, and coconut milk and are seasoned with *dendê* oil are known as *moquecas* in Brazil. The process of drying fish to preserve it was a familiar practice of the Africans and also the native Brazilians.

As in the rest of the Western Hemisphere where the Africans became the masters of the kitchens, here they merged their own ingredients and techniques with those of the Brazilian natives and the Portuguese colonists. From the Tupinamba Amerindians came knowledge of corn, native tropical fruits, and cassava, also known as manioc, from which comes *farinha de mandioca*, the toasted cassava meal that is the bread of Brazil. The Portuguese contributed the art of frying, making sweets, and utilizing pigs. The Africans seasoned it all with *dendê* oil and chiles, cooled it with okra and *couve* (greens), and thereby created the cooking style for which Bahia is renowned.

African culinary influence is strong all over Brazil, the largest country in South America. The national dish, a rice, bean, pork, and greens extravaganza called *feijoada completa,* descended from Bahian slave fare. Rio de Janeiro and São Paolo have elevated the simple rice-and-bean bowl to a culinary extravaganza of more pork cuts than were ever imagined by its slave creators. The recipe in this chapter is for a Bahian-style *feijoada*. Originally embellished with scraps of pork from the ears, tails, and feet, here it is updated with more easily accessible ham hocks, bacon, and pork shoulder.

The recipes that follow feature dishes made by African-Brazilians at home, sold by street vendors, and found in restaurants serving *cozhina típica*. Some of the recipes call for

dendê oil and the *malagueta* chile. They are found at Latin American or other specialty markets (see Resources).

As in Africa, coconut milk is a favored sauce for the simple poultry and fish sautés that comprise everyday cooking. It is widely available in cans, which is the easiest way to acquire it. Instructions for making it from fresh coconuts are given in the Glossary. There are also suggestions for using North American fish species that will approximate the firm, fleshy southern Atlantic fish enjoyed in Brazil.

The most common other ingredients are shrimp, chicken, onions, garlic, black beans, rice, chiles, peppers, limes, and cilantro. They are combined with coconut milk and *dendê* oil, with okra and *farinha de mandioca*—four embellishments worth seeking to bring the true flavors of Bahia into your kitchen.

Farofa · *Toasted Cassava Meal*

Farofa is the bread of Brazil. Bowls of toasted cassava meal are set out on the table for sopping up the spicy fish, chicken, meat, and coconut sauces. In Brazilian Portuguese, the meal is called *farinha de mandioca* and is available in Latin American markets, ready to eat. Once toasted, the meal becomes *farofa*, and it can be served plain as a table condiment or it can be elaborately embellished with vegetables and made into a pilaflike side dish.

Makes about 2 cups

1/2 *cup butter or vegetable oil*
2 *cups (1 pound) cassava meal*

In a skillet over medium heat, melt the butter. Stir in the cassava flour and cook, stirring constantly, until golden and crumbly, about 5 minutes.

Let cool and store in an airtight container in the refrigerator for up to a week or in the freezer for several months.

Farofa Amarela · *Yellow Farofa*

This is also known as *dendê farofa* because the cassava meal is sautéed in *dendê* oil, which turns it a rich yellow-gold. It is particularly nice with *Caruru* (page 79) and *Vatapá* (pages 80–81).

Makes about 2 cups

2 *cups (1 pound) cassava meal*
3 *tablespoons vegetable oil*
2 *tablespoons* dendê *oil*
salt and ground black pepper

In a skillet over medium heat, combine the cassava meal and vegetable and dendê oils and cook, stirring constantly, until the meal is golden and crumbly, about 8 minutes.

Let cool and store in an airtight container in the refrigerator for a week or in the freezer for a month.

Transforming the starchy tuberous cassava, called manioc *in Brazil, into a versatile flour was taught to the newcomers by the Amerindians, for whom it was a principal food. First, the dark thick skin was scraped off. Next, the white tuber was grated and the pulp pressed in a palm-leaf strainer. The pulp was then put into an earthenware vessel and stirred continuously over the fire until very dry. The toasty mixture resembled bread crumbs.*

Môlho de Pimenta · *Hot Sauce*

This is the hot sauce of Bahia, where it is found on every table to season each dish to taste. The *malagueta* chile is a small, extremely hot, thin, tapered chile used either red or green. It probably got its name from the Africans, who ate a small pungent berry from a shrub known as *aframomum melegueta*. Habanero (Scotch Bonnet), bird, or serrano chiles can be substituted. Use this sauce sparingly. It is *very hot*. To reduce the heat a little, remove the seeds and membranes from the chiles, but do so with rubber gloves on and don't put your fingers near your eyes.

Makes about 1 cup

6 malagueta, habanero (Scotch Bonnet), bird, or serrano chiles, minced
(see Glossary)
1 yellow onion, minced
1 garlic clove, minced
1/2 cup fresh lime juice
salt and ground black pepper

Combine all the ingredients, including salt and pepper to taste, in a bowl. Mix well. Alternatively, place in a blender or small food processor and purée. Let stand an hour for flavors to meld.

Transfer to a container with a tight-fitting lid and refrigerate for up to one week.

Môlho de Pimenta e Limão · *Hot Sauce with Lime*

Tânia da Paixão cooks at the Feijoada de Biu restaurant in Bahia. This is her combination for the ubiquitous seasoning served tableside to spike Bahian dishes. If you can find them, use *habanero* (Scotch Bonnet) chiles to make this sauce, or substitute serranos. To reduce the heat a little, remove the seeds and membranes from the chiles, but do so with rubber gloves on and don't touch your eyes.

Makes about 1 cup

6 fresh red or green chiles, minced (see Glossary)
1 red onion, finely chopped
2 garlic cloves, minced
1 bunch fresh cilantro, including stems, chopped
1/2 cup fresh lime juice
finely chopped tomatoes (optional)
salt

Combine all the ingredients in a bowl, including tomatoes (if using) and salt to taste. Stir well. Taste for seasoning. Let stand for at least 1 hour for flavors to meld.

Transfer to a container with a tight-fitting lid and refrigerate. Use within a day.

"I believe it may be stated that from the point of view of nutrition that the most salutary influence in the Brazilian's development has been that of the African Negro, both with respect to the valuable food products that, through him, have come to us from the land of his origin, and with respect to his own diet, which was better balanced than that of the white man—at least in this country under slavery."

Gilberto Freyre in
The Masters and the Slaves

Acarajés · *Black-eyed Pea Fritters*

On the street corners of Salvador, Bahian women, clad in the traditional white flounced dress of the region, strands of colorful beads around their necks, hair wrapped in colorful fabrics, cook these delicious fritters. A relative of the *akara* of Nigeria and the *kose* of Ghana, where they have been sold on the streets for centuries,sells *acarajés* rise to culinary heights in Bahia. Many women, like Maria Emilia Bettencourt, who sells *acarajés* on the beach at the Cabana da Amaralina, arrive early in the morning; some stay until after dark to cook *acarajés* and accouterments. Their customers eat the fritters like sandwiches, stuffed with fish and vegetable mixtures.

Every day, Maria Emilia sets up her charcoal burner just as mothers and grandmothers have done in Brazil and in West Africa for generations. These bready puffs, made from cooked puréed black-eyed peas, are great alone, but are best filled with the other typical Bahian dishes she has in front of her.

Listening to Maria Emilia name each dish is like being treated to a musical concert. The accent is usually on the last syllable and the choices include *acarajé, vatapá, camarão*, and *caruru. Vatapá* is a light orange purée of peanuts, dried shrimp, fish fillet, onions, bread, coconut milk, garlic, and *dendê* oil. *Camarão* are small dried shrimp with the texture of popcorn. Shrimp of this quality can be found through mail order in the United States (see Resources.) *Caruru* is stewed okra with dried shrimp. When filled, *acarajé* is a Bahian taco, with exotically delicious flavors and textures.

The fritters can be made the size of walnuts and served as appetizers or made sandwich-sized like Maria Emilia does. In both cases, spoonfuls of the black-eyed pea mixture are dropped into hot *dendê* oil and cooked until reddish golden and crisp. The fritters are retrieved and drained until cool enough to handle and fill. If small, eat them with *Môlho de Pimenta* (page 74), *Môlho de Pimenta e Limão* (page 75), or another favorite hot sauce. If larger, split them and fill with *Vatapá* (page 80), *Caruru* (page 79), *Salada de Bahia* (page 78), and/or dried shrimp.

One of the intricacies of making these fritters is the peeling of each bean. I have tried making them without peeling and have discovered they work fine, however. The texture is coarser and the black eyes are little flecks, but the taste is great.

Makes about 3 dozen walnut-sized fritters, or 6 sandwich-sized fritters

On a beach in Porto da Barra, Bahia, two young men spar with each other in a graceful dance of circling legs, arms, and torsos, eyes locked, never touching, a calibrated synchronicity adding rhythm to their movements. This is capoeira, a martial art disguised as dance that descended from the slaves, who were forbidden to fight.

1¼ cups (½ pound) black-eyed peas, rinsed and picked over
1 yellow onion, finely chopped
2 tablespoons (1 ounce) dried shrimp
salt
dendê oil for deep-frying (see note)

Place the peas in a bowl with water to cover by 4 inches and soak overnight. Drain. The traditional method requires peeling each bean. The skins are loose enough to come off after this soaking, so this step is tedious but manageable.

In a food processor or blender, combine the peas with the onion and dried shrimp and purée until smooth. Taste for seasoning (the dried shrimp is salty). Mix in salt to taste.

Pour oil to a depth of 4 inches in a deep-fryer or wok and heat to 350 degrees F. To make small fritters, drop by walnut-sized spoonfuls into the hot oil; do not crowd the pan. They will cook in 4–5 minutes. Using a slotted spoon, retrieve the fritters and place on a rack over paper towels to drain. Repeat until all the fritters are cooked.

To make sandwich-sized fritters, form the mixture into 3- or 4-inch patties. Use the slotted spoon to slide each patty into the hot oil; do not crowd the pan. Fry, turning if necessary to brown both sides, until cooked through, 6–8 minutes. Retrieve with a slotted spoon and drain on a rack over paper towels. Repeat until all the fritters are cooked.

Serve hot.

NOTE: Dendê oil is relatively expensive in the United States. To reduce the cost, mix 1 cup *dendê* oil with peanut oil for some color and the authentic flavor.

Another substitution is to color peanut oil with the Caribbean annatto seed. This bright red seed, which is found in Latin American markets, is often used to color cooking oil. It will produce the same color as *dendê*, but the flavor will be different. See instructions for making annatto oil in the Glossary.

VARIATION: *The* acarajé *mixture can also be spooned into banana leaves, folded into packets, and steamed rather than fried, in which case they are called* abarás. *Secure the banana leaves in place with kitchen string and place on a rack above simmering water. Cover and steam for 20 minutes. Unwrap the leaves, split each* abará *open, and fill with the same fillings used for* acarajés.

Salada de Bahia · *Brazilian Salad*

This combination of tomatoes, lettuce, and onions is typically served at *acarajé* stands, for stuffing into the black-eyed pea fritters with the other dishes. It can also be dressed with a little olive oil, lime juice, salt, and pepper and served as a side dish.

> Serves 6
>
> *6 small ripe tomatoes, sliced or chopped*
> *1/2 small red onion, finely chopped*
> *1 head butter or Bibb lettuce, shredded*

Combine all the ingredients in a bowl. Mix well, cover, and chill. Serve within a day.

Couve · *Sautéed Greens*

Couve is the word for greens, or, more specifically, large kalelike leaves grown in Bahia. Collard greens or spinach can be substituted. Unlike the long-cooked greens of the southern United States, *couve* is cooked until just tender-crisp and still brightly colored.

> Serves 6–8
>
> *2 pounds kale, collard greens, or spinach*
> *3 tablespoons vegetable oil*
> *1/2 yellow onion, finely chopped*

Lay the kale leaves one on top of the other. Roll them up and then cut crosswise into thin strips.

In a large skillet over medium heat, warm the oil. Add the onion and sauté until browned, about 5 minutes. Stir in the greens and cook, stirring all the while, until cooked through but still bright green and tender-crisp, 5–7 minutes.

Serve hot.

Fish is dried the same way in Brazil that it is in West Africa. First a hole or pit is dug. Rocks line the pit and grass and hay are thrown in and set on fire. The fish is set on grates down in the hole to receive heat from the fire and expedite the drying process so it becomes dry before it begins to deteriorate. "It has a special flavor which is really good when this is done right," says Ron Preston, African-American culinary historian and food service manager.

Caruru · *Stewed Okra with Dried Shrimp*

Seasoned with the Bahian pantry basics of dried shrimp, *dendê* oil, and peanuts, okra is cooked into a thick stew with rich depth. Some versions add cashews and fresh shrimp. *Caruru* is one of the fillings sold by Bahianas who vend *acarajés* at the beaches and on street corners and is served as a side dish with *Arroz con Coco* (page 82). I also like it with *Feijoada Completa* (page 84).

Serves 8 as a side dish; 12–15 portions in *acarajés*

2 pounds okra, sliced 1/2 inch thick
juice of 2 limes, or juice of 1 lemon and 1 lime
salt
2 tablespoons dendê *oil*
1 large onion, finely chopped
1 clove garlic, minced
1–2 ounces dried shrimp
1 teaspoon grated, peeled fresh ginger
3/4 cup (3 ounces) roasted peanuts, finely chopped or ground
1 cup water
Mólho de Pimenta *(page 74) or a bottled* habanero (Scotch Bonnet)
    sauce such as Papa Joe's brand
chopped fresh cilantro

Combine the okra and lime juice and a little salt in a bowl. Toss to mix.

In a skillet over medium heat, warm the *dendê* oil. Add the onion and garlic and sauté until browned, about 4 minutes. Add the dried shrimp, ginger, peanuts, and okra and stir to mix. Then add the water and cook, uncovered, over medium-low heat until thickened, about 30 minutes.

Season to taste with salt, hot sauce, and cilantro. Serve hot or at room temperature.

Vatapá · *Creamy Spiced Seafood and Peanuts*

Pronounced with the accent on the last syllable, this Bahian classic combines the West African basics of dried and fresh fish with ground peanuts and coconut milk. The results are a thick paste to serve in *Acarajés* (pages 76-77) or as a side dish with *Arroz con Coco* (page 82) or *Feijoada Completa* (page 84).

When using dried shrimp for any recipes in this book, find the best quality you can. The best in the United States are from Louisiana (see Resources). The amount can be varied, depending on your budget. Smell them first, if possible. They should not have any off odor and should be bright pink. In Bahia they are eaten like potato chips. Peeled and deveined fresh shrimp can be used in place of the fish fillets; they will give the dish a deeper color.

Serves 10–12

1 cup (6 ounces) roasted peanuts
¼–½ cup (2–4 ounces) dried shrimp
2 pounds rockfish, grouper, or sea bass fillets, cut into 1-inch pieces
juice of 1 lime or lemon
3 garlic cloves, minced
salt and ground black pepper
1 tablespoon olive oil
1 yellow onion, sliced
1 tablespoon grated, peeled fresh ginger
1 bay leaf
2 tablespoons chopped fresh cilantro
2 cups water
2 tablespoons dendê oil
1½ cups coconut milk
Môlho de Pimenta (page 74) *or* Môlho de Pimento e Limão (page 75)

In a food processor or blender, grind together the peanuts and dried shrimp until very fine.

Check the fish fillets for any small bones and remove. Then, in a bowl, combine the fish, lime juice, 1 of the minced garlic cloves, and salt and black pepper to taste. Stir to mix.

In a saucepan over medium-high heat, warm the olive oil. Add the onion and sauté until softened, about 5 minutes. Add the ginger, bay leaf, cilantro, and marinated fish, mix well, and stir in the ground peanuts and dried shrimp. Add the water and bring to a boil. Cook, uncovered, until the fish is cooked through, about 10 minutes. Drain the fish, reserving the cooking liquid.

Place the fish in a blender or food processor and purée until smooth, adding a little of the reserved cooking liquid if necessary to ease processing.

Transfer to a bowl and stir in the reserved cooking liquid, *dendê* oil, and coconut milk. Add hot-pepper sauce to taste. Serve at room temperature. Or transfer to a saucepan, reheat gently, and serve hot.

Tutu · *Creamed Beans*

Here is a dish that uses the leftover beans from *feijoada* to make refried beans for serving with reheated meats, sausage, or tongue and *Couve* (page 78).

Serves 4–6

2 ounces slab bacon, finely chopped
6–8 cups cooked beans from Feijoada Completa *(page 84)*
1 or 2 garlic cloves, minced
2–4 tablespoons Farofa *(page 73), plus additional* Farofa *for serving*

In a heavy skillet over medium-high heat, fry the bacon until crisp. Add the beans and their liquid (add a cup or so of water if necessary to make it soupy). Then stir in the garlic and cook, stirring, until heated through.

Stir in enough *Farofa* to thicken the mixture slightly, then serve. Pass additional *Farofa* at the table.

A r r o z *is the word for rice in Portuguese. The importance of rice in the Brazilian diet is illustrated by the fact that it is found in every course of a Brazilian meal, from soup to dessert.*

The abundance of coconuts *in Brazil makes their milk a handy and delicious staple. It is commonly cooked with rice, vegetables, soups, and stews, and forms the base for desserts like* Mousse de Coco *(page 95). For directions on extracting milk from fresh coconuts, see the Glossary. The benefits of canned coconut milk are consistency, ease, and convenience.*

Arroz à Baiana · *Rice, Bahian Style*

Rice holds as prominent a place on the table of African-Bahians, as it does wherever Africans are cooking. Here is a method for preparing rice as it is typically done in Bahia. The onion and garlic are optional, but you should sauté the rice for a couple of minutes even if you are preparing the dish without them.

Serves 6–8

2 cups long-grain white rice
2 tablespoons vegetable oil
$^1/_2$ yellow onion, finely chopped (optional)
1 garlic clove, minced (optional)
$^1/_2$ teaspoon salt
$3^3/_4$ cups hot water

Put the rice in a bowl and add water to cover by 1 inch. Stir well and let soak 1 minute to remove excess starch. Drain.

In a saucepan over medium heat, warm the oil. Add the onion and garlic, if using, and sauté until softened, about 3 minutes. Add the drained rice and cook, stirring frequently, until opaque, 4–5 minutes longer, being careful not to brown the rice. Stir in the salt and hot water and cook over medium heat, uncovered, until the water evaporates and little craters are forming in the surface of the rice, about 12 minutes.

Cover and remove from the heat. Let stand at least 10 minutes before serving.

ARROZ CON COCO: To make rice in coconut milk, substitute 3 cups coconut milk and $^3/_4$ cup water for the $3^3/_4$ cups water. Proceed as directed.

Ingredients for Brazilian soups and stews can be used interchangeably, depending upon what fresh or dried meat or fish and vegetables are on hand. For example pinto or Great Northern beans can be substituted for black beans in the Sopa de Feijão, next page. It can be made without any meat, and other vegetables, such as celery or pumpkin, could be included. This versatility is a trait of African cooking all over the world.

Many of the African slaves who dominated colonial kitchens in Brazil were high priestesses. Their experience of cooking ceremonial dishes for African deities was combined with Portuguese and Amerindian methods and ingredients to create the famed dishes of Bahia.

Sopa de Feijão · *Black Bean Soup*

This is an ancestor of *feijoada*, the national dish of Brazil. The earthy flavor, rich color, and high nutritive value are three reasons why black beans, native to the New World, are a daily staple.

At the grandiose *feijoada* buffets served on Saturday afternoons at hotels in Rio de Janeiro, a tiny cup of this delectable salty soup precedes the grand tasting of rice, beans, and an extravaganza of smoked, grilled, and braised pork and beef.

In Bahia, *Farofa* (page 73) and cassava biscuits are served with the soup. It would also be great with any of the breads in the Soul, Barbecue, or Louisiana Creole chapters.

Serves 4 as a main course, or 6–8 as an appetizer

1 cup (½ pound) black beans, rinsed and picked over
¼ pound salt pork, blanched 2 minutes in simmering water and chopped,
    or slab bacon, chopped
½ pound lean beef, coarsely chopped (optional)
1 carrot, washed well (or peeled) and finely chopped
2 yellow onions, finely chopped
1 fresh malagueta or other fresh or pickled red or green chile (see
    Glossary)
2–3 teaspoons salt
1 teaspoon dried sage, crushed
½ teaspoon ground mace or ground cloves
3 quarts water
ground black pepper

Soak the beans overnight in water to cover by several inches. Drain.

In a heavy saucepan or dutch oven over high heat, fry the salt pork and beef until they are browned, about 8 minutes. Pour off the grease. Add all the remaining ingredients, including the drained beans and black pepper to taste, and bring to a boil. Reduce the heat, cover, and simmer gently until the beans are very soft, about 1½ hours.

Pass the soup through a food mill or coarse-mesh sieve placed over a bowl. Return it to the saucepan, reheat, and serve piping hot.

Feijoada Completa · *Meat and Black Bean Stew*

Originally created from pork odds and ends by Bahia's African slaves, this delicious rice-and-bean combination has been elevated to Brazil's national dish. In Rio and São Paolo, a multifarious buffet of roasted and boiled meats accompany the rice and beans. This version is adapted from one made by Valmor Neto at his San Francisco restaurant, Bahia Brasil. Particular attention has been paid to reducing the salt and fat of the traditional dish.

You don't need to include all of the meats. Pick out the ones you like best and add them. If you leave them out altogether, the dish becomes simply black beans, to which you should add extra onions, celery, peppers, and other spices. I like to pass a clove or two of garlic through a press into the beans about 5 minutes before serving, to bring up the flavor.

Serve bowls of *Farofa (page 73)* on the side to sprinkle over the beans. *Feijoada* is also served with *Arroz à Baiana (page 82)*, *Couve (page 78)*, Cracklings *(page 148)*, and *Môlho de Pimenta (page 74)*.

Serves 8

2 cups (1 pound) black beans, rinsed and picked over
3/4 pound pork butt or shoulder, trimmed of fat
6 ounces slab bacon
1/2 pound smoked pork sausages
1/2 pound hot Portuguese sausage such as linguiça
1 or 2 pounds ham hock or shank, cut into 1-inch rounds
1 large yellow onion, chopped
2–4 ounces dried beef carne seca, minced (optional; see note)

For the seasonings:
3 garlic cloves, minced and sautéed in 1 tablespoon vegetable oil
6 green onions, including tops, chopped
1 yellow onion, chopped
large handful of chopped fresh parsley (about 1/2 cup)
2 bay leaves, crumbled
1 1/2 tablespoons dried oregano, crushed
salt and ground black pepper

chopped fresh cilantro or parsley

Soak the beans overnight in water to cover by several inches. Drain.

Place the drained beans in a saucepan and add water to cover by 3 inches. Bring to a boil, reduce the heat to low, cover, and simmer until the beans are tender, 2–2½ hours. Add additional water as needed to keep the beans covered.

While the beans are cooking, prepare the meats. Preheat an oven to 375 degrees F. Dice the pork butt or shoulder and the bacon into ½-inch cubes. Place the pork, whole sausages, and bacon in a large baking pan. Roast until well done. The sausages will be ready after 35–40 minutes and the other meats after 45–60 minutes.

Cook the ham hock at the same time as the meats are roasting. In a saucepan, combine the ham hock rounds and onion with water to cover. Bring to a boil, reduce the heat to a simmer, and cook until tender, about 1 hour. Remove the ham hock rounds from the water and remove the meat from the bones, if desired; set aside. Or leave the rounds intact for serving alongside the beans. Strain the cooking liquid into a bowl. Add the strained onions from the liquid to the beans. Add the cooking liquid to the beans if needed to keep them immersed.

Once the beans are almost cooked, check to make sure there is plenty of cooking liquid in the pot. It should be rather soupy at this point. Stir in the *carne seca*. Cut the sausages into rounds and add them and all the other cooked meats to the pot. Then add all of the seasonings to the pot, including salt and pepper to taste. Simmer for another 30 minutes, or until the beans are very tender.

Taste and adjust the seasonings. Sprinkle with chopped cilantro or parsley just before serving.

NOTE: Using dried beef adds complexity to the richness of this dish, but its inclusion is optional. If dried beef isn't available at your butcher, Armour makes a ground compressed dried beef sold in 2½-ounce jars. Soak it in warm water to cover for 15 minutes to rinse off some of the salt.

Cozido · *Spicy Mixed Meat and Vegetable Stew*

A *cozido* is a vegetable-and-meat mélange typical of African one-pot meals that include okra, such as the Senegalese *tiebe yape*. It gets its Brazilian accent from pumpkin, cilantro, and a healthy dose of cassava meal. Serve this with *Arroz à Baiana* (page 82) and *Môlho de Pimento e Limão* (page 75).

Serves 8–10

2 yellow onions, chopped
4 green onions, including tops, chopped
2 garlic cloves, minced
juice of 2 or 3 limes
1 malagueta, serrano, or other fresh or pickled small hot chile (see
    Glossary), or 1 teaspoon red pepper flakes
salt and ground black pepper
2$1/2$–3 pounds beef brisket and/or pork shoulder, trimmed and cut into
    1-inch cubes
2 ounces slab bacon, minced (optional)
$1/4$ cup vegetable oil
2 sausages such as linguiça, sliced $1/2$ inch thick
6 cups water
$1/4$ cup chopped fresh cilantro
$1/4$ cup chopped fresh parsley
black peppercorns
1 pound sweet potatoes or yams, peeled and cut into cubes
4 cups cubed mixed vegetables (about 3 pounds total) such as peeled
    sweet potatoes or yams; peeled plantains; peeled pumpkin, chayote,
    or other squash; peeled carrots; and peeled turnips
$1/4$ head green cabbage, shredded
4 tomatoes, chopped
3 ears of corn, cut into 2-inch rounds or kernels removed
$1/4$ pound green beans, cut into 2-inch lengths
$1/4$ pound okra, thickly sliced or left whole if small
$1/2$ cup cassava meal
Môlho de Pimenta e Limão *(page 75)*

In a large bowl, combine the yellow and green onions, garlic, lime juice, chile, ¹/₂ teaspoon salt, and a dose of ground black pepper. Add the pork and/or beef cubes and toss to coat with the seasoning. Let stand 30–60 minutes.

In a large heavy pot over high heat, fry the bacon until crisp, if using. Remove the bacon and drain on paper towels. Throw out the grease. In the same pan, heat the oil over high heat until almost smoking. A few pieces at a time, brown the meat with the onions, then transfer to a plate when browned. Add the sausage slices to the same pan and brown on all sides. Return the reserved bacon and the browned meat and onions to the pan and cook until all the liquid evaporates. Pour off any fat.

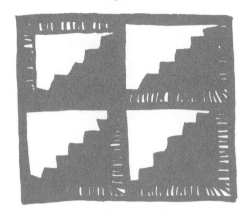

Add the water, cilantro, parsley, a few black peppercorns, and salt to taste. Bring to a boil, reduce the heat to low, and simmer, uncovered, until the meat is tender, about 1¹/₂ hours. Skim off any fat.

Stir in the cubed mixed vegetables, cabbage, and tomatoes and cook until tender, 20–30 minutes. Stir in the corn, green beans, and okra. Cook another 10 minutes.

Using a slotted spoon, remove the meat and vegetables and arrange on a large platter or scoop into a soup tureen. Stir the cassava meal into the liquid remaining in the pot and cook until thickened, 3-4 minutes. Pour over the vegetables and meat.

Serve hot. Pass the hot-pepper sauce.

Xinxim de Galinha · *Chicken with Peanuts and Shrimp*

Dona Canceição de Reis has been preparing typical Bahian dishes for twenty-five years. Her restaurant, Casa de Gamboa in Salvador, is located in a beautiful colonial residence that creates the feeling of eating in someone's home. When you arrive, an appetizer of tiny stuffed Brazilian crabs is put in front of you. It is a spicy mélange of ground crab legs and seasoning served with a refreshing fruit juice cocktail known as a *batida*, such as a *caipirinha* made with *cachaça* (Brazil's sugarcane rum) and limes.

This is one of Bahia's most famous dishes the way Dona Canceição showed me how to prepare it. She precooks the chicken and finishes it in a sauce of peanuts, onions, coconut milk, and shrimp. *Dendê* oil adds color and a strictly Brazilian accent, but the dish can be made without it.

Serves 6

1 large chicken, disjointed and each piece cut in half (see Glossary)
1 can (16 ounces) whole or chopped tomatoes, with their juice
1 yellow onion, sliced
2 fresh mint sprigs
3 cups water
2 tablespoons olive oil
¼ cup ground dried shrimp
¼ cup toasted peanuts, ground
¼ cup finely minced or puréed white onion
2 teaspoons finely minced, peeled fresh ginger
4–6 tablespoons dendê oil
12 large or medium shrimp, peeled and deveined
½ cup coconut milk

Combine the chicken, tomatoes, yellow onion, mint sprigs, and 2 cups of the water in a large pot. Bring to a boil, then reduce heat to medium, and cook, uncovered, until the chicken is until almost done, about 10 minutes. Using tongs, retrieve the chicken pieces and, when cool enough to handle, remove the skin. Set aside. Save the broth for soup or other uses.

In a large skillet over medium-high heat, warm the olive oil. Add the dried shrimp, nuts, white onion, ginger, and *dendê* oil and sauté until fragrant, 3–4 minutes. The *dendê* oil will turn all the ingredients a beautiful orange.

Add the chicken pieces to the skillet and turn to coat with the seasonings. Stir in the remaining 1 cup water. Add salt to taste and bring to a boil. Cook for 10 minutes or so to finish cooking the chicken and blend all the flavors.

Add the fresh shrimp and cook until they turn bright pink and curl, another 3 minutes. Stir in the coconut milk. Heat through and serve.

Siris Recheados · *Stuffed Crab*

In Bahia, the legs and meat are removed from tiny spider crabs, mixed with other ingredients, and restuffed into the back shells for delicious little appetizers. In the American South, blue crabs are used for making a similar dish.

Serves 6

2 gallons water
2 teaspoons salt, plus salt to taste
6 small blue crabs
2 tablespoons vegetable oil
1 malagueta, *bird, or serrano chile, minced (see Glossary)*
3 green onions, including tops, minced
2 tomatoes, seeded and chopped
1 garlic clove, minced
juice of 1 lime
1/3 cup cassava meal or fine dried bread crumbs
2 or 3 fresh cilantro sprigs, chopped
1/2 cup coconut milk
2 tablespoons dendê oil (optional)
ground black or cayenne pepper

In a large pot, bring the water to a boil and add the 2 teaspoons salt. Drop in the crabs and cook until the color turns, 15–20 minutes. Remove from the heat and drain. Let cool until they can be handled.

Preheat an oven to 350 degrees F.

Pull off legs from the crabs. Smash the leg shells and remove as much meat as possible. Place in a bowl. A little of the shell mixed in with the meat gives an added amount of calcium and adds to the texture.

Lift off the backs of the crabs and remove the liver and lungs and discard. Remove the meat from the back cavities and clean the shell. Add all the crab meat to the crab meat in the bowl.

In a skillet over medium heat, warm the oil. Add the chile and green onions and sauté a few minutes until just soft. Stir in the crab meat and all the remaining ingredients, including pepper to taste. Mix well and remove from the heat. Stuff the mixture into the crab backs. (This dish can be prepared up to this point and refrigerated up to 8 hours before baking.)

Arrange the stuffed crabs in a shallow baking pan, stuffing side up, and bake until heated through, about 10 minutes. Serve hot.

Religion *exudes a strong hold on Bahia. On All Saints' Day in 1501, the first Portuguese settlers landed on the spot explorer Pedro Alvares Cabral had claimed for Portugal a year earlier. They named it Salvador, which means "savior." The bay where they landed was christened Todos os Santos, or All Saints Bay. Salvador is reputed to have 365 churches, one for each day of the year, and at least one holiday every month. No wonder the Brazilians say Bahia is the soul of their country.*

Peixe Grelhado · *Grilled Grouper*

With most of the population living along the Bahian coastline, it's no wonder seafood plays such an important role in the diet. When stewed, the fish is mixed with seasonings and stretched to feed a crowd. When the catch is big, whole fish or fillets are cooked simply. A favorite way to prepare them is on a grill. At outdoor *acarajé* stands, small troutlike fish are grilled over the coals or wrapped in banana leaves and steamed over them.

Serves 4

4 grouper or sea bass fillets, 4 or 5 ounces each
6 tablespoons olive oil
1 garlic clove, minced
1 small fresh red or green chile, minced (see Glossary)
juice of 1 lime
salt and ground black pepper
1 red bell pepper, seeded and sliced lengthwise
1 green bell pepper, seeded and sliced lengthwise
1 yellow bell pepper, seeded and sliced lengthwise (optional)

Place the fish in a single layer in a shallow dish. In a small bowl, combine 4 tablespoons of the olive oil, the garlic, chile, lime, and salt and black pepper to taste. Sprinkle the mixture over the fish and rub it in on both sides. Let marinate while you cook the bell peppers and build the fire.

In a skillet over low heat, warm the remaining 2 tablespoons oil. Add the bell peppers and sauté until wilted and very soft, 10–12 minutes. Add salt and black pepper to taste. Set aside.

Build the charcoal fire for the barbecue and let the coals burn down. Lift the fish from the marinade, reserving the marinade, and place on the grill rack. Grill, turning once, until cooked through when pierced, 4–5 minutes on each side, depending upon the thickness of the fillet.

Just before the fish is ready, pour the marinade ingredients over the bell peppers and reheat 2–3 minutes. Spoon over the grilled fish and serve.

STOVE TOP VARIATION:
Marinate the fish and sauté the bell peppers as directed. Remove the peppers from pan. Put the fish and marinade ingredients in the same hot pan over high heat and cook 4–5 minutes on each side. Return the peppers to the pan, season with salt and pepper, and serve.

With over five thousand miles of coastline and twenty-eight thousand miles of waterways, Brazilians have been blessed with an abundance of fish and crustaceans from which their diet has benefitted.

Bolinhos de Bacalhau · *Codfish Croquettes*

This sublime fritter, similar to those made in other regions of African culinary influence, makes the best of the salty flats of cod.

Makes about twenty 2-inch fritters

1 pound salt cod
1 pound potatoes, peeled and cut into 2-inch chunks
2 tablespoons olive oil
2 green onions, including tops, finely chopped
1 garlic clove, minced
1 green or red bell pepper, seeded and finely chopped
1 fresh malagueta, *bird, or other small fresh chile, seeded and minced*
   (see Glossary)
¹/₂ cup chopped fresh parsley
¹/₂ cup chopped fresh cilantro
2 eggs, beaten
2–4 tablespoons all-purpose flour
salt and ground black pepper
peanut oil for deep-frying

Soak the salt cod in cold water to cover 10–12 hours. To maximize desalting, change the water every few hours. Drain well. Remove the skin and bones and flake the fish into a bowl with a fork or your fingers.

Place the potatoes in a saucepan with water to cover and bring to a boil. Boil until tender, about 10 minutes. Drain and pass through a food mill placed over a bowl or place in a bowl and mash with a potato masher or fork.

In a skillet over medium-high heat, warm the olive oil and sauté the green onions, garlic, bell peppers, and chile until soft, about 2 minutes. Stir in the salt cod and cook another 3–4 minutes. Add to the potatoes along with the parsley, cilantro, and eggs. Add enough flour to form a stiff dough. Season to taste with salt and pepper and mix well. Using your hands, shape the mixture into football shaped croquettes about 2 inches long.

In a deep, heavy pot, pour in peanut oil to a depth of 3 inches and heat until almost smoking. Add the *bolhinos*, a few at a time, and fry until dark brown, 4–5 minutes. Using a slotted spoon, transfer the *bolhinos* to a rack or paper towels to drain and cool slightly. Repeat with the remaining *bolhinos*.

Serve hot.

Goiaba *is Portuguese for guava, the small, round native Brazilian fruit that is pale green to gold and full of tiny seeds. It is eaten fresh when ripe and sweet, but most often it is cooked into a gelatinous paste or jelly. Guava paste, or* goiabada, *is sliced and typically served with a mozzarella-like cheese for dessert and for breakfast.*

Saltcod, *once a mainstay in the diets of Africans and Europeans alike, was traded by the Portuguese for African slaves and then fed to the slaves in the New World. It is still an important ingredient in tropical countries.*

Moqueca de Peixe · *Fish Stew in Coconut Milk*

One of the prized dishes of Bahia, *moqueca* is a quickly made fish stew. I learned to make this version from chef Tânia da Paixão, who prepares it in an earthenware pottery skillet that doubles as a serving dish. It is served with *Arroz à Baiana* (page 82), *Farofa* (page 73), and *Môlho de Pimenta* (page 74).

Serves 4

4 firm fish fillets such as halibut or grouper, about 5 ounces each, or
*   1 1/2 pounds medium shrimp*
3 garlic cloves, minced
1 malagueta, bird, or serrano chile, minced (see Glossary), or cayenne
*   pepper to taste*
1/2 teaspoon salt
2–3 tablespoons dendê oil
1 1/2 cups coconut milk
3 green onions, including tops, cut into long pieces
1 green bell pepper, seeded and slivered
1 tomato, sliced
1/2 red onion, sliced
chopped fresh cilantro
1 lime, cut in half

Cut each fish fillet into thirds. If using shrimp, peel and devein them.

In a shallow dish, combine the fish or shrimp, garlic, chile, and salt and toss to coat on all sides. Let stand 10 minutes.

In a skillet, heat the *dendê* oil until almost smoking. Add the fish or shrimp and quickly brown on both sides. Pour the coconut milk over the fish. Reduce the heat to medium-high and bring to a boil. Cover, reduce the heat to low, and cook about 5 minutes.

Uncover and top the fish with the green onions, bell pepper, tomato, red onion, and cilantro to taste. Add a little water if the pan seems too dry. Cover and continue to cook until the fish is cooked through and feels firm, about 10 minutes. Tânia does not stir the dish. She simply cooks it over low heat long enough to steam all the flavors together.

Before serving, squeeze the lime halves over the top and add more freshly chopped cilantro, if desired. Serve immediately.

Moqueca *comes from the Tupinamba Indian word* pokeka, *which means a stew of fish seasoned with hot peppers. The African influence comes in with the addition of* dendê *oil and coconut milk.* Dendê *oil gives the dish a golden cast and distinctive Brazilian accent, but it can be made with olive or safflower oil instead.*

Camarão à Baiana · *Spicy Shrimp in Coconut Milk*

This recipe is reminiscent of Louisiana creole and Caribbean shrimp dishes. In addition to the onions, peppers, tomatoes, and chiles are *dendê* oil and coconut milk, two distinctive Bahian ingredients. Serve it with *Arroz à Baiana* (page 82).

Serves 6

2 pounds medium shrimp, peeled and deveined
1/3 cup fresh lime juice
1 clove garlic, minced
1 fresh malagueta *or other small fresh chile, minced (see Glossary)*
salt and ground black pepper
2 tablespoons vegetable oil
1 green bell pepper, seeded and chopped
1 yellow onion, chopped
6–8 large ripe tomatoes, peeled, seeded, and chopped
1 bay leaf, crumbled
1 cup water
1 1/2 cups coconut milk
2 tablespoons dendê oil

In a bowl, combime the shrimp, lime juice, garlic, chile, and salt and black pepper to taste. Let marinate while preparing the sauce.

In a skillet over medium-high heat, warm the vegetable oil. Add the bell pepper and onion and sauté until soft, 4–5 minutes. Add the tomatoes, bay leaf, water, and salt and black pepper to taste. Simmer 15 minutes.

Stir in the shrimp and their marinade and cook, stirring, for 2 minutes. Add the coconut milk and *dendê* oil and cook another 5 minutes, to thicken the sauce and blend the flavors. Serve immediately.

Mousse de Coco · *Coconut Mousse*

Snowy white and silky smooth, here is a company dessert that epitomizes the essence of coconut. Make it for a party big enough to serve both this dessert and *quindins* (page 98), because egg yolks left over from this recipe can be used in the other one.

Serves 12–16

2 envelopes (¼ ounce each) unflavored gelatin
2 tablespoons water
3 cups coconut milk
6 egg whites
¾ cup sugar

In a small saucepan, stir the gelatin into the water. Place over medium-low heat and stir until it dissolves, 1–2 minutes.

Pour the coconut milk into a bowl and stir in the hot gelatin until well mixed. Strain through a fine-mesh sieve into another bowl.

In a large bowl, beat the egg whites until they are frothy and begin to become shiny and hold their shape. Then beat in the sugar, a little at a time. Keep beating slowly and adding the remaining sugar until stiff, glossy peaks form. Do not overbeat. Slowly beat the coconut milk mixture into the stiff egg whites. When fully incorporated and the mixture is beginning to set, pour into an oiled 6-cup bundt pan or gelatin mold. Cover and chill until set, at least 8 hours or overnight.

To unmold, dip the mold into a bowl of warm water and loosen the edges with a thin knife. When it begins to pull from the sides, place a plate over the top and invert it. Lift off the mold. Cut into wedges and serve.

At acarajé stands in Bahia, you will find cocada, a round, flat caramelized disk laced with grated coconut, and pé-de-moleque (boy's foot), a similar disk made with peanuts. These candies are similar to the tablette (page 62) of the Caribbean and the peanut brittle of the southern United States (page 151).

Cocada Branca · *White Coconut Compote*

Here, coconut and sugar are quickly combined to make a sweet finishing touch to a Bahian meal. The compote is light and fragrant with coconut.

Serves 6

1 1/2 cups sugar
1 1/2 cups milk
2 whole cloves
1 large coconut, peeled and grated (see Glossary), or 4 cups unsweetened
medium-thread dried coconut
1 teaspoon vanilla extract

In a saucepan, combine the sugar, milk, and cloves. If using dried coconut, add it at this point. Bring to a boil, stirring frequently, and, if using fresh coconut, stir it in once the boil is reached. Reduce the heat to low and simmer gently, stirring occasionally, 10 minutes. Stir in the vanilla.

Remove from the heat and pour into a bowl. Let cool and remove and discard the cloves. Serve cold.

Bolinhos de Estudante · *Tapioca Fritters*

These chewy fritters, traditionally made from finely ground cassava flour
(see Glossary), are found at roadside snack stands like the one Maria Emilia
Bettencourt operates in Amaralina. Named for the students who like to snack
on them, they are sprinkled with cinnamon and sugar.

Makes six 3-inch *bolinhos*

1/2 cup quick-cooking tapioca
1/2 cup sugar
1/2 cup unsweetened finely grated dried coconut
dash of salt
1 cup water
1/2 cup milk
1/2 teaspoon vanilla extract
peanut oil for deep-frying
sugar and ground cinnamon for dusting

In a saucepan, combine the tapioca, sugar, coconut, salt, water, and
milk. Place over medium heat and bring almost to a boil, stirring all the while.
When bubbles begin to form around the edges, reduce the heat to low and cook
until thickened, about 5 minutes. Stir in the vanilla extract. Remove from the
heat and let cool. Form the cooled mixture into six 3-inch-long football shapes.

In a deep-fryer, heavy pot, or wok, pour in oil to a depth of 3 1/2 inches.
Heat the oil to 375 degrees F. Drop in the fritters, 1 or 2 at a time, and fry until
browned, about 3 minutes. Using a slotted spoon, transfer to a rack or paper
towels to drain and cool slightly. Repeat with the fritters.

Sprinkle with sugar and cinnamon and serve.

Quindins de Yaya · *Tiny Coconut Custards*

An egg-rich treat whose roots can be traced to the Middle East, where this kind of sweet, dense custard originated. Arabs shared their desserts when trading with both the Portuguese and the West Africans. The Bahian version is named for *yaya*, the young African girl slaves who often sold their sweets on street corners and split the proceeds with their masters.

Makes 24 servings

1 cup sugar
1 cup butter, at room temperature
9 egg yolks plus 3 whole eggs
1/2 cup corn syrup
1 teaspoon vanilla extract
2 cups unsweetened grated dried coconut
boiling water, as needed

Preheat an oven to 325 degrees F.

In a bowl, beat together the sugar and butter until light and fluffy. Beat in the egg yolks, one at a time. Then beat in the whole eggs, corn syrup, and vanilla. Stir in the coconut until well mixed.

Oil 24 muffin-tin cups, each 1½ inches in diameter, or one 9-inch cake pan. Divide the batter evenly among the muffin cups or pour into the cake pan. Set the muffin tins or cake pan in a large baking pan and pour boiling water into the baking pan to reach 1–2 inches up the side of the muffin tins or cake pan.

Bake until set and a skewer inserted in the middle comes out clean, 25–35 minutes. Remove the pans from the water and let cool.

Invert the cake pan onto a serving platter. The muffin tins can be inverted onto a flat baking sheet and then the custards moved with a spatula to a serving platter. Serve at room temperature.

Brazilian drinks include beer, guava nectar, coffee, and cachaça. Cachaça, like rum, is a clear potent liquor distilled from sugarcane. Coffee beans are a major export product and Brazilian coffee, known as cafezinho, is served in demitasse cups throughout the day.

Dolce de Leite · *Sweet Milk Pudding*

This milk-and-sugar pudding is served as an afterschool snack or for dessert with fresh fruit. It has a lumpy consistency and can be made with or without eggs. Here are both versions.

Serves 6–8

For the eggless version:
1 cup sugar
¼ cup water
1 can (15 ounces) evaporated milk
2 cups milk
2-inch-length vanilla bean, or 1 teaspoon vanilla extract

For the egg version:
2 cups milk
2 cups water
4 egg yolks
½ cup sugar
ground nutmeg and ground cinnamon
½ teaspoon vanilla extract

To make the eggless version, in a heavy saucepan over high heat, combine the sugar and water. Bring to a boil, stirring to dissolve the sugar. Reduce the heat to medium and cook, stirring constantly, until the sugar caramelizes and turns golden brown and syrupy, about 10 minutes.

Meanwhile, in another pan, combine both milks and heat over medium heat until warm to the touch. Gradually pour the warm milk into the hot sugar, stirring constantly. Add the vanilla bean. (If using vanilla extract, add at the end of cooking.) Cook over medium-low heat, stirring frequently, until thickened, about 1 hour. Remove from the heat and pour into a serving dish. Remove and discard the vanilla bean (or stir in the vanilla extract). Let cool and serve cold.

To make the egg version, in a heavy saucepan, combine the milk and water and bring just to a boil.

Meanwhile, in a large bowl, beat together the egg yolks and sugar. Whisk the hot milk mixture, a little at a time, into the egg yolks. Return the egg-milk mixture to the pan and add the nutmeg and cinnamon to taste. Cook over medium heat, stirring constantly, until very thick, 4–5 minutes. Stir in the vanilla. Remove from the heat and let cool. Serve cold.

soul food

"Soul has to do with a style associated with black culture. It's family food. Each family adds its own touch to dishes, but they are all closely related by the ingredients, as are all African-inspired cuisines," says Edward Hamilton, dining instructor at San Francisco City College's restaurant management training facility.

Edna Lewis, doyenne of southern cooking, says, "In the sixties the young people in the cities were missing something they thought was in the South. They coined the term *soul food* and nobody challenged it."

However you define it, soul food is the popular term for well-spiced, inexpensive dishes developed by African-Americans in the southern United States. It uses cheap cuts of meat in small amounts. It incorporates fish that's been called "trash." It combines pungent sauces and gravies with a healthy mix of greens, grains, and legumes. Soul food is not faddish or trendy. It is timeless.

"When you cook from the soul, the food is very tasty," explains Marsha Polk-Townsend, proprietor of RSVP Catering in Alameda, California. "You get this feeling for cooking that is for taste and from memories."

When the first shipload of slaves arrived in Virginia in 1619, cooking in the American South, as we know it today, began. The Africans brought their proficiency in metallurgy, pottery, leatherwork, and weaving. They came with an expertise on rice cultivation that had been practiced in Africa since before the first century. They carried okra, sesame, and watermelon seeds, black-eyed peas, African yams, and a penchant for spices and seasonings.

Once here, as in other parts of the New World where they were enslaved, their role of culinary coordinator commenced. "They were ordered to cook although they were not permitted to learn to read and write," says Edna Lewis. "The mistress of the house would go into the kitchen and read a recipe and expect them to prepare the dish." Their knowledge of food, what they cooked at home, and their own creativity are what created southern cooking.

This chapter is not about southern cuisine in plantation kitchens. It is about the food cooked at home, originally by slaves living off the leftovers and scraps and supplemented by their gardens.

For nearly two hundred and fifty years, from 1619 until 1865, African-Americans were enslaved in the United States. A typical daily menu on a plantation in Georgia meant milk and bread for breakfast, peas (black-eyed or other bean) and corn bread for dinner, and milk and bread for supper. A reputable plantation would also have dried fruit, collard greens, meat, snap beans, potatoes, milk, and butter. And there would be time to hunt squirrel, coon, possum, rabbit, and wild turkey.

The slaves "made an effort to mold whatever was available into something a little better. The great complaint of slaves," writes Eugene D. Genovese, in *Roll, Jordan, Roll: The World the Slaves Made*," was the monotony of their assigned diet. They responded by varying it themselves."From the Native Americans they learned about corn and its uses, which was incorporated into every aspect of the meal. Dried ground corn, known as hominy, became a filling mush called grits. Cornmeal cooked with water became couche couche; its African antecedent, *fufu*, is a paste made from mashed yams. Cornmeal cooked into unleavened loaves over rocks by Narraganset Indians developed into adaptations for oven-baked and fried corn breads known as spoon bread, hoecakes, corn pone, and hush puppies. Fried corn cooked in its own milk served as vegetable or main dish. Sweetened and baked with eggs, it is corn pudding.

Beans, indigenous to Africa and to America, became important sources of protein. Black-eyed peas from Africa or red beans from America were simmered in cast-iron pots over the open hearth. The beans were seasoned with pig's tails or feet, ham hocks, or salt pork.

Pigs, rarely known in Africa because of the Muslim influence, came with the Spaniards and flourished in the mild North American climate. The meat was preserved by smoking and salting, techniques exchanged and shared by African, Amerindian, and European. Pork was the most important meat in the United States until after the Civil War, when beef took the lead. African-Americans used smoked and salted pork odds and ends to season beans, greens, bread, and pastries.

In rural southern communities, hog butchering is still cause for a get-together, with music and socializing accompanying the business of slaughtering and preserving. The whole community shares the tasks. And everyone shares in the meat, even if they can't attend the butchering. Since plantation days, when the chops, hams, and loins went to the Big House and the slaves got the leftover ears, tails, feet, fat, ribs, and innards, all parts of the pork are used. Knowing that the tastiest morsels of meat are those found next to the bone, African-Americans created their famous pork recipes such as smoked ham hocks, pickled pig's feet, and barbecued ribs, as well as chitterlings from the small intestine.

Lard, the heavy white fat rendered from hogs, was the only oil for cooking. African fish, vegetable, and corn fritters became specialties. Fried chicken, flaky pie crusts, and light, tender biscuits all started with lard.

The pigs were fed on the corn husks and other refuse from the gardens. African-Americans came from an agricultural heritage, and the importance of the garden cannot be overemphasized. The vitamin-and-nutrient-rich greens, okra, beans, peas, squash, and melons that composed their diet in West Africa also contributed to the soul food kitchen. So did sugarcane and sorghum, crops grown in personal as well as plantation gardens. They provided syrup and sugar for sweetening desserts and for flavoring savory dishes.

Seasoning in soul food cooking often means simultaneously combining salt and sugar with the spike of black pepper or chiles. Bacon and ham hocks typically provide the salt. Hot comes from ground black pepper or fresh, dried, ground, or pickled chiles. "Salt, pepper, and sugar, these are necessary to the taste," decrees Herocine Williams, cook at Walnut Hills

Restaurant in Vicksburg, Mississippi. They double as palate stimulators and satisfiers, appeasing all the taste buds.

The recipes in this chapter have been gathered from cooks and other resources all over the United States. They were developed using the methods and ingredients that make them soul food classics. Fat, sugar, and salt have been cut to make them more amenable to current dietary needs. In the spirit of African-American cooking, however, these recipes are packed with flavor. They are based on healthful grains, vegetables, fruits, and legumes and seasoned with onions, peppers, celery, herbs, and spices. Except where noted, the recipes are only guidelines—not precise formulas. Amounts, vegetables, grains, and spices can be varied according to personal taste and what's on hand.

In this chapter, you'll find which spices and ingredients impart the most flavor and how to use them. These dishes are everyday and company fare. Spicing is easy. It's up to you to add the soul.

Pepper Vinegar Sauce

Everywhere people of African heritage have set the table, this condiment has become a fixture. Easy to make and a potent seasoning, it perks up ordinary food, turning it into fiery bites. Jars of these pickled chiles are found in markets in Bahia and on the tables of soul food restaurants in the South. When the little dynamite-hot chiles are in season in the summer, they are easily preserved this way. The chiles can be used for any of the recipes in this book. Shake the vinegar on greens and other vegetables, chitterlings, and other meats.

Tiny bright red chiles are sometimes referred to as "rooster spur peppers" and the sauce as "rooster spur pepper sauce."

> *fresh red and/or green* malagueta, *bird, or serrano chiles (see Glossary)*
> *boiling water, as needed*
> *sugar*
> *salt*
> *distilled white vinegar*

Tightly pack fresh chiles into one or more sterilized canning jars. Pour boiling water over them and let stand 20 minutes. Drain off the water.

Add a touch of sugar and salt to each jar. In a saucepan, bring vinegar to a boil and pour over the chiles to cover. Seal with a canning jar lid according to the manufacturer's instructions and store up to 1 year in a cool place.

VARIATION: *Pack chiles into a small sterilized vinegar bottle instead of a canning jar. Add the sugar, salt, and boiling vinegar as directed above and, using an ice pick, punch a hole or two in the lid. Store in the refrigerator up to 3 months. Add additional vinegar as needed to keep the chiles covered.*

Gravy

Gravy is a soul food signature. Every cook has his or her own gravy recipe. Originally, gravy always started out with pork fat, or lard, to give the sauce a meaty flavor. Now canola or safflower oil is used with flour, salt, and pepper. Water, or sometimes stock or milk, is added and the mixture is cooked until it thickens. It can also begin with a roux (page 166). Gravy goes on rice, potatoes, bread, pork, chicken, or fish. It can be made with the pan drippings of whatever meat or fish was sautéed or fried and can be enriched with stock or wine. Here is a basic recipe.

Makes about 1 cup

2 tablespoons vegetable oil or olive oil, pan drippings, butter, or bacon drippings
2 tablespoons all-purpose flour
1–1 1/2 cups water, milk, stock, or wine (see note)
salt and ground black pepper

Heat the oil or other fat in a skillet over medium heat. Stir in the flour and cook, stirring until the flour is browned, about 5 minutes. Slowly stir in the liquid and cook and stir until thickened, about 5 minutes longer. Season to taste with salt and pepper.

NOTE: If using milk, cook the gravy at a low temperature and do not let it boil. Just simmer until thickened, 5–10 minutes. If using wine, dilute with half stock or water if desired, and cook until it is reduced by half. Taste before adding salt, as wine has a salty quality. If using canned stock, taste before salting.

Paprika, the dried powder of a sweet red pepper, helps brown anything it is sprinkled on, making it especially good when you want to quickly brown fish or chicken.

Seasoned Flour

This staple mixture is used for breading fish, chicken, pork chops, and even vegetables.

Makes ½ cup; enough for about 2 pounds meat or fish

½ cup all-purpose flour
½ teaspoon salt
½ teaspoon ground black pepper

Suggested seasonings:
lemon pepper
cayenne pepper
dry mustard
paprika
dried herbs such as basil, oregano, thyme, and/or sage, crushed
ground spices such as allspice, coriander, cumin, and/or ginger

In a bowl, combine the flour, salt, and black pepper. Add as many of the suggested seasonings to taste as desired.

Plain Rice

Every southern cook I talked to rinsed rice before cooking it. They do it because rinsing keeps the grains separate and results in pots of fluffy rice.

Makes 3 cups; serves 4

1 cup long-grain white rice
2 cups water
1 teaspoon salt

Put the rice in a bowl and fill it with water. Swirl it around a couple of times and drain the rice in a colander.

In a saucepan, bring the water to a boil and then add the salt. Stir in the rice, reduce the heat to low, cover, and cook until tender, about 20 minutes. Remove the lid and fluff up the grains with a fork before serving.

Rice was first grown in what is today the United States in 1685, in Charleston, South Carolina. A load of rice was being transported on a ship from Madagascar when the ship got in trouble and stopped at the port of Charles Towne. The captain left some rice in gratitude. This rice, which thrived, has become known as Carolina Gold.

Rice Pilau

This popular way of cooking rice with vegetables and/or meats and fish in South Carolina is sometimes called *perlew* or *purloo*. Its relatives include Jollof Rice (page 259) in Senegal, Jambalaya (pages 184–185) in Louisiana, and *pelau* in the Caribbean. In the Middle East it is known as pilaf. It can be a side or main dish, depending upon what goes in it. Here is a basic recipe with suggestions for variations.

> Serves 4
>
> 2 ounces slab bacon, minced (optional)
> 2 tablespoons vegetable oil
> 1 small yellow onion, chopped
> 1 cup long-grain white rice, rinsed and drained
> 2 cups water
> 1/2 teaspoon salt, or to taste

In a cast-iron or other heavy, wide 10-inch skillet over high heat, fry the bacon (if using) until crisp. Pour off the fat. Add the oil to the same skillet, reduce the heat to medium, and the onion. Sauté until soft, 3–4 minutes. Stir in the rice and cook and stir 1 minute. Add the water and salt and bring to a boil. Reduce the heat to low, cover, and cook until the rice is tender, 18–20 minutes.

Remove the lid and fluff up the grains with a fork before serving.

OKRA-TOMATO PILAU: After the bacon is browned and the fat is drained, add 1/4 pound okra, sliced, with the onion and oil. Sauté 4 minutes and then add the rice and cook 1 minute. Stir in 1 cup finely chopped fresh or canned tomatoes and cayenne pepper to taste. Add the water and salt to taste and proceed as directed.

SHRIMP-PEPPER PILAU: After the bacon is browned and the fat is drained, add 1/2 red or green bell pepper, seeded and chopped, with the onion and oil. Sauté until soft, about 4 minutes. Then, add 1/4 pound medium shrimp, peeled, deveined, and cut into thirds, and 1 garlic clove, minced. Sauté 1 minute. Stir in the rice and cook 30 seconds. Add the water and salt and proceed as directed.

In the South in spring, a tender bitter green known as poke salet grows wild along the roads. It is also the term for a variety of wild greens, including dandelion, pig weed, turnip tops, and land cresses. Louise Haney, a cook in Florence, Alabama, remembers her grandmother cooking it. "She mixed it with eggs and made everyone eat it. It smells like medicine when it's cooking and I never liked it."

To cook it, young poke sprouts are gathered and soaked in cold water. Then they are drained and put in a saucepan, covered with water, and cooked until tender, then drained again. Next, a little bacon grease is heated in a skillet, eggs are mixed with the cooked poke, and they are scrambled in the grease until done.

The single most important possession for a slave, and later freed blacks, was the kitchen garden or garden patch. Okra and yams, the staples of West African gardens, were transported across the Atlantic. So, too, were black-eyed peas, sesame seeds, collards, and watermelons.

Gardens were allowed, and even encouraged, by some slaveholders because they helped both to reduce the cost of feeding slaves and to maintain a healthy labor force. In some instances the slaves, as an incentive, were allowed to sell their produce. It is felt

Oven Rice

Dye Rhodan cooks at the Colleton River Plantation Golf Course in Hilton Head, South Carolina, while saving to open her own restaurant. She grew up on a farm in nearby Ridgefield, where she still raises hogs with her father. Here is her fail-safe way to make fluffy rice in the oven.

Serves 6–8

2 cups long-grain white rice, rinsed and drained
2 cups water
1 or 2 tablespoons butter
$1/2$ teaspoon salt
ground black pepper

Preheat an oven to 325 degrees F.

Combine all the ingredients in a buttered shallow 2-quart baking dish. Cover with aluminum foil and bake for 20 minutes. Uncover, fluff up the grains with a fork, re-cover, and continue cooking until tender, 25 minutes longer. Serve hot.

that, from the eighteenth century on, black southerners had a better diet than many whites because they raised and ate so many vegetables.

The Encyclopedia of Southern Culture: Volume 1 includes an excellent description of these indispensable gardens: "The techniques of growing vegetables, as well as the plants themselves, were another aspect of the Afro-American tradition. A 19th century planter on the Sea Islands off the coast of Georgia described a slave's garden as 'a small patch where arrowroot, collards, sugarcane, ground nuts, benne, gourds, and watermelons grew in comingled luxuriance.' The comingled look . . . was a form inherited from West Africa. . . . The mixture of plant types together, rather than separated in orderly rows, seems to create an effective 'garden climate'. . . By layering plants, through planting two or three plants growing to different heights next to each other, the insect population apparently can be reduced, weeds decreased through shading them out, and soil nutrients and ground water conserved."

Red Rice

Red rice is cooked with tomato sauce and bell peppers and is similar to Spanish rice. It is popular in Georgia and South Carolina, where it is served with Low Country Boil (page 133).

Serves 6–8

2 ounces slab bacon, minced (optional)
2 tablespoons vegetable oil
1/2 yellow onion, chopped
1 celery stalk, chopped
1/2 green bell pepper, seeded and chopped
2 cups long-grain white rice, rinsed and drained
1 cup canned tomato sauce
1/2 teaspoon salt
ground black pepper

In a cast-iron or other heavy, wide 10-inch skillet over high heat, fry the bacon (if using) until crisp. Using a slotted spoon, remove the bacon and drain on paper towels. Discard the fat.

In the same pan over medium heat, warm the oil. Add the onion, celery, and bell pepper and sauté until softened, about 5 minutes. Stir in the rice and return the bacon to the pan. Cook and stir 1 minute. Stir in the tomato sauce. Fill the tomato sauce can with water twice and pour it in with the salt and pepper to taste. Raise the heat to high, bring to a boil, stir, and cover. Reduce the heat to low and cook until the rice is tender, about 20 minutes.

Remove the lid and fluff up the grains with a fork before serving.

Stewed Okra

The stewed okra Dot Hewitt cooks at her restaurant, Dot's Place, in Austin, Texas, is among the best anywhere. Similar to this one, it comes out thick and flavorful, perfect with Fried Chicken (pages 134–135), Glazed Ham (page 139), or Fried Catfish (page 128).

Serves 6

2 tablespoons vegetable oil or bacon drippings
1 yellow onion, halved and sliced
2 pounds tomatoes, seeded and sliced
1/2 pound okra, sliced
1/2 teaspoon sugar
1 teaspoon salt
1 teaspoon ground black pepper

In a heavy saucepan over medium heat, warm the oil. Add the onion and sauté until just soft, about 3 minutes. Put the tomatoes on top of the onions and then add the okra. Sprinkle the sugar, salt, and pepper over all.

Bring the mixture to a boil, cover, and cook, stirring occasionally, until very tender and thick, about 1 hour or so. Add water if necessary to keep the pan from going dry. The dish will become a thick, stewy mélange when ready.

Taste and adjust the seasoning, then serve.

Okra's botanical name is Hibiscus esculentus. *It is* gwan *in the Bambara language,* ngombo *in Angola,* nkruma *in Ghana,* gombo *in French (Martinique), and* derere *in Zimbabwe. It is a good source of potassium, low in calories, and fat-free.*

Alberta Beckwith's tip on how to keep okra from getting slimy is to soak it in a little milk before using it. Other cooks recommend sautéing it in oil before adding to gumbos or stews.

Okra is best cooked in a nonstick or stainless-steel pan. A cast-iron pot tends to discolor it.

Fried Okra

Here is everyone's favorite way to eat okra. Even those who have no love for okra are tempted by this dish.

Serves 4

1 cup cornmeal
1 teaspoon paprika
1/2 teaspoon salt
1/4 teaspoon ground black pepper
1 pound okra, sliced into 1/2-inch-thick rounds
1/4 cup vegetable oil

In a bowl or small paper bag, combine the cornmeal, paprika, salt, and pepper. Drop in the okra, a few rounds at a time. Roll the okra around in the cornmeal mixture in the bowl or shake the bag to coat well. Remove the okra to a plate and continue with the remaining rounds.

In a cast-iron or other heavy skillet over high heat, warm the oil. Add the okra and fry, turning to cook on all sides, until tender and golden, 5–7 minutes. Using a slotted spoon, remove the okra to paper towels to drain. Serve hot.

Glazed Yams

This recipe comes from Bob Owens, a wine distributor in Los Angeles. It emphasizes the sweetness of yams without being cloying. The orange wedges develop a tart caramelized glaze from the sprinkling of sugar. These are perfect with Glazed Ham (page 139), Fried Chicken (pages 134–135), and Fried Catfish (page 128).

Serves 6

2 tablespoons vegetable oil
3 garnet or red jewel yams, peeled, cut in thirds crosswise, and then into 1 1/2-inch wedges
1 teaspoon sugar
salt and ground black pepper

In a nonstick skillet over medium heat, warm the oil. Add the yams and sauté until the orange brightens. Sprinkle with the sugar and salt and pepper to taste. Reduce the heat to low, cover, and cook, stirring occasionally, until tender, 5–8 minutes.

Only in the United States does the confusion between sweet potatoes and yams exist. In the Caribbean and Africa, a yam is a hard, white- or yellow-fleshed, dark-skinned hairy tuber, from the genus Dioscorea, and a staple food. The orange garnet, red jewel, and other "yams" in American produce bins are actually all sweet potatoes (Ipomoea batatas) from the morning-glory family (Convolvulaceae), which are native to the Caribbean. Yams in the Soul Food and Louisiana Creole chapters is used in the vernacular, which means the garnet and jewel varieties are the correct ingredients. White potatoes are commonly called Irish potatoes in the South and in the Caribbean.

Kwanzaa is an African-American holiday created by Dr. Maalana Karenga of Southern California in 1965. It is celebrated every year for seven days between December 26 and January 1 to commemorate African-American heritage and seven principles: umoja *(unity),* kujichagulia *(self determination),* ujima *(collective work and responsibility),* nia *(purpose),* kuumba *(creativity), and* imani *(faith).*

Remove the cover, raise the heat, and cook and stir until a shiny glaze forms, about a minute or so. Serve hot.

Twice-Baked Sweet Potatoes

These were one of the potluck items served at a Kwanzaa Celebration at Downs United Memorial Methodist Church in Oakland, California. Small sweet potatoes were baked, seasoned, and stuffed back into their shells.

Serves 8

4 sweet potatoes or garnet or red jewel yams
1 teaspoon ground allspice
$1/2$ teaspoon ground nutmeg
4–6 tablespoons butter, at room temperature

Preheat an oven to 400 degrees F.

Prick the potatoes with the tines of a fork and place them on the rack in the oven. Bake until very tender, about 45 minutes. Remove from the oven and reduce the oven temperature to 375 degrees F.

When cool enough to handle, cut the potatoes in half, and scoop out the pulp into a mixing bowl, keeping the skins intact. With a potato masher or fork, mash the pulp and season with the allspice and nutmeg. Stir in the butter. Spoon the pulp back into the skins. Or, for a more decorative presentation, spoon the potato mixture into a pastry bag fitted with a large fluted tip and pipe potato rosettes into the skins. Arrange the stuffed potatoes in a shallow baking pan. (The recipe can be done up to this point 6 hours ahead of time.)

Return to the oven and bake until the edges are lightly browned and crisp, about 20 minutes. Serve hot.

The use of sugar in flavoring savory dishes is found in the cooking of many cultures. In African-American cooking, because sugar was usually available, often as cane syrup, it was used to flavor the daily food from beans to cabbage, potatoes to stews. One thing about adding a little sugar to a dish that also incorporates salty, hot, bitter, and tart flavors, as the Chinese discovered thousands of years ago, is that all the taste buds are satisfied. And you don't come away wishing for dessert.

Smothered Potatoes

Mary Johnson, the cook at the King's Tavern, the oldest restaurant in Natchez, Mississippi, shared this way of cooking smothered potatoes. You end up with the most delicious pot of potatoes with a sweet essence. The potatoes don't brown; instead they steam and soak up the flavor. Mary uses bacon drippings rather than oil; they add a wonderful taste and should be used if you can afford the cholesterol. Season the potatoes well with black pepper if you want an extra zip. If you like potatoes, this is the ultimate in comfort food.

Serves 4

1 tablespoon vegetable oil or bacon drippings
3 baking potatoes, peeled and cut into 1-inch pieces
1/2 yellow onion, chopped or sliced
salt and ground black pepper
1/2 cup water or chicken stock (see Glossary)
chopped fresh parsley (optional)

In a heavy saucepan over medium-high heat, warm the oil. Add the potatoes and onion, sprinkle with salt and pepper to taste, and sauté, turning with a spatula, until the onions are soft, about 5 minutes. Pour in the water, cover, and reduce the heat to medium-low. Cook until the potatoes are tender, about 15 minutes.

Serve hot, sprinkled with parsley, if desired.

Smothered Cabbage

Rosemary Kennedy is a friend and former coworker who is now retired from the Alameda County Probation Department in California. Her tender cabbage is colored with flecks of sweet red peppers and seasoned with red onion, salt, and lots of black pepper.

Serves 8–10

1 head green cabbage, chopped
1 red bell pepper, seeded and chopped
1 red or white onion, chopped
ice cubes
2 tablespoons vegetable oil
salt and ground black pepper

Combine the cabbage, bell pepper, onion, and a bunch of ice cubes in a plastic bag. Put in the refrigerator until 30 minutes before planning to serve (or up to 3 hours).

In a nonstick skillet over high heat, warm the oil. Pour in the vegetables. Stir, then sprinkle with salt and plenty of the black pepper. Cover and reduce the heat to medium. Steam, stirring frequently, until the onion begins to brown but the cabbage is still crisp, about 15 minutes. This is also delicious if cooked over high heat until the onion browns and slightly caramelizes, about 10 minutes longer. Taste for seasoning and serve hot.

Cabbage is related to collards and kale and is one of the world's oldest cultivated vegetables. It was used in early African-American kitchens to wrap around potatoes or other foods for roasting in the ashes of hearth fireplaces.

Large open fireplaces were the stoves of the first African-Americans. Everything was cooked over coals, even coffee. Big iron pots hung over the fire, while the ashes served as an oven in which potatoes and corn bread were roasted and baked. In old recipes many dishes are referred to as being cooked "in ashes."

Alabama Hot Slaw

This slaw, which is more like a relish, gets its heat two ways. One is from cooking and the other is from cayenne pepper. Hot slaw served at the Hollywood Inn in Florence, Alabama, is a spicy complement to greens, beets, and beans, but it goes equally well with barbecue. It keeps in the refrigerator several weeks.

Makes about 1 quart; serves 8–10

1 large head green cabbage, shredded
3 carrots, peeled or scrubbed and grated
2 yellow onions, chopped
2 green or red bell peppers, seeded and chopped
1 cup distilled white vinegar
$1/2$ cup yellow mustard
1 cup sugar
1 teaspoon salt
$1/4$ teaspoon cayenne pepper, or to taste
2 teaspoons paprika
1 tablespoon ground black pepper

In a large enameled or other nonreactive pot, combine all the ingredients. It won't look like there is enough liquid, but cabbage gives off a lot of its own water when heated. Cook over medium heat, stirring occasionally so it doesn't scorch, until the cabbage is tender, the liquid evaporates, and the mixture is thickened, about 20 minutes. Remove from the heat and let cool.

Serve at room temperature. Store tightly covered, 3–4 weeks in the refrigerator.

Fried Green Tomatoes

When the first full-sized tomatoes are still green and you can't wait any longer, this is the natural thing to do. Pick them before they get a bit of red but are still as big as they are going to get. Their firm texture is almost meatlike, which accounts for some old recipes recommending a milk gravy be served with them.

Serves 6

3 full-sized green tomatoes
1/2 cup cornmeal
3/4 teaspoon salt
3/4 teaspoon ground black pepper
1 teaspoon paprika
1 teaspoon all–purpose flour
3 tablespoons vegetable oil

Core the tomatoes and then cut them crosswise into thick slices. In a shallow bowl, combine the cornmeal, pepper, paprika, and flour. Dredge the tomato slices in the cornmeal mixture and set in single layer on a plate. You will not use all of the coating; reserve the remainder. Put the plate in the freezer for 5 minutes to allow the moisture from the tomatoes to soak up the coating.

In a nonstick skillet over medium-high heat, warm the oil. Remove the tomatoes from the freezer and dredge in the remaining cornmeal mixture. Fry the tomatoes, turning once, until browned on both sides, about 3 minutes on each side. Serve hot.

Southern Green Beans

One summer in the late sixties, I stayed in Laurinburg, North Carolina, for three weeks with three elderly sisters. We ate green beans from the garden everyday. Usually they were simply steamed with a little salt, but this, their company recipe, uses a couple slices of bacon for seasoning.

For a meatless version, I've found crisply fried garlic slivers add a tart, almost "meaty" embellishment that is wonderful.

Serves 4

1 pound green beans
2 ounces (1 or 2 slices) lean bacon, minced
4–6 green onions, including tops, finely chopped
2–4 tablespoons water
ground black pepper

Trim the green beans and leave them whole or cut into 2-inch lengths.

In a skillet large enough to hold the beans in a single layer, fry the bacon over medium-high heat until crisp. Using a slotted spoon, remove the bacon to a paper towel to drain. Pour off all but 1 tablespoon of the bacon drippings from the skillet. Add the onions to the skillet and sauté over medium heat until softened, about 4 minutes. Stir in the beans and 2 tablespoons water. Cover and cook over medium-high heat for 3 minutes. Uncover (and do not re-cover); the beans will be bright green. If they seem too crisp, add the remaining 2 tablespoons water and continue cooking, uncovered, stirring frequently until all the water evaporates and the beans are tender.

Serve with a liberal dose of pepper and the bacon sprinkled on top. Toss and serve hot.

VARIATION: *Slice 3 or 4 garlic cloves lengthwise into thin slivers. In a skillet large enough to hold the beans in a single layer, heat 2 tablespoons vegetable oil over medium heat. Add the garlic and fry until golden brown. Using a slotted spoon, remove the garlic and drain on paper towels. Cook the green beans in the pan as directed, adding salt to taste. Sprinkle with the garlic slivers instead of the bacon, toss, and serve hot.*

Uncovering *a green vegetable in the middle of cooking tends to change the color. Cook according to the time given and, if you have to peek, don't put the lid back on. Glass lids are helpful for steaming and cooking green vegetables.*

Collard Greens

Here is a basic pot of greens the way Alberta Beckwith, a professional cook in Florence, Alabama, makes them. Collards have a texture and are close to the type of greens used in similar dishes in West Africa, but kale, chard, mustard, turnip, and beet greens can be substituted. The kale and chard will take about the same amount of time to cook as the collards; the other greens will take only about 20 minutes.

These greens, which are high in iron and vitamin C, are typically cooked with a bit of ham hock or salt pork (with smoked turkey necks gaining in popularity) in plenty of boiling water. By today's standards the greens are over-cooked. Nothing is lost, however, because the "pot likker" is a nutritional bonus served with the flavorful greens. And when Corn Dumplings (page 146) are cooked in the pot likker, the dish becomes a satisfying entrée.

Serves 6

1 pound ham hocks or shanks, cut into 2-inch pieces, or 1 whole smoked
*   turkey neck*
ground black pepper
1 large bunch collard greens

In a heavy pot, combine the ham hocks and water to cover. Add a liberal dose of black pepper. Bring to a boil and simmer for 1 hour.

Stack the greens one on top of the other. Roll up and slice crosswise into thin strips. Add the greens to the meat and cook until very tender, 30–40 minutes. Serve hot with the pot likker.

Collard greens have a wealth of folklore associated with them. Served with black-eyed peas and hog jowl on New Year's Day, they promise a year full of good luck. Leaving a leaf hanging over your door all year long will ward off evil spirits. Placing a fresh collard leaf on your forehead will help cure a headache. The great jazz musician, Thelonius Monk, wore a collard leaf in his lapel when he played the New York City clubs.

Corn Pudding

The versatility of corn is exemplified in puddings like this that double as a main course or a side dish. It combines the texture of whole corn kernels with just a touch of paprika for color or cayenne pepper for a bit of heat. The flecks of green and red pepper give it a colorful appearance. Use the freshest corn you can find, or, if corn is out of season, frozen may be substituted. This pudding can be cooked on top of the stove or in the oven.

Serves 4 as a main course, 6–8 as a side dish

3–5 tablespoons cornmeal, depending upon water content of corn
$3/4$ teaspoon salt
$1/2$ teaspoon paprika or cayenne pepper
$2^1/2$ cups milk
1 tablespoon butter
2 cups corn kernels (from 3 or 4 ears)
$1/2$ red and/or green bell pepper, seeded and finely chopped (optional)
2 eggs, beaten

Preheat an oven to 350 degrees F. Butter an 8-inch square baking dish or a pie pan.

In a saucepan, combine the cornmeal, salt, and paprika or cayenne. Stir in the milk. Over medium heat, cook and stir until the mixture thickens, about 5 minutes. Remove from the heat and stir in the butter, corn, bell pepper, and eggs.

Pour into the prepared baking dish or pan and set it inside a slightly larger pan. Pour in hot water to come halfway up the sides of the dish or pan. Bake until set in the center, about 45 minutes.

Alternatively, to cook on top of the stove, place it in the hot-water bath and cover with aluminum foil. Cook over medium-low heat until the center sets, 40–50 minutes.

Serve hot.

Corn and peanuts were grown by African-Americans in garden patches all over the South. Parched corn and peanuts were snacks to eat when the harvest was being brought in, and later, throughout the winter. To parch corn kernels or shelled peanuts, put them in a skillet with a little vegetable oil and fry over the fire until they turn brown.

The Louisiana Creoles call their rice-based dressing Dirty Rice (page 188).

A restaurant that specializes in soul food, such as Walnut Hills in Vicksburg, Mississippi, typically offers the following dishes: fried catfish, rice and gravy, fresh hull (shell) or lima beans, fried corn, collard or mustard greens, coleslaw, fried chicken, fried or stewed okra, corn bread, hush puppies, biscuits, and cobbler or potato pie for dessert. The food is served at a large round table, with all the dishes on the table at once.

Corn Bread Dressing

Dressing doesn't just mean what is stuffed into the holiday bird. Turkeys were few and far between in the soul food kitchen of the past, but the dressing was cooked anyway. On buffets in the South today corn- and rice-based "dressings" are among the dishes eaten with Fried Chicken (pages 134–135) or Smothered Pork Chops (pages 138–139). This dressing is like the one cooked by Cora Lee Conway at the Agricultural Museum Restaurant in Jackson, Mississippi. You can use the corn bread recipe on page 239 for the bread cubes. Cut it into cubes, toast them in a 300 degree F oven for 30–40 minutes, and let cool before using.

Serves 6–8; enough to stuff a 15-pound turkey

1 yellow onion, chopped
4 green onions, including tops, chopped
2 celery stalks, chopped
6 cups corn bread cubes
2 teaspoons ground sage or dried sage leaves, crushed
1 1/2 teaspoons ground thyme or dried thyme leaves, crushed
1/2 cup chopped fresh parsley
2 eggs, lightly beaten
1/4 cup butter, melted
salt and ground black pepper
1–1 1/2 cups chicken or turkey stock (see note)

Preheat an oven to 375 degrees F. Butter a 4-quart baking dish if not using to stuff a turkey.

In a large bowl, combine all the ingredients, except the stock, seasoning to taste with salt and pepper. Mix well. Pour in enough stock to achieve desired moistness and again mix well. (If stuffing the mixture into a turkey, use the smaller amount of stock.)

Put the dressing in the prepared baking dish (or stuff the bird). Cover and bake for 30 minutes. Uncover and bake until it just begins to brown on top, another 30 minutes. Serve hot.

NOTE: See the Glossary for directions for making stock or, to make a quick stock, in a saucepan combine the wing tips and neck from the chicken or turkey with some celery tops, onion, bay leaf, black peppercorns, and 4 cups water. Bring to a boil, reduce the heat, and simmer 40–60 minutes. Strain. You will have more stock than required; the rest can be used to make gravy, covered and stored in the refrigerator for up to 5 days, or frozen for up to 6 months.

"The importance of seasoning in our cooking can't be overemphasized," says Kennell Jackson, a teacher of black studies at Stanford University. "The right seasoning balances the bitterness of greens with the salt and smokiness of ham. Every vegetable has its own formula so nothing overruns the whole pot."

Hominy or Grits

In old recipe books, grits are referred to as hominy. Today, hominy, however, commonly refers to dried and hulled corn. When the corn is coarsely milled it becomes "grits," named for the gritty particles. Most southern cooks prefer cooking regular grits, but quick-cooking ones are more widely available. If you can find regular grits, they take longer to cook, but seem to have a fresher flavor.

Since they are made the same way as polenta, but from white instead of yellow corn, grits can be prepared in exactly the same way. Serve them hot and creamy, or let cool and then bake or fry.

Serves 4

4 cups water
1/2 teaspoon salt
1 cup grits
1 tablespoon butter

In a saucepan, bring the water to a boil and add the salt. Stir in the grits. Reduce the heat to medium-low and cook, stirring regularly, until thick and the spoon stands up in the middle, about 10 minutes for quick grits, 20–40 minutes for regular grits.

The word grits comes from the Middle English gyrt for "bran." Grits are boiled and served as a side dish or cereal. They are available "regular," which are full-sized granules that take up to 40 minutes to cook, "quick," which are smaller granules and cook in 15–20 minutes, or "instant," which require the addition of boiling water only. Look for stone-ground grits for the best flavor.

Baked Grits

These have been nicknamed Christmas grits at my house because they include flecks of red and green peppers and because they go so well with the Christmas ham. They could also be served for breakfast. Leftovers are sublime fried in a little oil. This recipe uses quick-cooking grits because they are more widely available than regular grits. If you prefer regular grits, prepare them according to the recipe on page 122 and add the other ingredients as directed here.

Serves 6

3 tablespoons butter
$^1/_2$ yellow onion or 3 green onions, tops included, chopped
$^1/_2$ green bell pepper, seeded and chopped
$^1/_2$ red bell pepper, seeded and chopped
1 fresh red or green chile, seeded and minced (see Glossary)
3 cups water
dash of salt
1 cup quick-cooking grits
$^1/_4$ cup shredded Cheddar cheese
$^1/_4$ cup milk
paprika

Preheat an oven to 350 degrees F. Butter an 8-inch square baking dish or 8-inch cast-iron skillet.

In another skillet over medium-high heat, melt the butter. Add the onion, bell peppers, and chile and sauté until just softened, 3–4 minutes.

Meanwhile, in a saucepan, bring the water to a boil. Add the salt and slowly add the grits, stirring all the while. Cook over medium heat, stirring constantly, for 5–10 minutes, or longer if you want a finer texture. Stir in the onion mixture, cheese, and milk and mix well. Taste for seasoning.

Place in the prepared baking dish. (At this point, the dish may be covered and refrigerated up to overnight.) Sprinkle with paprika and bake until set and just beginning to brown on the top, 25–30 minutes. Serve hot.

Or let cool completely, slice, and fry in a little oil in a nonstick pan, turning once, until crisp. Serve as a side dish or for breakfast.

Pot of Beans

Basically every pot of beans starts out the same way. To shorten cooking time and, some say, to reduce the presence of flatulence-causing carbohydrates, beans are soaked in water, preferably overnight. See glossary for quick-soak directions and other pertinent bean information. You can also try the following variation for Benny Clewis's Gas-Free Beans, made that way by adding carrots. Any dried bean may be used in this recipe from speckled Appaloosas to dark red, light red, or white kidney beans, from baby green or baby white limas to tongues of fire beans, from old-fashioned field peas to colorful calypso beans. Call Beans and Beyond (see Resources) in Oakland, California, to receive their catalog listing over a hundred organic and other commercial bean varieties. Beans always taste better if cooked a day before they are served.

Serve these beans with Hush Puppies (page 145), Basic Corn Bread (page 239), or Corny Corn Bread Muffins (page 144).

Serves 6–8

2¹/₂ cups (1 pound) dried beans, rinsed and picked over
8–10 cups water
1 pound ham hocks; 3 ounces salt pork, blanched 5 minutes and drained; 4 ounces slab bacon, whole or cut into pieces; or 1 smoked turkey neck (optional)
salt and ground black pepper

Soak the beans overnight in water to cover by several inches. Drain.

In a large pot, combine the drained beans, 8 cups of the water, and the meat, if using. Bring to a boil, reduce the heat to low, cover partially, and simmer, stirring occasionally, until tender. Add more water as needed. Timing will vary between 45 minutes and 2 hours, depending upon age and type of bean. Lima beans take only a short time, red beans about 1 hour, and black beans about 1¹/₂ hours. These are approximate times only, as beans have varying degrees of natural tenderness, even among the same variety.

When the beans are tender, the meat, if using, can be removed from the pot. If ham hocks were used, the meat can be cut off the bone and stirred back into the beans. The bacon, too, can be cut into small pieces and served in the beans. I recommend discarding the salt pork and turkey neck, as there is more flavor than meat on them.

Season to taste with salt, if needed, and pepper to taste. Serve hot.

Monday became the traditional day in the South to cook a pot of beans, mainly because it was a good way to use the leftover ham bone from Sunday's dinner. Beans were an important source of protein and fiber in the diet of West Africans long before they came to the New World. Lentils, black-eyed peas, favas, and garbanzo beans were eaten in Africa. In America, lima, black, red, and many other kinds of beans were added to the repertoire. They can be eaten pods and all when young, shucked when mature, and dried for long storage. There are over a hundred different varieties, shapes, colors, and flavors of beans. See the Glossary for more information on the different types of beans and Resources for sources.

BENNY CLEWIS'S GAS-FREE BEANS: Texas cook Benny Clewis learned from his mother that one way to "kill the gas in red beans" was to cook them with carrots. He recommends serving these when your friends or the local "society group drops in for dinner or supper." Combine 2½ cups (1 pound) soaked and drained red beans; 2 yellow onions, chopped; 1 carrot, peeled and cut into ½-inch cubes; a dollop of celery seeds; 2 garlic cloves, minced; and 1 teaspoon of sugar in a large, heavy pot with at least three times as much water as beans. Bring to a boil, reduce the heat to low, and simmer until the beans are tender enough to serve, about 1½ hours. Then add a dash of salt, 3 tablespoons Worcestershire sauce, and a dash of hot-pepper sauce and cook 10 minutes or longer to blend the flavors. Serve hot.

SOUL BROTHERS BEANS: Rip Wilson, proprietor of Soul Brothers Kitchen in Berkeley, California, serves a pot of black-eyed peas that are so packed with flavor you don't miss the pork one bit. To make them, in a heavy saucepan, heat 2 tablespoons vegetable oil over medium heat and add 1 cup chopped celery; 1 bell pepper, seeded and chopped; and 1 yellow onion, chopped. Sauté until softened, about 5 minutes. Add 2½ cups (1 pound) soaked and drained black-eyed peas (or other dried beans) and water to cover by at least 2 inches. Bring to a boil, cover, reduce the heat to low, and cook, stirring occasionally, until tender, about 1½ hours. Season to taste with salt and pepper, stir in the chopped parsley, and serve.

Ham Hocks, Greens, and Black-eyed Peas

Here is the classic way of cooking beans, soul food style. Use collard greens, or Caribbean callaloo if you can find it fresh. Otherwise, beet tops, kale, or turnip greens will be fine. This is one of those dishes that tastes even better the next day. Serve it with Corny Corn Bread Muffins (page 144), Skillet-Baked Corn Bread (page 194), or Baking Powder Biscuits (pages 142–143).

Serves 6

1¼ cups (½ pound) dried black-eyed peas, picked over and rinsed
1–2 pounds ham hocks, cut into 2-inch rounds
1 yellow onion, chopped
2 garlic cloves, minced
1 fresh or pickled red or green chile (see Glossary)
9 cups water
1 pound collard, kale, turnip, beet, or mustard greens, sliced or leaves
   left whole
ground black pepper
Pepper Vinegar Sauce (page 105)

Soak the black-eyed peas in water to cover by several inches overnight. Drain.

In a heavy saucepan, combine the ham hocks, onion, garlic, chile pepper, and water and bring to a boil. Skim off any foam that forms on top. Stir in the drained black-eyed peas and bring to a boil again. Reduce the heat to medium and simmer until the peas are tender, about 45 minutes.

Add the greens and cook until very tender and all flavors have taken on a richness, about 20 minutes. Season to taste with black pepper. Remove the chile and discard.

Ladle into soup bowls and serve. Pass the Pepper Vinegar Sauce.

H a m   h o c k s and shanks are cut from the center of the round leg bone, next to the picnic shoulder. Usually sold smoked, the shanks are skinless and the hocks still have their skins on. These tasty morsels are fabulous to cook with a pot of beans or greens. Or cook them with onions and garlic as in the Brazilian recipe for Feijoada Completa (pages 84–85).

Southern Goober Soup

High-protein peanuts appear in savory as well as sweet dishes created by African cooks whether their kitchens are in Mississippi, Georgia, Martinique, or Senegal. These leguminous plants, related to peas, grow underground and are also called ground nuts or ground peas. Peanut-rich soups are found in West Africa and in the American South, where they are still a major crop.

Serves 6–8

2 tablespoons vegetable oil
1 yellow onion, chopped
1 celery stalk, chopped
1 green bell pepper, seeded and chopped
1 red or green pickled chile, chopped (see Glossary)
1 teaspoon paprika
1 teaspoon ground cumin
1 teaspoon ground coriander
6–8 cups chicken stock (see Glossary)
1/2 cup long- or short-grain white or brown rice
1/2 cup creamy peanut butter
salt and ground black pepper
chopped fresh parsley

In a large, heavy saucepan over medium heat, warm the oil. Add the onion, celery, and bell pepper and sauté until softened, about 5 minutes. Stir in the chile, paprika, cumin, and coriander and cook 1 minute. Stir in the chicken stock and bring to a boil. Add the rice and stir well. Cook, uncovered, until the rice is tender, 15–20 minutes.

Spoon a little of the hot soup into the peanut butter to thin it, then stir the peanut butter into the soup. Season to taste with salt and pepper. Cook another 5 minutes or so to blend flavors. Ladle into soup bowls, sprinkle with parsley and serve hot.

George Washington Carver, an agricultural chemist whose efforts to improve the economy of the South included crop diversification, developed hundreds of uses for the peanut (as well as the sweet potato and the soybean). The United States produces 10 percent of the world's peanuts and makes greater use of them for food than any other country. Two-thirds of the peanut production goes into roasted peanuts, peanut butter, and confectionary products. The rest is crushed for oil and for animal feed.

Peanuts were a portable and nourishing food for both armies during the Civil War, when they inspired the song "Eating Goober Peas." Their popularity with the soldiers created a national market for them. Today, peanuts are the ninth most valuable crop in the United States.

Fried Catfish

Firm and meaty, catfish tastes much better than its whisker-faced appearance suggests. Catfish have long been the primary fresh fish eaten by southern blacks. In the past they were pulled out of streams and rivers. Raymond Washington, who grew up outside of Austin, Texas, used to eat plenty of catfish from the rivers, but now the waters are too polluted. "Catfish are scavengers," he laments.

To satisfy his own love of catfish, Raymond and his father, Clarence, built a catfish farm that is fed by rainwater reservoirs. To share their bounty, Raymond runs a fifty-seat restaurant called Catfish Hill on the farm. On weekends he serves fried or baked catfish with pinto beans, coleslaw, and hush puppies. Seasoned Flour (page 107) can be substituted for the flour, cornmeal, paprika, salt, and cayenne pepper. Other firm fish fillets can be used in place of the catfish.

Serves 4

1/4 cup all-purpose flour
1/4 cup yellow or white cornmeal
2 teaspoons paprika
1 teaspoon salt
dash of cayenne pepper
4 catfish (or other firm fish) fillets, 3 to 6 ounces each, cut into
   serving-sized pieces if large
1/4–1/2 cup vegetable oil
lemon wedges, Creole Rémoulade (page 168), or West Indian Hot Sauce
   (page 23)

In a shallow plate combine the flour, cornmeal, paprika, salt, and cayenne pepper. Coat the fish fillets with the mixture, patting it on to get as much to adhere as possible. Lay the fish on a plate or baking sheet in a single layer and place in the freezer for 5 minutes or the refrigerator up to 2 hours. This will help to make the coating stick.

In a nonstick or cast-iron skillet, pour in oil to a depth of 1/4 inch. Heat to 325 degrees F, or until the oil looks hazy and is moving on the surface. Take the fish from the freezer and slide it into hot oil. Fry, turning once, until well browned, 3–5 minutes on each side; the timing depends upon the thickness of the fillet and the type of fish. Catfish will take about 4 minutes on each side.

Serve with lemon wedges or sauce.

VARIATIONS: *The fish fillets can be soaked in buttermilk or dipped in beaten egg before dipping them into the cornmeal mixture.*

Stuffing the shells, or "bark," of small blue crabs with crab meat and seasoning is done in Bahia, in the Caribbean, and along the Low Counties of South Carolina and Georgia. The undisputed champion cooks of this dish in the South, however, are the Gullahs, who live on the Sea Islands off the coast of South Carolina. As with barbecue sauces and sweet potato pies, everyone puts a personal twist on the recipe to make the crab special and they don't divulge the secret. Try the recipe for Siris Recheados (page 90) from Bahia or season the crab meat with green onion, dry mustard, and Tabasco sauce, and bind it with bread crumbs and heavy cream or mayonnaise to give it a southern accent. Then, bake or fry it.

Since 1960, hundreds of acres of soybean and cotton fields in Mississippi, Alabama, and Arkansas have been converted into commercial catfish ponds. Mississippi catfish farms supply 65 percent of the catfish eaten in the United States, about 200 million pounds a year. The most popular way to eat catfish is fried and served with ketchup, hush puppies, coleslaw, and French fries.

Baked Catfish

Raymond Washington bakes his catfish this way. It comes out flaky, fat-free, and really shows off the essence of this delicious fish. Any firm white fish fillet can be substituted. It can be served with Creole Rémoulade (page 168), Pepper Vinegar Sauce (page 105), or Creole Sauce (page 167).

Serves 4

4 catfish fillets, 3–6 ounces each, cut into serving-sized pieces if large
salt and ground black pepper
lemon pepper

Preheat an oven to 375 degrees F.

Place the catfish fillets in a shallow baking pan or dish. Sprinkle on both sides with salt, pepper, and lemon pepper. Bake 15 minutes, then turn and bake until cooked through, about 5 minutes longer. Serve immediately.

She-crab soup was made popular by William Days in 1920 when he and other African-American street vendors began selling it in Charleston, South Carolina. What makes it so special is the inclusion of the eggs from the female crab, which give it an added richness. It is expensive because there are more male crabs than female crabs.

Catfish Stew

If the catch wasn't as big as you hoped for all the mouths you want to feed, making a stew is the best way to stretch a small amount of meat or fish. Catfish stew is so good, however, it's worth making no matter how much fish you have.

Serves 6–8

For the stock:
1 whole catfish, 2–3 pounds, cleaned
1 teaspoon black peppercorns
2 celery stalks, coarsely chopped
1 yellow onion, chopped
2 fresh parsley sprigs
2 fresh thyme sprigs, or 1 teaspoon dried thyme leaves, crushed
1 bay leaf
5 cups water

2 ounces slab bacon, minced (optional)
2 tablespoons vegetable oil, or 2 tablespoons butter
1 yellow onion, chopped
2 tablespoons all-purpose flour
2 large baking potatoes, peeled and cut into 3/4-inch cubes
1 cup milk
salt and ground black pepper
chopped fresh parsley

To make the stock, fillet and skin the catfish. Cut the fillets into 1-inch pieces and reserve in the refrigerator. Place the head, tail, and bones of the fish and the peppercorns on a piece of cheesecloth and tie securely to make a bundle. Place in a saucepan. Add the celery, onion, parsley, thyme, bay leaf, and water. Bring to a boil, reduce the heat to low, cover partially, and simmer for 30 minutes. Remove the cheesecloth package and discard. Reserve the stock in the pan.

If using the bacon, in a skillet over medium heat, fry until crisp. Using a slotted spoon, remove to paper towels to drain. Pour off the fat. In the same skillet over medium heat, warm the oil. Add the onion and sauté until soft, about 3 minutes. Add the flour and and cook slowly, stirring, for 2 or 3 minutes. Stir in the potatoes and cook 1 minute. Stir in a little of the reserved stock and

Garfield Wright, Jr., started cooking at Tuminello's Restaurant, a seventy-five-year-old establishment in Vicksburg, Mississippi, when he was fifteen. That was over thirty–five years ago and he hasn't lost his enthusiasm for his profession. Now he is in charge of the kitchen at Maxwell's, where he puts his personal stamp on the upscale southern food there. His favorite seasoning for fish and for vegetables is lemon pepper.

stir well. Add salt to taste and cook over medium heat until the potatoes are done, about 10 minutes. Stir in the milk and reserved catfish and simmer until the fish is cooked, another 5 or 6 minutes.

Adjust the seasonings and serve topped with chopped parsley.

Salmon Patties

These patties are typically made with canned salmon stretched with bread crumbs. Any cooked salmon can be substituted and leftover barbecued salmon is a divine alternative. A squeeze of fresh lemon juice or a little yellow mustard spread on top is just the right condiment for the canned salmon version. If using fresh salmon, try the Creole Rémoulade (page 168) or one of the Caribbean hot sauces.

Geneva Francais, owner-chef of the African Brown Bag Restaurant in Atlanta, Georgia, serves salmon cakes with whole cooked sweet potatoes and a spicy red sauce. Serve these with Sweet Potato Biscuits (page 149).

Serves 4–6

1/2 yellow onion, chopped
2 eggs, beaten
1/2 cup fine dried bread crumbs
1/4 cup finely chopped fresh parsley
salt and ground black pepper
1 pound cooked salmon fillet or canned salmon, picked over for bones
  and flaked
1/4 cup Seasoned Flour (page 107) or cornmeal
3–4 tablespoons vegetable oil

In a bowl combine the onion, eggs, bread crumbs, parsley, salt and pepper to taste, and salmon and mix lightly. Using your hands, form into 3-inch patties about 1/2 inch thick. Place the flour on a shallow plate and dredge the patties in it.

In a heavy skillet, warm the oil over medium-high heat. Add the patties and fry, turning once, until heated through and browned, 3-4 minutes on each side. Serve piping hot.

The islands off the coasts of South Carolina and Georgia harbor the Gullah-speaking Geechees and a unique African-American heritage. It is here that postslavery African-American history began because the slaves here were the first to be freed. In 1862, they built the first black school, and they became the first African-American landowners. They were never sharecroppers. It is thought that the name Gullah came from the Gola tribe between Sierra Leone and the Ivory Coast, or was shortened from Angola.

The Geechees, who had come from different tribes, developed their own Gullah language in order to communicate with one another. The blend of African and English patois is still spoken by thousands of descendants who live in the Low Country.

St. Peter's Fish and Peppers

"This is a farm-raised fish called tilapia, but we also call it St. Peter's because it is the same one Peter served to feed the multitudes," says chef Geneva Francais.

In Africa there are over three hundred species of tilapia, an economical fish destined to become more available at markets in the United States. Serve it with steamed rice or Corn Bread Dressing (page 121).

Serves 6

For the coating:
1/4 cup cornmeal
2 tablespoons all-purpose flour
1/4 teaspoon cayenne pepper
1/4 teaspoon ground turmeric
salt and ground black pepper

6 tilapia or other white fish fillets, 3–5 ounces each
3 or 4 tablespoons vegetable oil
2 bell peppers, a mixture of colors, seeded and sliced
1/2 yellow or white onion, thinly sliced
dash of sugar
dash of cayenne pepper
salt
1 tablespoon fresh lemon juice
1 tablespoon water

To make the coating, combine all the ingredients in a shallow plate. Dredge the fish fillets in the cornmeal mixture, coating evenly.

In a heavy skillet or nonstick pan, heat 2 tablespoons of the oil until almost smoking. Add the fish and brown quickly on both sides. Remove to a plate.

To the same skillet over medium heat, adding more oil if needed, add bell peppers, onion, sugar, cayenne, and salt to taste. Sauté until peppers are tender, about 6 minutes. Return fish to the pan to finish cooking, about 2 minutes.

Remove the fish from the skillet to a heated serving platter.

To the same skillet over medium heat, add lemon juice and water and stir to mix with the peppers. Taste for seasoning. Spoon over the fish and serve.

Low Country Boil

I met Joelene Campbell at the King Tisdell Museum in Savannah, Georgia, where she is one of the guides. She told me about the tradition of making Low Country boil on the beach with her friends. Low Country is the name given to the marshy plains from Savannah up through the middle of the South Carolina coast.

To make the boil the old-fashioned way, you need a cast-iron pot with feet. Joelene uses an aluminum footed pot, but any pot you can use over an open flame will do. This seafood boil flavored with unshelled peanuts can also be made on the kitchen stove. When making it at home, it is best to make the base a day in advance to allow the flavors to develop. Serve with Red Rice (page 110).

Serves 8

1 yellow onion, chopped
3 quarts water, or as needed
6 ounces green peanuts in the shells
8–12 small new potatoes, unpeeled
2 or 3 blue crabs or 1 Dungeness crab, uncooked or cooked and cleaned
1 pound smoked sausages, cut into 2-inch lengths
4 ears of corn, cut into 2- or 4-inch lengths
1/2–1 pound medium shrimp in the shell
salt and cayenne pepper
Pepper Vinegar Sauce (page 105), Tabasco sauce, or other
    hot-pepper sauce

In a large, heavy pot or aluminum footed tub, combine the onion and the water. Bring to a boil, drop in the peanuts, and boil for 10 minutes. Add the potatoes and cook another 10 minutes, then drop in the uncooked crabs. (If using cooked crabs, put them in after the shrimp.) Add the sausages at this point, too. After another 10 minutes, put in the corn. Cook 10 more minutes and add the shrimp (and the cooked crab). Cook until the shrimp turn pink, 5–10 minutes longer. Add salt and cayenne pepper to taste.

Using a slotted spoon, retrieve the cooked food and divide evenly among individual bowls or place in one large serving dish or bowl. Ladle the soup over everything. Take the peanuts out last and set them aside separately so they can cool and be shelled. Pass the hot sauce.

Chitterlings or chittlins are considered quintessential soul food. In the spirit of nothing is wasted, they show how good the offal meats can be, if you have the time to prepare them. Fortunately, chitterlings can be found already cleaned, tenderly cooked, and frozen. I met Ann Stirgis's husband, Jim, at lunch at the Walnut Hills restaurant in Vicksburg, Mississippi, and he said to call her because she makes the best chitterlings in the world: In a 2-quart saucepan combine 1 pound cleaned and cooked chitterlings, cut into small pieces; 2 tablespoons vinegar; 1 tablespoon fresh lemon juice; 1 yellow onion, chopped; 1 potato, peeled and cubed; and dried thyme, oregano, and cayenne pepper to taste with about 1 cup water. Bring to a boil and cook until the vegetables are tender, 20–30 minutes. Serve these savory morsels with hot sauce on the side to six people.

Fried Chicken

Making greaseless fried chicken depends on maintaining the high heat of the oil so the crust does not absorb it. Chef Dye Rhodan, from Hilton Head, South Carolina, shares her method and advises, "Fry it hot and fast, until the juices run out clear." She also recommends a quick fry in hot oil and finishing it in the oven to reduce the amount of oil absorption. Peanut or vegetable oil may be used to fry the chicken, but the most tasty and crisp results will come from shortening or lard.

Before frying, the chicken is soaked in water or buttermilk to keep it moist. After it is dredged in the spicy coating, it should be placed in the refrigerator for 15 minutes or as long as overnight, a step that helps keep it crisp when frying.

Serves 4

1 chicken, 3–4 pounds, cut into serving pieces, or 3–4 pounds
   chicken parts

For buttermilk fried chicken:
1 1/2 cups buttermilk
1 egg

For southern fried chicken:
large bowl of ice water

For coating:
1 cup all-purpose flour
1/2 teaspoon sugar
1 teaspoon salt
1/2 teaspoon ground black pepper
1/2 teaspoon garlic powder
1 teaspoon paprika
1/4 teaspoon cayenne pepper

2 1/2 cups vegetable shortening, lard, or peanut or vegetable oil

If making the buttermilk fried chicken, place the chicken pieces in a bowl with 1 cup of the buttermilk. Cover and refrigerate overnight.

If making the southern fried chicken, soak the chicken pieces in ice water for 15 minutes. This seals in the juices.

Martha Murphy, of Richmond, California, defines soul food as originally being the food that held the body and soul together. "The greens that slaves were allowed to grow in their gardens, the parts of livestock rejected by the big house, such as the intestines, the feet, the back, the neck, head, and tails, were nutritious and helped them survive. Consequently, a style of cooking developed while each cook added a personal spice or other seasoning. The cooking style continues to evolve and change with what is available, as exemplified with the use of wine as a contemporary ingredient."

For both recipes, make the coating. Combine the flour, sugar, salt, black pepper, garlic powder, paprika, and cayenne pepper in a brown paper bag for the southern fried chicken or on a shallow plate for the buttermilk fried chicken.

If making the southern fried chicken, retrieve the chicken pieces, one at a time, from the ice water and drop into the bag, close, and shake well to coat all over. Remove and set on a baking sheet. When all the chicken is coated, place it in the refrigerator for at least 15 minutes.

If making the buttermilk fried chicken, in a shallow bowl, beat the egg and then beat in the remaining 1/2 cup buttermilk. One piece at a time, retrieve the chicken from the buttermilk, dip in the flour mixture, dip in the egg mixture, and then dip again in the flour mixture. Set on a baking sheet. When all the chicken is coated, place it in the refrigerator for 15 minutes.

To fry both the southern and the buttermilk versions, melt the shortening in a deep-fryer or deep, heavy pan over high heat to 325–350 degrees F. To test, dip a corner of the chicken in the hot oil; if it immediately sizzles, it is ready. Fry the chicken, a few pieces at a time, turning frequently, until golden and cooked through, 15–20 minutes. Remove and drain on a rack or on paper towels. Continue until all chicken is cooked. Serve hot.

Alternatively, fry the chicken just until the batter is set, 7–8 minutes. Then put it on a baking sheet and finish cooking in an oven preheated to 375 degrees F. Turn the pieces occasionally until cooked through, about 30 minutes. Serve hot.

Chicken and Dumplings

One chicken feeds many when cooked and stretched with light biscuity dumplings. The flavors are pure and comforting—as simple as a boiled hen with the dumplings cooked in the broth, or more elaborate, such as this version from Lottie Kennedy of Savannah, Georgia. Use a stewing hen; it will take longer to cook than a fryer but keeps its texture better. The chicken can be cut into serving pieces on the bone before cooking or left whole and carved as you would a roasted bird. It could also be boned after cooking and returned to the broth before the dumplings are added for a company presentation.

Serves 4–6

1 stewing or fryer chicken, about 3 pounds, skinned and cut into serving
   pieces if desired (see recipe introduction)
2 celery stalks, chopped or sliced
2 carrots, peeled and sliced or chopped
1 bell pepper, seeded and chopped
1 yellow onion, chopped
2 garlic cloves, minced
1 bay leaf
1 teaspoon dried thyme, crushed
2 teaspoons salt
$1/2$ teaspoon ground black or white pepper
Baking Powder Dumplings, Old-Fashioned Dumplings, or Egg Dumplings
   (recipes follow)
chopped fresh parsley

In a large, heavy stockpot, place the chicken and all the remaining ingredients except the dumplings and parsley. Add water to cover and bring to a boil. Reduce the heat to low and simmer until the chicken is tender, $1^{1}/2$–2 hours for a stewing hen, 45–60 minutes for a fryer. When cooked, remove the chicken. If you are serving the chicken whole to be carved at the table, simply set the chicken aside. If you are cutting it up, let it cool until it can be handled and then cut it into serving pieces on the bone, or bone it and cut the meat into pieces. (Save the bones for making stock.) Reserve the broth in the pot.

While the chicken is cooking, select a dumpling recipe and make the dough. Return the broth to a boil. Drop spoonfuls of the dumpling dough into the boiling broth. Sprinkle with parsley, cover, and cook until the dumplings are tender, 10–20 minutes depending upon the recipe.

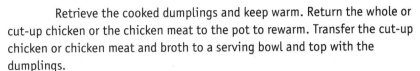

Retrieve the cooked dumplings and keep warm. Return the whole or cut-up chicken or the chicken meat to the pot to rewarm. Transfer the cut-up chicken or chicken meat and broth to a serving bowl and top with the dumplings.

If serving the chicken whole, transfer it to a platter and carve at the table. Spoon the broth and dumplings over chicken when serving. Sprinkle with more fresh chopped parsley if desired.

Baking Powder Dumplings

Like biscuits and very satisfying, these are classics.

Serves 4–6

1 cup all-purpose flour
2 teaspoons baking powder
$^1/_2$ teaspoon salt
$^1/_2$ cup milk

In a bowl, mix together the flour, baking powder, and salt. Pour in the milk and stir well, then beat with an electric mixer or wooden spoon until stiff. Drop by teaspoonfuls into the boiling broth. Cover and cook until puffed and done, 10–15 minutes.

Old-Fashioned Dumplings

These little doughy pieces taste like fat noodles.

Serves 4–6

$1^1/_2$ cups all-purpose flour, or as needed
$^1/_2$ teaspoon salt
$^1/_2$ cup water, chilled

In a bowl, mix together the flour and salt. Stir in the water to form a dough and then dump the dough onto a floured board. Knead until the dough becomes pliable and firm, adding more flour if the dough is too sticky. On the floured board, roll out about $^1/_4$ inch thick. Cut into $1^1/_2$-inch squares. Drop the dough squares into the boiling broth, cover, and cook until done, about 10 minutes.

Egg Dumplings

A bready texture characterizes these dumplings. Cook them covered without moving them for the whole 15 minutes.

Serves 4–6

1 cup sifted all-purpose flour
2 teaspoons baking powder
1/2 teaspoon salt
1 egg
1/4 cup milk

In a bowl, mix together the flour, baking powder, and salt. In another bowl beat together the egg and milk. Stir the wet ingredients into the dry ingredients to form a stiff dough. Drop by spoonfuls into the boiling broth. Cover the pot and cook until done, about 15 minutes.

Smothered Pork Chops

Smothered meats and vegetables are made by first browning the ingredients and then finishing them in a liquid, usually water, but stock may be used as well. They are actually smothered in steam until tender. This is how Leannie Moore of Berkeley, California, cooks them. Serve with Glazed Yams (page 112) and Plain Rice (page 107).

Serves 4

4 pork chops, shoulder or center-cut
1/4 cup all-purpose flour
1 teaspoon garlic powder
1/2 teaspoon salt
1/4–1/2 teaspoon ground black pepper
3 tablespoons vegetable oil
1 cup water or chicken stock (see Glossary)

Pat the pork chops dry with a paper towel. In a paper bag or on a shallow plate, combine the flour, garlic powder, salt, and pepper. One at a time, add the chops to the bag or plate and shake or dredge to coat with the flour mixture.

Making a silk purse from a sow's ear must have been coined because of dishes like chitterlings (page 133), sandwiches filled with pig's ear (page 227), and hog head cheese. They exemplify the African specialty for taking leftovers and creating highly seasoned richness. Not really a cheese, the hog head is cooked with the pig's gelatinous feet until the meat falls off the bones. Then it is seasoned with pepper and spices and formed into a pâtélike loaf.

In a skillet large enough to hold all 4 chops in a single layer, warm the oil over high heat. Add the chops and brown well on both sides. Pour off any oil. Pour in the water, cover, and cook, turning once or twice, until "smothered down," about 20 minutes. Adjust the seasonings and serve hot.

Glazed Ham

Brown sugar, honey, and dry mustard give the Sunday, holiday, or company ham a rich mahogany sheen and melt into a salty-sweet sauce that complements the pink meat. Kids love this ham as much as grown-ups do. Serve it with Oven Rice (page 109), Glazed Yams (page 112), Collard Greens (page 119), and Baking Powder Biscuits (pages 142–143).

Serves 10–12

1 bone-in ham, 5–8 pounds, ready to cook
6–8 whole cloves
1 cup firmly packed brown sugar
3/4 cup honey
1 heaping tablespoon dry mustard

Preheat an oven to 325 degrees F.

Place the ham in a roasting pan. Cut diagonal slashes over the surface of the ham and stud with the cloves. In a small bowl, combine the sugar, honey, and mustard and mix well. Using a spoon or pastry brush, spread the mixture all over the surface of the ham, and place the ham in the oven.

Bake, basting frequently with the glaze until it is dark mahogany and sticks to the ham. Plan on 20 minutes per pound.

Transfer to a platter, let cool slightly, and then slice and serve with the pan juices on the side.

Hams come from the large hind pork leg. Fresh hams have a bone running through the center and a thick layer of meat covered with fat and skin. They can be roasted, smoked, or braised in liquids. Hams that are smoked have been cured and must be roasted or baked before eating. "Country" hams are heavily salted and must be soaked before cooking.

Oxtail or Shortrib Stew

Martha Murphy, who lives in Richmond, California, shared this recipe. Martha's mother came from New Orleans and her father, also a cook, came from another part of Louisiana. "Both cooked differently, Mother used tomatoes where Dad used more garlic," says Martha, whose style is a combination of both. She describes her cooking as being "somewhat like a running brook that diverts from the mainstream and takes on its own configuration." Whereas Martha cooks with wine, her mother never did. Serve with Plain Rice (page 107) or Oven Rice (page 109).

Serves 4–6

3 tablespoons vegetable oil
3 pounds oxtails, cut into 1½-inch sections, or 3 pounds short ribs
1 yellow onion, finely chopped
3 garlic cloves, chopped
2 large or 4 small bay leaves
½ teaspoon grated nutmeg, preferably freshly grated
1 tablespoon fresh lemon juice, red wine, or wine vinegar
2 cans (16 ounces each) peeled tomatoes with their juice
2 celery stalks, including leaves, finely chopped
½ green bell pepper, seeded and finely chopped
salt and ground black pepper

In a heavy pot, heat the oil over high heat and brown the meat well on all sides. Add all the remaining ingredients except the celery, bell pepper, and salt and pepper. Cover, reduce the heat to medium, and cook until tender, 1½–2 hours.

When the meat is tender and beginning to pull away from the bones and the sauce is cooked down, add the celery and bell pepper and season to taste with salt and pepper. Cook 10 minutes longer. This brief cooking ensures a crunch at the end. Serve hot.

NOTE: This dish can also be cooked in a pressure cooker. It will take about 40 minutes.

Wild game has always played an important role in African-American dining. Lottie Kennedy, who lives in Savannah, Georgia, has hunter friends who occasionally bring by a freshly killed raccoon. Here is how she prepares it: Once cleaned and cut up into serving-sized pieces, the coon is combined with celery, garlic, bell pepper, onions, red pepper flakes, and water in a large stockpot and boiled an hour or so until tender. Then it is removed from the broth and placed in a hot oven to brown well, which takes another half hour or so. Some cooks soak the coon overnight in salt water or vinegar, but Lottie prefers this method of twice-cooking to rid the animal of its gamey flavor.

Benny's Hoecake

Benny Wade Lewis is a Texas cook who lives near Houston. His father taught him to make hoecake bread, which is cooked on top of the stove and goes "along with almost any meal." This quick bread was one of the first recipes Benny learned to cook when he was a very young child and he remembers syrup always being served with the meal, usually Brother Rabbit Blue Label Molasses.

Serves 6–8

2 cups all-purpose flour
1 tablespoon baking powder
1/4 teaspoon salt
1/2 cup shortening or bacon drippings
2 teaspoons sugar dissolved in 2/3 cup milk

In a bowl, stir together the flour, baking powder, and salt. Add the shortening and cut in with a pastry blender, 2 knives, or your fingers until the mixture resembles coarse crumbs. Make a well in the center; add the milk mixture all at once. Now, stir just until the dough clings together in a rough mass. Turn out onto a lightly floured surface and knead gently 10–12 strokes.

On the floured surface, roll out the dough into a round about 9 inches in diameter and 1/2 inch thick. Take an ungreased cast-iron well-seasoned skillet (see page 268) and put the dough round in it. Pat the dough until it touches the wall all the way around the inside of the skillet.

Turn a burner to medium and place the skillet on it. After 4 or 5 minutes, lift the round to see if it has browned. If so, flip it or gently turn it with a wide spatula. Cook another 5–10 minutes on the second side. To check if it is done, take a wooden toothpick and insert it in the center. If it comes out clean, it's done. If the dough is too thick or the heat too high it will burn a little, but, as Benny says, "this only helps to season the taste of the hoecake."

Cut it into wedges and serve hot.

Hoecakes are also made with cornmeal and cooked into small pancakes to eat with syrup as a snack, side dish, or for breakfast. To make them, in a bowl, combine 2 cups yellow or white cornmeal, 1 cup all-purpose flour, dash of salt, and 2 tablespoons sugar. Cut in 1/2 cup shortening until the mixture is mealy, then stir in 1 1/4 cups buttermilk to make a stiff batter. In a smoking-hot cast-iron skillet, heat the oil and drop in spoonfuls of the batter to make 3-inch cakes, spacing the cakes an inch or so apart. Cook until browned on one side, flip them, and cook on the second side. Keep warm while repeating with the remaining ingredients. Serve hot.

Baking Powder Biscuits

Biscuits are the ultimate quick bread. Everyone who makes great biscuits has a special knack. Whether it's using lard, shortening, or butter; keeping the fat cold and working it into the flour just right; or adding an extra dash of salt or sugar, the best biscuits are flaky and melt in your mouth.

This dough can either be patted together, kneaded lightly, and rolled or patted out on a lightly floured board before being cut, or the biscuits can be formed by pulling off pieces of dough and shaping them by hand. That's how Georgian Lottie Kennedy makes them and it's also how Fanny Marie Harris, who learned the technique from her grandmother in Shreveport, Louisiana, makes them. Fanny prefers tiny hand-formed biscuits because "you get more of the crispy outside that way." Lottie, who raised her nine children on homemade buttermilk biscuits, always rubs margarine over the hot tops when they come out of the oven and serves them with sugar syrup made from cane or sorghum.

This recipe makes a big batch, and with the addition of sugar, becomes great shortcake (see variation).

Makes twenty-four 2-inch biscuits

4 cups all-purpose flour
3 tablespoons baking powder
³⁄₄ teaspoon salt
¹⁄₂ teaspoon sugar (optional)
¹⁄₃ cup shortening, lard, unsalted butter, or margarine
1¹⁄₄ cups milk or buttermilk
¹⁄₄ cup butter or margarine (optional)

Preheat an oven to 450 degrees F.

In a bowl, stir together the flour, baking powder, salt, and sugar (if using.) Add the shortening and, using a pastry blender, 2 knives, or your fingers, cut in until the mixture is mealy. Pour in the milk and stir until the dough holds together in a rough mass. On a lightly floured surface, gently knead to form a loaf.

To form the biscuits by hand, pinch off walnut-sized pieces of the dough. Form into balls by pinching the dough ends under the balls to make smooth tops. Place on greased baking sheets and flatten slightly.

To cut out the biscuits, on a lightly floured surface, pat or roll out the dough ¹⁄₂–³⁄₄ inch thick. Using a biscuit cutter or glass 2 inches in diameter, cut

SHORTCAKE VARIATION: Add ¹⁄₂ cup sugar to the dry ingredients and make the dough as directed. On a lightly floured surface, pat out the dough about ³⁄₄ inch thick. Using a biscuit cutter or glass 3 inches in diameter, cut out rounds. Place them on a greased baking sheet. Gather up the scraps and pat them out, then cut out as many more 3-inch rounds as possible. Bake as directed until puffed and lightly browned, about 25 minutes. Makes about 10 shortcakes. Top with berries and whipped cream.

out rounds. Place the rounds on greased baking sheets. Pat the scraps together and cut out as many more rounds as possible. The last biscuit is made by hand.

Bake until risen and lightly browned on top, 15–20 minutes. If you like, rub the butter over the tops as soon as the biscuits come out of the oven. Serve warm.

Beaten Biscuits

These chewy little breads were invented before baking powder and baking soda made biscuit rising easy. Originally the dough was actually beaten with a mallet or cleaver handle, sometimes outdoors against a tree stump. For a modern interpretation and to show how a quite nice little biscuit can still be made without a rising agent, these are "beaten" in an electric mixer fitted with a dough hook. When the biscuits are baked, each one develops an indentation where it can be pulled apart and slathered with butter, honey, or cane syrup.

Makes 12 biscuits

3 cups sifted all-purpose flour
1/2 teaspoon salt
3/4 teaspoon sugar
1/3 cup lard or shortening
1/2 cup milk

Preheat an oven to 350 degrees F.

Resift the flour with the salt and sugar into a mixing bowl. Add the lard and, using a pastry blender, 2 knives, or your fingers, cut in until crumbly. Stir in the milk to make a stiff dough.

In an electric mixer fitted with a dough hook, beat the dough until it "blisters," 15 minutes. The tiny air pockets in the blisters are what will cause it to rise. The dough will be shiny and elastic.

Turn the dough onto a floured surface and roll out 1/2 inch thick. Using a biscuit cutter or glass 2 inches in diameter, cut out rounds. Arrange on a greased baking sheet and stick the tops of each with the tines of a fork in a couple of places.

Bake until lightly risen and just beginning to brown, about 30 minutes. Serve hot.

After the Civil War, news about the slaves' freedom traveled west at various speeds. Although the war ended April 9, 1865, it wasn't until June 19 that the slaves in Texas found out they were free. A black folktale surmises that Texas landowners were holding off announcing emancipation until the end of the summer harvest. Juneteenth became a holiday for black Texans from that moment, and has since been shared as an African-American holiday in states all across the South.

Texas cook Benny Clewis says a typical menu for a Juneteenth celebration includes barbecued goat, red and yellow watermelons, potato salad, red beans, cat head biscuits, and to drink, home brew mash beer, white lightning whiskey, and chalk wine. Cat head biscuits are made with flour, eggs, milk and sugar. They have no rising agents, so when they are rolled and cut they come out looking like little cat heads.

Corny Corn Bread Muffins

In this recipe from Rosemary Kennedy, creamed corn and canned jalapeños are added to basic corn bread to give it extra oomph. The muffins are great cold, which makes them perfect for taking to potlucks. Try making them in mini muffin tins for bite-sized treats.

Makes 12 large muffins or 36 mini muffins

1¹/₂ cups yellow cornmeal
1¹/₂ cups all-purpose flour
1 tablespoon baking powder
¹/₂ teaspoon salt
1 egg
1 can (16¹/₂ ounces) cream-style corn
¹/₂ cup milk
¹/₂ cup (3¹/₂ ounces) canned chopped green chiles (optional)
¹/₄ cup vegetable oil, or ¹/₄ cup butter, melted

Preheat an oven to 375 degrees F. Grease 12 muffin-tin cups.

In a bowl, stir together the cornmeal, flour, baking powder, and salt. In another bowl, beat the egg. Stir in the corn, milk, chiles, and oil. Stir the wet ingredients into the dry ingredients just until moistened; do not overbeat. Pour into the prepared muffin-tin cups, filling about two-thirds full.

Bake until slightly browned on top, 20–25 minutes. Remove from oven and let cool a few minutes before removing from the tin. Serve hot.

Hush Puppies

Hush-puppy stories vary by location and reason, but it is unanimously agreed these fried corn cakes got their name from being tossed to the dogs to keep them quiet. Whether it was fishermen frying their catch or slaves sitting around a campfire after processing sugar for syrup and grinding, when the dogs got restless from the good cooking smells, their namesakes were created. Now they are commonly served with fried catfish.

The egg makes these cornmeal fritters light, but can be omitted. Adjust the amount of buttermilk to compensate. The flour also makes them lighter, but it too can be omitted, in which case use less liquid. Seasoning with cayenne, green onions, and parsley makes these crisp fritters tasty accompaniments to Fried Catfish (page 128), Catfish Stew (pages 130–131), or Fried Chicken (pages 134–135).

Makes about twenty-four 2-inch fritters

2 cups yellow cornmeal
1/2 cup all-purpose flour
1 teaspoon baking soda
2 teaspoons baking powder
1 1/2 teaspoons salt
1/4 teaspoon cayenne pepper
1 egg, beaten
1 1/3 cups buttermilk
4 green onions, including tops, minced
3 tablespoons chopped fresh parsley
peanut oil for deep-frying

In a mixing bowl, stir together the cornmeal, flour, baking soda, baking powder, salt, and cayenne. In another bowl, beat the egg and add the buttermilk, green onions, and parsley, mixing well. Stir the wet ingredients into the dry ingredients and mix well.

In a deep-fryer or deep, heavy pot, pour in oil to a depth of 3 inches. Heat to 375 degrees F. Working in batches, carefully drop the batter, either by rounded spoonfuls or formed into 3-inch long "pones" into the hot oil. Fry, turning with a slotted spoon, until crisp and golden, about 5 minutes. Using the slotted spoon, retrieve the fritters and drain on a rack or paper towels. Serve hot.

Corn Dumplings

Fanny Marie Harris of Shreveport, Louisiana, shared this method for making what is also known as hot-water corn bread and is cooked in the pot likker left from a pot of greens (page 119). These dumplings are equally delicious substituted for the flour dumplings in Chicken and Dumplings (pages 136–137). Fanny says, "Whatever you don't use in the pot can be fried in a skillet."

Serves 4

2 cups water
1 cup yellow cornmeal
pinch of baking powder
1/2 teaspoon salt
1 egg

Have the pot of greens boiling on the stove (see recipe introduction) and ready a bowl of cold water.

In a saucepan, bring the water to a boil. Add the cornmeal, baking powder, and salt, stirring vigorously. (A whisk works well for this step.) Keep stirring until the cornmeal is incorporated. Then, take it off the burner, add the egg, and quickly beat it in. Keep stirring fast-fast-fast to beat the egg well into the batter.

Put your hand into the bowl of cold water and then scoop up a walnut-sized piece of dough and form it into a ball. Drop the ball into the boiling pot of likker. Repeat, forming as many dumplings as you want. Cook, turning to heat on all sides, until they float and are set, about 5–7 minutes. Serve hot. Fry any remaining batter in oil, if desired.

VARIATION: *In a saucepan combine 2 cups cold water, the cornmeal, baking powder, and salt. Mix well and bring to a boil. Cook, stirring continuously, until thickened, 8–10 minutes. Remove from the heat and beat until lukewarm. Beat in the egg. Drop by spoonfuls into the boiling pot likker, cover, and cook until set and cooked through, 10–15 minutes. Serve hot.*

Crackling Bread

Louise Haney, who grew up on a farm outside of the beautiful town of Florence, Alabama, described the pig butchering she helped do when she was growing up, which was similar to the description given by Sara Brook in *You May Plow Here*, right. Crackling bread, like other breads, used to be only cooked in cast-iron skillets over coals in a big open fireplace. A lid was put on top of the skillet, then hot coals were piled on the lid to ensure even heat.

Serves 6

1 cup Cracklings (page 148), finely cut
1 1/2 cups yellow or white cornmeal
3/4 cup whole-wheat flour
1/2 teaspoon baking soda
1/4 teaspoon salt
1 egg
1 cup buttermilk or sour milk (see note)

Preheat an oven to 400 degrees F. Grease a 9-inch cast-iron skillet or 9-inch baking or pie pan.

In a bowl stir together the cracklings, cornmeal, flour, baking soda, and salt. In another bowl, beat the egg and stir in the buttermilk. Stir the wet ingredients into dry ingredients. Pour into the prepared skillet or pan.

Bake until lightly browned on top, 20–25 minutes. Let rest a few minutes before cutting into wedges. Serve hot.

NOTE: To sour milk, stir 1 tablespoon distilled white vinegar into 1 cup milk and let stand 30 minutes at room temperature.

"Before you smoke the meat you trim the fat off, and the fat would go for lard, and the skin that the lard came out of was cracklins. We'd cut the fat and skins up and put em . . . in a big black pot with three legs on it sitting on a brick. Then we'd make a fire . . . and somebody would sit there with a cracklin stick . . . carved from white oak—and they would stir it and it would cook and cook and cook until it turned brown. When it turned brown and go to the bottom, that's cracklins. . . . My mother would put them in a sack and let em drip to get the rest of the fat out. Then she'd put em in big old crocks in the kitchen on the tables, and whenever we want to make cracklin bread, you go and sift some cornmeal, put in salt and soda . . . and then you'd crumble up a lot of cracklins . . . and put some buttermilk and put it in the pan in the stove and cook it.*

Sara Brooks in* You May Plow Here

Cracklings

Nothing ever went to waste, says Louise Haney, not even the little crisp bits left from the fatback after the lard was rendered. These cracklings, or cracklin's, sprinkled with a little salt, are delicious, but pure cholesterol. Pork skin comes in big flats and is cooked long and slow to both render out the fat and tenderize what's left. In the Spanish Caribbean these are called *chicharrónes*.

Makes about 2 cups

1 pound pork skin, cut into thin strips

Preheat an oven to 350 degrees F.

Lay the strips of pork skin in a single layer on baking sheet. Place in the oven and cook, turning occasionally, until crisp and golden, about 1½ hours. Using a slotted spoon, remove from the pan and drain on paper towels. Let cool.

Store in an airtight container in the refrigerator 1½ weeks or freeze several months. To recrisp, place in a preheated 350 degree F oven for 5 minutes.

Sweet Potato Biscuits

These doughy morsels are delicious with Fried Chicken (pages 134–135) or Glazed Ham (page 139), and sublime with Southern Goober Soup (page 127) or Salmon Patties (page 131). This makes a very wet dough and a wonderful biscuit that is soft and potatoey in the center and crisp on the outside.

Makes about twenty 2-inch biscuits

2 sweet potatoes or garnet yams (about 1 pound)
³/₄ cup milk
3 cups all-purpose flour
1 tablespoon baking powder
¹/₂ teaspoon salt
¹/₄ cup shortening
2 tablespoons butter, melted

Preheat an oven to 375 degrees F.

Using a fork, prick the sweet potato skins in several places. Place them on the oven rack and bake until tender, about 45 minutes. Remove from the oven and, as soon as they are cool enough to handle, peel the sweet potatoes. Place them in a bowl and mash with a potato masher or fork or pass them through a food mill placed over a bowl. Stir in the milk, mixing well.

In another bowl stir together the flour, baking powder, and salt. Add the shortening and cut in with a pastry blender, two knives, or your fingers until the mixture looks mealy. Stir in the sweet potato mixture and mix well to form a soft dough.

Turn the dough out onto a floured work surface and pat out ³/₄ inch thick. To keep the moist dough from sticking, sprinkle it with flour and dust a biscuit cutter or glass 2 inches in diameter with flour before cutting. Cut out rounds and place on a lightly greased baking sheet. Brush with the melted butter, and bake until lightly browned, about 25 minutes. Serve hot.

Tea Cakes

A cross between pound cake and shortbread, these light sweets are popular from Alabama to Oklahoma. Alabaman Louise Haney remembers these as her childhood cookies. To grate the nutmeg she wrapped the whole nutmeg in cloth and pounded it with a hammer. The tea cakes were cooked in a wood–fired oven.

Lillie Brown grew up on a farm in Bonita, Louisiana, where she lived until she was fourteen. She learned to cook from her mother when she was six years old. The first taste she remembers as a child was grating nutmeg for tea cakes. "Brown sugar came in blocks then and we had to grind it, too."

Serve the cakes with coffee or tea, or use them as the base for fruit and cream shortcakes.

Makes about 20 cakes

2 cups sugar
1 cup butter or shortening, at room temperature
3 eggs
³/₄ cup buttermilk
1¹/₂ teaspoons vanilla extract
5–6 cups all-purpose flour
¹/₄ teaspoon ground allspice
¹/₄ teaspoon grated nutmeg, preferably freshly grated
2 teaspoons baking powder
¹/₄ teaspoon baking soda

Preheat an oven to 350 degrees F. Line a rimmed baking sheet or jelly roll pan with parchment paper and oil the paper.

In a bowl and with an electric mixer set on medium speed, beat together the sugar and butter until creamy. Beat in the eggs, one at a time, and then, the buttermilk. Add the vanilla. In another bowl, mix 1 cup of the flour with the allspice, nutmeg, baking powder, and baking soda. Add the flour mixture to the batter and mix well. Add another cup of flour and beat in. Then, beat in enough of the remaining flour to make a firm dough.

Turn the dough out into the prepared pan and pat into the pan to distribute evenly. Dip a sharp knife or cleaver into flour and cut the dough to form 20 pieces, 5 lines one way and 4 lines the other way. This won't separate the dough, but it will score it for easy removal after baking.

The grinding of sugar used to be a regular communal activity. On fall evenings, neighbors gathered together to feed the sugarcane into a one-mule treadmill. After collecting the juice, they poured it into a large kettle to be boiled into sugar. At the end of the evening, everyone gathered around the open fire, which now had an iron pot full of hot fat suspended over it. They slipped freshly caught fish and hush puppies into the fat to fry until golden.

Bake until puffed and set, 25–30 minutes. Do not allow the cakes to brown. They should be fully cooked but still an even pale gold. Let cool in the pan, then cut along scored lines to separate into cakes. Transfer to a serving dish and serve. Store leftover cakes in an airtight container up to 3 days.

Goober Brittle

Peanuts were adopted early by cooks in West Africa and in the southern United States. In both places they grow well and provide a source of protein and oil. Nut brittles and pralines are found in African-influenced kitchens in Brazil, where *pé-de-moleque* is made, in the Caribbean, and the southern United States. See the recipes for Coconut Candy (page 62) in the Caribbean chapter, Pralines (page 197) in the Louisiana Creole chapter, and Groundnut Toffee (page 264) in the Recent African Immigrants chapter.

Makes four 3-inch rounds

1¹/₂ *cups shelled raw peanuts*
2 *cups sugar*
1 *lemon, or 2 tablespoons fresh lemon juice*

Preheat an oven to 350 degrees F.

In a wide, shallow ungreased pan, spread out the peanuts in a single layer. Place in the oven to roast, stirring once or twice, until lightly browned, 5–7 minutes. Set aside.

Put the sugar in a heavy saucepan and melt it over low heat. To help keep it from sticking to the pan sides and caramelizing too fast, put a whole lemon on the end of a fork and stir the sugar with the lemon. Alternatively, add lemon juice to the sugar. Stir in the mixture constantly so the sugar doesn't burn and melts evenly.

When it has become a thin golden syrup, remove from the heat and stir in the nuts. Pour onto the parchment-lined baking sheet in 4 mounds. With knives or spoons, shape and flatten each mound until it is about 3 inches across and perfectly round. This must be done quickly before the syrup has cooled. Don't touch it with your hands as it is very hot and will blister your fingers.

Let cool and harden. Wrap individually in plastic wrap and store in an airtight container for up to 1 week.

Native to South America, probably Brazil, the peanut got the name goober *when African slaves associated it with other subterranean foods they knew and called it* nguba, *a Gedda word from the Congo. Peanuts were planted in the gardens of slaves and free blacks for personal use and for sale. They stored well and were roasted to eat throughout the year. During the cotton harvest and ginning, peanuts were boiled; the "peanut boilings" were community social events. In the winter they were more often roasted.*

Pie Crust

The secret to making flaky pie crust is to keep all the ingredients as cold as possible. Ice water and chilled shortening, lard, or butter, plus chilling the dough after it is rolled and placed in the plate, keep the fat and flour layers separate to ensure flakiness.

Makes one 9-inch unbaked pie crust

1½ cups all-purpose flour
¼ teaspoon salt
⅓ cup vegetable shortening, lard, or butter, chilled
¼ cup ice water

In a bowl stir together the flour and salt. Add the shortening and, using a pastry blender, two knives, or your fingers, cut in the shortening until well blended and the mixture holds together when pinched. Pour the water into the flour, stirring to mix. When the dough pulls together in a mass, dump it onto a floured surface.

Roll out the dough into a round to fit a 9-inch pie plate, and transfer the round to the pie plate, easing it in gently and trimming off the overhang. Crimp the edges between two fingers. Place in the freezer for 15 minutes or in the refrigerator, covered with plastic wrap, up to 24 hours.

Sweet Potato Pie

Every good cook has a special touch that makes his or her "potato pie" taste better than the neighbor's. I tasted plenty and found the tartness of a little lemon extract to be my favorite addition. Either the pale golden sweet potatoes or the orange sweet potatoes we call yams can be used. The sweet potato is less sweet and has a mealier texture, while the red garnet yam is quite sweet and smoother. The sweet potatoes may be boiled or baked, but I think the texture is better when baked. They don't absorb the water they do in boiling.

Serves 8

$1^1/_2$ pounds sweet potatoes or yams
Pie Crust (page 152)
3 tablespoons butter, at room temperature
$^1/_2$ cup sugar
2 eggs
$^1/_4$ teaspoon natural lemon extract
$^1/_2$ teaspoon ground allspice, preferably freshly ground
$^1/_2$ cup milk or heavy cream

Preheat an oven to 400 degrees F.

Using a fork, prick the sweet potato skins in several places. Place them on the oven rack and bake until tender, about 45 minutes.

Remove from the oven and, as soon as they are cool enough to handle, peel the sweet potatoes. Place them in a bowl and mash them with a potato masher or fork or pass them through a food mill placed over a bowl. Let cool. Leave the oven set at 400 degrees F. Meanwhile, make the crust as directed.

Line the crust with aluminum foil and spread a layer of dried beans over the foil (see note). Bake for 10 minutes to set it and keep it from getting soggy. Remove the beans and foil and bake another 5 minutes. Let cool. Reduce the oven temperature to 350 degrees F.

In a bowl, beat together the butter and sugar until light and fluffy. Beat in the eggs, one at a time. Add the cooled mashed potatoes and mix well. Add the lemon extract, allspice, and milk and mix well. Pour into the cooled pie shell. Bake until filling is firm and the crust is browned, 40–50 minutes. Cool on a rack and serve at room temperature or chilled.

NOTE: The beans keep the dough from rising and forming air pockets. They may be saved and reused for lining pies, but not for cooking and eating.

Fried Pies

Similar to fritters, these little flat half-moon fruit pies are family favorites from Mississippi to Texas. Sometimes called "sweetie pies," they were originally made from the scraps of pie dough and leftover pie filling. They are best fried in a little oil in a very hot cast-iron skillet. The filling might be anything from dried apples, apricots, or prunes to mixed fruits.

Cora Lee Conway, who cooks an excellent Southern buffet at the Agricultural Museum in Jackson, Mississippi, makes deliciously tart apple-filled fried pies, which inspired these.

Makes eight 6-inch fried pies

6–8 ounces dried apples
1/2 cup sugar
1 tablespoon fresh lemon juice
1/2 teaspoon ground cinnamon
1/4 teaspon ground allspice
1/4 teaspoon natural lemon extract (optional)
Pie Crust dough (page 152)
vegetable oil for frying

In a saucepan combine the apples, sugar, lemon juice, and water to cover by 1 inch. Bring to a boil, reduce the heat to medium and simmer uncovered, stirring frequently, until the fruit is soft and mushy and the liquid has evaporated, about 20 minutes. Add more water if necessary. Stir in cinnamon, allspice, and lemon extract (if using). Let cool.

Make the pie dough. On a lightly floured board, pinch off a walnut-sized piece (one-eighth) of the dough and roll out into a round 1/8 inch thick. Repeat until all dough is rolled into rounds. (Alternatively, roll out all the dough at once and, using a circular cutter 4 or 5 inches in diameter, cut out 8 rounds.) Spread an eighth of the filling in the center of each round, being sure to leave an edge for sealing. Fold each round in half, press the edges, and seal with the tines of a fork.

In a cast-iron skillet, pour in oil to a depth of 1/4 inch and heat over medium-high heat. When it is hot, add the pies, a couple at a time, and cook, turning once, until browned, about 3 minutes on each side. Using a spatula, remove to a rack or paper towels. Serve hot or at room temperature.

VARIATION: *Omit the spices and substitute dried apricots, prunes, or mixed dried fruits for the apples. Reconstitute them by combining with sugar and water and cooking until softened to a paste. Fill and bake as directed.*

Banana Pudding

Bananas were known in Africa long before they made it to the New World in the 1500s. Here is an easy banana pudding that is low in calories and high in flavor. Add a dollop of whipped cream when serving to give a rich dimension.

Serves 4

2 cups milk
$^1/_3$ cup sugar
3 tablespoons cornstarch
dash of salt
1 teaspoon vanilla extract
1 teaspoon butter
2 bananas, sliced
whipped cream (optional)

Pour the milk into a saucepan over medium-high heat and warm until bubbles just begin to form around the edges. Add the sugar, stirring to dissolve, and simmer 3–4 minutes.

In a bowl, stir together the cornstarch and salt. Pour a little of the hot milk into the cornstarch mixture, stir well, and add the diluted cornstarch to the saucepan. Cook over medium heat, stirring continuously, until thickened, about 5 minutes. Stir in the vanilla, butter, and bananas.

Pour into individual serving dishes, or into a 1-quart decorative dish. Let cool, cover, and chill. Serve with whipped cream (if using).

P o n e comes from the Algonguin Indian word for bread. Perhaps because yams are as important to Africans as bread is to Europeans, they adopted this word from the Native Americans and used it, not only for corn bread sticks, but also for the sweet potato dessert they created in the South and in the Caribbean. For a recipe, see Sweet Potato Pone (page 65) in the Caribbean chapter.

Benne Cookies

Sesame seeds, known as benne by the slaves, were brought from Africa, where they are eaten like grain. Benne seeds are reputed to be bearers of good luck and were commonly planted in gardens along the southeastern coast. In South Carolina they are still popularly made into cookie and candy confections (see Resources).

Makes about 48 cookies

3/4 cup sesame seeds
1/2 cup butter, at room temperature
1 cup firmly packed brown sugar
1 egg
1 teaspoon vanilla extract
1 cup all-purpose flour
1/4 teaspoon baking powder
dash of salt

Preheat an oven to 350 degrees F. Spread the sesame seeds on a baking sheet and bake until toasted, 5–7 minutes. Let cool. Reduce the oven temperature to 325 degrees F.

In a bowl, beat together the butter and brown sugar until light and fluffy. Beat in the egg and then stir in the vanilla. In another bowl, stir together the flour, baking powder, and salt. Stir the dry ingredients into the wet ingredients and mix. Stir in the sesame seeds and mix well.

Place small spoonfuls of the batter, 2 inches apart, on well-greased baking sheets. Bake until slightly spread out and lightly browned, 6–8 minutes. Let cool on on baking sheets, or remove to wire racks to cool. Store in an airtight container up to 5 days.

Gingerbread

Ginger, the spicy root with the stomach-soothing powers, is a favorite in many parts of the world. It grows well in West Africa and the Caribbean and is used as a seasoning and in confections by African cooks everywhere. The British, who settled the eastern United States and are also known for their affection for ginger, are most likely the coinfluence in desserts like this one.

When molasses wasn't available, as it wasn't in early African-American kitchens, other syrups such as cane or sorghum were used. Here is a recipe in which any of the three can be added. Cane syrup and molasses are strong flavored, while sorghum has a lighter aroma and taste. This cake is for people who love the taste of ginger. It is moist and delicious hot or cold. Serve it with whipped cream or ice cream if you like. Or try the variation that follows and add a spicy sugar topping.

Makes 9 large squares, or twelve 2-inch squares

2 1/2 cups sifted all-purpose flour
1 1/2 tablespoons ground ginger
1 teaspoon ground cinnamon
1/4 teaspoon ground cloves
1/2 teaspoon salt
1 1/2 teaspoons baking soda
1/2 cup firmly packed brown sugar
1/2 cup butter, melted
2 eggs
1 cup molasses, cane syrup, or sorghum syrup
1/2 cup hot water

Preheat an oven to 350 degrees F. Grease and flour an 8-inch square cake pan.

In a medium bowl, stir together the flour, ginger, cinnamon, cloves, salt, and baking soda. In a large bowl, beat together the brown sugar and melted butter until well mixed. Beat in the eggs. In a small bowl or measuring cup, combine the molasses and the hot water.

To the butter mixture, alternately add the dry ingredients and the molasses mixture, one third at a time, beating well after each addition. Pour into the prepared pan.

Bake until puffed and golden, 35–40 minutes. Let cool in the cake pan at least 15 minutes before cutting.

VARIATION: *For the spicy sugar topping, in a bowl, mix together 1/2 cup firmly packed brown sugar; 1/4 cup butter, at room temperature; 1 teaspoon ground ginger; and 2 teaspoons ground cinnamon. Sprinkle on the gingerbread after it has baked for 30 minutes. Return to the oven and continue baking until done, another 5 minutes or so.*

Fruit Cobbler

You can use almost any fruit in season for this cobbler. The simple biscuit-style crust is pushed into the fruit to help thicken it. The crust can either be dropped by spoonfuls onto the fruit in the old-fashioned way or it can be rolled out and cut into rounds or strips for a contemporary presentation. Vary the amount of sugar depending on the sweetness of the fruit. You do not have to peel the peaches, nectarines, or apples. Just pit and cook.

Serves 6 to 8

8–10 cups peeled (if desired), pitted, and stemmed fruit such as
    peaches, nectarines, or berries
$1/2$–$3/4$ cup sugar
1 tablespoon fresh lemon juice
$2^{1}/_{2}$ tablespoons cornstarch or all-purpose flour
1–2 tablespoons butter

For the crust:
$3/4$ cup all-purpose flour
2 tablespoons sugar
$1^{1}/_{2}$ teaspoons baking powder
dash of salt
dash of ground cinnamon
$1/4$ cup butter or shortening, chilled
3–5 tablespoons milk
$1/2$ teaspoon vanilla extract (optional)

Preheat an oven to 350 degrees F. Butter a 9-by-11-inch baking dish.

Slice the fruit (leave the berries whole) and place in the prepared dish. Stir in the sugar to taste. Add the lemon juice and cornstarch, adjusting the amount of cornstarch according to the juiciness of the fruit. Dot with the butter and cover with aluminum foil. Bake for 20 minutes.

Meanwhile, to make the crust, in a bowl, mix together the flour, sugar, baking powder, salt, and cinnamon. With a pastry blender, two knives, or your fingers, cut in the butter until the mixture resembles coarse meal. In a small mixing bowl, combine the milk and vanilla. Use the smaller amount of milk if you are going to roll out the dough and the larger amount if you are dropping it by spoonfuls onto the fruit. Stir the wet ingredients into the dry ingredients, mixing well.

The South's signature fruit-and-biscuit-dough desserts may have been called cobblers because their lumpy uneven biscuit crust texture resembles a cobblestone street. San Francisco cook Freddie Strong's cobbler encases the sweet fruit in layers of dense biscuit crust. Growing up in Forest City, Arkansas, where he learned to cook at age seven, he remembers, "Sometimes we only had peaches and flour but we could create a great dish."

To roll out the dough, place it on a lightly floured surface and roll it out ½ inch thick. Using a round cutter or inverted glass, cut out rounds. Or cut the dough into strips to make a lattice topping.

Remove the baking dish from the oven and arrange the pastry evenly over the top, pressing gently into the fruit. Alternatively, drop the dough by spoonfuls over the hot fruit.

Return the cobbler to the oven and bake until the pastry is browned and puffed, about 35 minutes. Let cool 20 minutes or so before serving.

Homemade Ice Cream

An extravagance of riches makes this the quintessential cap to a celebration, be it Fourth of July, Juneteenth, or a family reunion. Hand churning is a multigenerational activity that begins with the kids when the paddle turns easily and ends with the grown-ups as the cream freezes and thickens. Although electric ice cream makers are easier to use, the hand-churned maker may be one tradition that should continue, as it results in a thorough appreciation for the amount of work necessary for such a delicious result. This basic recipe can be made as vanilla ice cream or flavored with fresh fruit.

> Serves 8–10
>
> For the custard base:
> 4 cups (1 quart) milk
> 2 cups heavy cream
> 4 eggs, beaten
> 2 cups sugar
> 2 tablespoons all-purpose flour or cornstarch
> pinch of salt
> 1 tablespoon vanilla extract
> 8 large peaches, peeled, pitted, and chopped or puréed, or 4–6 cups
>   mashed berries (optional)
>
> 5 pounds ice cubes or chunks
> 1 pound coarse rock salt

Make the custard base the day before you are going to churn the ice cream. In a saucepan, combine the milk and cream over medium heat and warm until small bubbles begin to form around the edges.

In a bowl, using a whisk or an electric mixer set on medium speed, beat together the eggs, sugar, flour, and salt until stiff and the mixture folds back on itself like a ribbon.

Slowly pour the hot cream mixture into the eggs, whisking all the while. Return the mixture to the saucepan and cook over medium heat, stirring constantly, until it just thickens and coats the back of a spoon, about 5 minutes. Remove from the heat and let cool slightly. Stir in the vanilla and fruit (if using). Pour into a bowl, lay a piece of plastic wrap directly onto the surface of the custard (this will keep a skin from forming), and chill overnight.

Coffee and tea were expensive and hard to come by during slavery and after. Many poor people made ersatz coffee by roasting corn or other grains. Teas made from wild herbs were common for medicinal use and for drinking with meals. Working in sugarcane fields meant cane syrup was plentiful, so to make the "tea" taste good, a heaping dose of sweetener was added. This custom may account for the preference for sweetened tea that is predominant in the South.

To churn the ice cream, pour the chilled custard into the ice cream canister to fill about two-thirds full. Place the paddle and lid on and set it in the ice cream maker. Layer the ice alternately with the rock salt in the machine. (The salt increases the coldness of the ice and helps freeze the cream and give it a smooth texture.) Start turning the handle slowly at first and then pick up speed to expose the entire custard mixture to the sides of the tin, which will help set and freeze it into ice cream. Continue churning until the mixture feels stiff. It will take 20–50 minutes to thicken to ice cream; the timing depends upon the strength and stamina of the churners.

Peek inside to see how it is doing. When ready, serve immediately. To store, pack in covered plastic containers for up to 1 month.

NOTE: If there is more of the custard than you have time to churn, it may be poured into a shallow roasting pan, frozen, and cut into squares to serve.

louisiana creole

The word creole, *which means mixed heritage, can be used to describe any of the African-inspired cooking styles in the Americas. For this chapter, in keeping with the word's geographical usage in the United States, creole refers to African-American home cooking in Louisiana.*

When African slaves were installed in the kitchens of French and Spanish immigrants in Louisiana, they arguably created the world's most refined example of creole cooking. The blend of African, French, Spanish, Caribbean, and Native American ingredients and techniques is typified by such tantalizing everyday fare as pots of bubbling gumbo, iron skillets of jambalaya, plastic tubs of crawfish, and lumpy rounds of sweet pralines.

The development of creole cooking in Louisiana began in the 1700s, when the French settled their small landholding in continental North America. During the Spanish era, 1769–1803, large numbers of slaves were imported to Louisiana. The slaves labored in the cotton fields, rice fields, sugarcane fields, and in domestic service. Those in the kitchens developed creole cooking from the blend of cultures that became uniquely Louisianan.

With the French came butter, green peas, eggplant, celery, and rice. They contributed the technique of thickening soups and stews with a roux. This blend of butter or oil and flour cooked together became a creole staple that begins many definitive dishes such as gumbo. Names of many dishes, like oysters en brochette and bouillabaisse de bayou, reflect their French derivatives.

With the Spanish came olive oil, cows, and pigs. A significant African contribution here as elsewhere was their one-pot rice dishes that combined grains, meat, and seafood. The Jollof rice of Senegal and the paella of Spain were translated into Louisiana's jambalaya. Gumbo, which takes its name from an African word for okra, loosely defines a variety of soupy stews served over rice.

Here, as in other parts of the Americas, Native Americans introduced and shared their knowledge on the uses of corn. The Choctaws in Louisiana also shared file, the ground leaves of the indigenous sassafras plant. File became one of the distinguishing seasonings in creole gumbos. Added at the end of cooking, it thickens and bestows a distinctive greenish depth. Pecans were another Louisiana contribution to the creole table.

Chiles and green peppers for seasoning and spicing creole sauces came from the Caribbean. Black pepper, which had long seasoned pots in Africa and Europe, was carried by traders from around the world.

The Gulf of Mexico provided a rich source of oysters, pompano, redfish, snapper, crabs, and shrimp for the seafood dishes West Africans knew best. The bayous and rivers held trout, catfish, and crawfish (crawdads or crayfish)—little "mud bugs" that thrived in the rice fields as well as in the bayous. These are what were once, like garfish, called "trash" fish, some because they fed on garbage and others because they were throwaways. They have become synonymous with creole cuisine.

Game abounded in the forests and played a role in the diet of the slaves. Although hunting wasn't allowed, small animals were trapped, and alleviated the monotony of salt pork, the main meat in their diet. Today, squirrels, possums, and rabbits are occasionally hunted, then cooked in sauces seasoned the creole way with onions, celery, garlic, green peppers, chiles, and tomatoes.

The recipes in this chapter were compiled to give a taste of creole family cooking as it has evolved in Louisiana. Seasoned with onions, tomatoes, and peppers, the dishes are the classics of New Orleans and the bayou country and comprise a legacy of creole cuisine, as it has been passed on by African-American Creole cooks through home and restaurant kitchens for nearly three hundred years.

Roux

The ingredient for thickening the soups, stews, and gravies that typify Louisiana creole cooking is made by slowly cooking oil or butter with flour until it is lightly browned. A big batch may be made in advance and stored in the refrigerator. Here are three methods; each yields 1 cup.

STOVE-TOP METHOD: In a small skillet over medium heat, warm 1 cup vegetable oil. (For a richer flavor use ½ cup butter and ½ cup oil.) Stir in 1 cup all-purpose flour and cook over medium heat, stirring constantly, until beginning to brown, about 15 minutes.

OVEN METHOD: In a small bowl, stir together 1 cup oil and 1 cup all-purpose flour. Spread out on a baking sheet, making sure the flour doesn't touch the edges of the pan, and put in a preheated 325 degree F oven until toasted, about 1 hour. Stir the mixture occasionally as it toasts. Roux may be made like this in large quantities and kept in an airtight container in the refrigerator a week or two.

FAT-FREE METHOD: A fat-free roux can be made by toasting the flour alone in the oven. Spread 1 cup all-purpose flour on a baking sheet or in a cast-iron skillet. Place in a preheated 325 degree F oven for 20–30 minutes, stirring frequently. The object is to toast the flour to give it a cooked taste, which helps it incorporate into the sauce. Always add this flour to a dish after the vegetables have been sautéed. Then add the liquid.

Making roux is a time-consuming task, one that must be tended to diligently. Kevin Belton, a former football player for the San Diego Rams and now a full-time cooking teacher at the New Orleans School of Cooking, has fond memories of his mother making roux that he shares with his students. "My mama made her roux at a high temperature so it didn't take as long. But she couldn't leave it, no matter if the doorbell rang or anything. That meant I had a good fifteen minutes to jump on the bed and she couldn't catch me because she was making the roux. I learned to judge the time by the aroma coming from that roux. Just as it begins to brown, the flour has a nutty fragrance that means it's almost done. I could smell it changing and I knew when to get off the bed."

Creole Sauce

This versatile sauce combines the essence of creole flavors. It can be be used with the bits of onions and peppers to add texture or it can be cooked down and puréed to make a smooth sauce. A must with Creole Meat Loaf (page 193), it also goes well over rice or eggs and makes a quick dinner when sautéed chicken breast or fish fillets are finished cooking (smothered) in it. Stanley Jackson, the chef at Kabby's in the Riverside Hilton in New Orleans, uses sauces like this to smother down swamp fish and calls them "sauce piquant."

Double or triple the recipe to have some on hand in the refrigerator. It will keep 2 weeks. Use Creole Sauce in place of ketchup.

Makes about 2 cups; 6–8 servings

1 tablespoon vegetable oil
1/2 yellow onion, finely chopped
1/2 green bell pepper, seeded and finely chopped
2 garlic cloves, minced
1 teaspoon Worcestershire sauce
1 teaspoon brown sugar
1 tablespoon red wine vinegar
1/2 teaspoon dry mustard
2 cups canned tomato sauce
2–3 tablespoons chopped fresh parsley
Tabasco or other favorite Louisiana hot-pepper sauce

In a skillet over medium heat, warm the oil. Add the onion and bell pepper and sauté until softened, about 5 minutes. Add the garlic and cook 1 minute.

Stir in all the remaining ingredients, including hot-pepper sauce to taste, and bring to a boil. Reduce the heat to medium-low and simmer until thickened, about 20 minutes. Serve hot.

C r e o l e rather than Cajun cooking is presented in this book because the Cajun culture descends primarily from a group of French settlers who arrived in Louisiana in the 1700s. They came from Nova Scotia, an area that had been called Acadia for a hundred years. The word cajun is a corruption of Acadian. Cajuns who settled in southwestern Louisiana brought a peasant style cooking that evolved over the years through their close proximity to the Creoles. Similar ingredients and methods exemplify both cooking styles. Some dish names, like maque chou, are Cajun originals.

Rémoulade Sauce

Perfect with Garfish Boulettes (page 192), Fried Catfish (page 128), or any sautéed or grilled fish, this is a mayonnaise relish jazzed up with tart pickles, chopped parsley, sweet shallots, hot chiles, and savory tarragon. Use commercial mayonnaise or homemade from the recipe below.

Makes about 1 cup; 6–8 servings

1 cup commercial or homemade mayonnaise (see note)
2 tablespoons finely chopped tart pickles
2 tablespoons minced fresh parsley
1 shallot, minced, or 2 green onions, including tops, minced
½–1 pickled red or green chile, seeded and minced (see Glossary)
3 tablespoons fresh lemon juice or vinegar from pickled chiles
1 tablespoon dry or prepared yellow mustard
*1 tablespoon chopped fresh tarragon, or 1 teaspoon dried tarragon,
    crushed*
ground black pepper

In a bowl, combine all the ingredients and stir to mix well. Let stand at least 30 minutes for flavors to blend before serving. The sauce may be refrigerated, well covered, up to 1 week.

NOTE: To make mayonnaise, in a bowl, blender, or food processor, blend together 1 egg, 1 teaspoon dry mustard, 3 tablespoons fresh lemon juice, and 1 teaspoon salt. With the motor running or while whisking constantly, slowly, ever so slowly, drizzle in 1¼ cups vegetable oil, drop by drop at first, blending all the while. Then, as the mixture thickens, drizzle in the oil in a thin, steady stream. Continue to beat until a mayonnaise consistency forms.

Stewed Squash

Any summer squash can be used for this easy recipe, but the most authentic creole flavor will come with using Louisiana's mirliton. This pear-shaped, pale green squash, native to Central America, is also known as chayote in Latin America, *christophene* in Martinique, chocho in Jamaica, and vegetable pear in the English Caribbean. Serve the squash with Redfish Creole (page 191) or Creole Meat Loaf (page 193).

Serves 6

1 pound summer squash such as chayote, zucchini, pattypan, or
    crookneck
½ yellow onion, chopped
salt and ground black pepper
1–2 tablespoons butter (optional)

Slice or cube the squash. Place in a saucepan with the onion. Pour in just enough water almost to cover. The squash has a lot of natural moisture so you don't need to flood it. Bring to a boil, reduce the heat to medium-low, and simmer until it is tender and stewy looking but still has texture, about 10 minutes. Season to taste with salt and pepper and then swirl in butter (if using). Serve immediately.

Fried Eggplant Fingers

Any vegetable can be fried this way. Eggplant, known as aubergine by French-speaking creoles, needs to be soaked in salted water or sprinkled with salt and drained on paper towels to rid it of any bitterness. Putting the breaded pieces in the freezer or refrigerator before cooking helps the coating to adhere better when cooked.

Serves 6–8

1 perfectly unblemished eggplant, cut into 2-inch "fingers"
1/2–3/4 cup fine dried bread crumbs
1 tablespoon dried basil, crushed
1 teaspoon dried oregano or marjoram, crushed
1 teaspoon garlic powder
1/2 cup vegetable oil
salt

Soak the eggplant in cold salted water to cover for 15 minutes. Put a plate on top to keep the pieces from floating.

On a plate or shallow dish, stir together the bread crumbs, basil, oregano, and garlic powder. Dredge a wet piece of eggplant in the bread crumb mixture, coating evenly, and place on a baking sheet. Repeat with remaining fingers. Place in the freezer or refrigerator 10–20 minutes.

In a nonstick or cast-iron skillet, heat the oil until almost smoking. Remove the eggplant from the freezer and fry, a few pieces at a time, until browned, about 4 minutes. Turn the eggplant as needed to brown all sides.

Using a slotted spoon or spatula, remove the eggplant and place on paper towels to drain. Sprinkle with salt and eat hot.

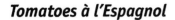

Tomatoes à l'Espagnol

Although tomatoes grow well in Louisiana, there aren't many recipes for using them alone. Fresh off the vine, green tomatoes are sliced and fried. Red tomatoes are sliced and served natural, but are more frequently a seasoning ingredient for gumbos, jambalaya, and other creole dishes. Here is an old recipe for baked tomatoes showing the Spanish influence on Creole cooking.

Serves 6–12

6 large firm tomatoes
salt and ground black pepper
1 teaspoon sugar
1/2 teaspoon cayenne pepper
1 garlic clove, minced
2 tablespoons vegetable oil or butter
1 large green bell pepper, seeded and finely chopped
1/2 yellow onion, finely chopped
3/4 cup fine dried bread crumbs mixed with chopped fresh parsley and
        2 tablespoons vegetable oil or melted butter

Preheat an oven to 350 degrees F.

Cut the tomatoes in half crosswise. Squeeze out seeds and set cut side up on a buttered baking dish large enough to hold all 12 halves. In a tiny bowl combine the salt and black pepper to taste, sugar, cayenne, and garlic. Sprinkle evenly over the tomato halves.

In a skillet over medium heat, warm the oil. Add the bell pepper and onion and sauté until soft, about 5 minutes. Stuff into the tomatoes. Top evenly with the crumb mixture. Bake until heated through, about 20 minutes. Serve hot.

Stuffed Bell Peppers

In the summer, Louisiana gardens are full of peppers, which is one reason they are a creole staple. You'll find stuffed peppers on the menu of The Praline Connection in New Orleans as well as on buffet tables throughout the South.

To make them into perfect edible containers for stuffing, first the peppers are parboiled until tender. Or, they may be filled raw and baked as directed in the variation below. They are filled with rice mixtures (also known as dressings) such as Dirty Rice (page 188) or one of the dressings given here.

Serves 6

6 large bell peppers
Eggplant Dressing (page 173) or Corn Dressing (page 174)
1 cup fine dried bread crumbs
1 tablespoon butter, cut into bits

Preheat an oven to 375 degrees F.

Select a large pot, big enough to hold all the peppers, and fill three-fourths full with water. Bring to a boil. Cut the peppers in half lengthwise or cut the very tops off crosswise. Remove the veins and seeds. Drop into the boiling water and cook until tender, 10–15 minutes. Drain.

Stuff with the dressing of choice and place on a lightly oiled baking sheet or baking dish. Divide the bread crumbs evenly among the tops and dot with the butter. Bake until heated through and the crumbs are lightly browned, 20–30 minutes. Serve hot.

VARIATION: After cutting, deseeding, and deveining the peppers, fill them with the selected dressing and place on a lightly oiled baking sheet or baking dish. Cover with aluminum foil and bake until peppers are softened, about 20 minutes. Remove foil, divide bread crumbs evenly among the tops, and dot with butter. Return to the oven to brown the crumbs, an additional 15–20 minutes.

Eggplant Dressing

Helen Comeaux of Lafayette, Louisiana, shared this recipe, which is equally delicious stuffed into the bell peppers, at left, or baked as a casserole as it is prepared here. Serve with Skillet-Baked Corn Bread (page 194).

Serves 6

1 large globe eggplant or 6 Japanese eggplants, cut into small cubes
salt
1 pound ground beef or ground pork (see variation)
3 tablespoons olive or vegetable oil
2 yellow onions, finely chopped
$1/4$–$1/2$ teaspoon cayenne pepper
3 garlic cloves, minced
$1^1/2$ tablespoons mixed dried herbs such as marjoram, thyme, sage, oregano, and basil, crushed
ground black pepper
2 cups canned tomato sauce
$1/2$ cup water
1 cup fine dried bread crumbs
1 tablespoon butter, cut into bits

Preheat an oven to 375 degrees F.

Lay the eggplant cubes on paper towels and sprinkle with salt. Let stand for 20 minutes to drain off bitterness. Beads of liquid will form on the cubes. Pat them dry with paper towels.

In a skillet over high heat, brown the meat, breaking it up with a spatula. Remove to a paper towel–lined plate. Pour off the fat from the pan.

In the same skillet over medium-high heat, warm the oil. Add the onions and eggplant cubes and sauté until tender, 6–7 minutes. Sprinkle with cayenne to taste and sauté 20 seconds. Return the beef to pan. Add the garlic, herbs, salt and black pepper to taste, tomato sauce, and water. Cover and cook over low heat to blend flavors, 10–15 minutes. Taste for seasoning. Let cool slightly.

Place the dressing in a buttered 2-quart baking dish, top with the crumbs and butter and bake to heat through and lightly brown the crumbs, 20–30 minutes. Serve hot.

VARIATION: Omit the meat and add 1 egg, beaten, after the vegetables have been sautéed.

Coup de main is the Creole phrase for helping hand. It refers to community gatherings for the purpose of putting up the summer's produce. On a late-summer Saturday, all the neighbors would get together to help one another prepare produce for canning.

On these harvest days, the whole family picked the garden. Field peas were laid out to dry or packed into jars for canning. The last watermelons surrendered their rinds to be pickled in sweet syrup. Corn kernels mixed with salt, water, and tomatoes became creole maque chou, a spicy vegetable mélange. The women dominated the bean snapping and string pulling.

The feeling was festive. Wilbert Guillory tells about the time his godfather brought along his accordian to play. His son took the washboard out of the tub to strum, and someone else grabbed a pair of spoons to clap against his thigh. "The music that resulted we called zydeco. It sounds just like its name and the name means snap bean," says Wilbert, who started producing the Southwest Louisiana Zydeco Music Festival in 1982.

Corn Dressing

This is the quintessential summer dish to make when the garden is bursting with corn, tomatoes, and peppers. The addition of Spanish olives gives it a tangy bite. It can also be stuffed into bell peppers (page 172).

Serves 6

6 ears of corn
3 tablespoons butter or olive oil plus 1 tablespoon butter, cut into bits
2 yellow onions, chopped
$1/4$–$1/2$ teaspoon cayenne pepper
8 ripe tomatoes, chopped
$1/2$ teaspoon brown sugar
$2^{1}/_{2}$ cups cooked white rice
6–8 pimiento-stuffed Spanish green olives
salt and ground black pepper
$1/4$ cup chopped fresh parsley
1 cup fine dried bread crumbs

Preheat an oven to 375 degrees F.

Cut off the kernels from the ears of corn (see note). Set aside.

In a skillet over medium heat, warm 2 tablespoons of the butter or oil. Add the onion and sauté until soft, about 5 minutes. Add the cayenne pepper to taste and cook 30 seconds. Add the tomatoes, corn kernels, and brown sugar. Cook, stirring occasionally, 10 minutes. Turn off the heat and mix in the rice, olives, salt and pepper to taste, and parsley.

Place the dressing in a buttered 2-quart baking dish, top with the crumbs and butter, and bake to heat through and lightly brown the crumbs, 20–30 minutes.

Serve hot.

NOTE: The least messy way to cut the corn kernels off a cob is to hold the cob upright in a deep, wide bowl and run the knife down the cob. Then scrape the cob with the knife to extract the corn juices, or milk.

Rebecca's Maque Chou

Rebecca Henry is a folk medicine specialist who writes for the magazine *Creole* in Lafayette. She is known for keeping the formulas for the old home remedies and other aspects of the Creole heritage alive and is writing a book about them. Maque chou is an original Acadian name. This blend of corn, peppers, and tomatoes is cooked into a thick stew, which is traditionally preserved in canning jars for the winter larder. Serve this with Stuffed Bell Peppers (page 172) filled with Eggplant Dressing (page 173), Redfish Creole (page 191), or Glazed Ham (page 139).

Serves 6

12 ears young, tender corn
$1/4$ cup vegetable oil or margarine
1 large yellow onion, chopped
1 green bell pepper, seeded and chopped
1 garlic clove, minced
4 ripe tomatoes, chopped
salt and ground black pepper

Cut off the kernels from the ears of corn (see note, at left). Set aside.

In a heavy pot or dutch oven over medium-high heat, warm the oil. Add the onion, bell pepper, and garlic and sauté until tender, 6–7 minutes. Stir in the corn kernels and tomatoes. Season to taste with salt and pepper. Reduce the heat to medium and cook, stirring frequently, until the mixture is thickened and mushy, 1–1$1/2$ hours. If necessary, press more milk from the corn cobs into the pot from time to time to keep the mixture soft. It is done when it forms a thick corn stew, delicious and naturally sweet from the peppers, corn, and tomatoes. Serve hot.

Cornmeal Mush

This bowl of cornmeal and water, known and spelled as couche couche, cush cush, and coosh coosh, is known all over the South. A staple for children growing up in slavery, it was once a mainstay for many African-Americans. Its ancestor is *fufu*, a starchy paste made of yams or grains and eaten as bread in West Africa.

Typically couche couche is made with finely ground cornmeal, cooked to a paste. It can be served right away with a little sugar or cane syrup and milk. Or it can be cooled, cut, and fried. Grits or polenta could be substituted for a coarser texture. For the best flavor use stone-ground cornmeal from a natural-foods store rather than the boxed cornmeal.

This recipe was shared by Rebecca Henry of Opelousas, Louisiana. She says a creole way to serve the soft mush is with caille, also known as clabber or curdled milk, spooned over the top. Or you can let the mush cool completely until firm, cut it into squares or strips, and then fry the pieces on a greased griddle, turning to brown on both sides. Soft or fried, it can be served with cane syrup and sausage or Creole Sauce (page 167).

Serves 6

2 cups cornmeal (see recipe introduction)
1 teaspoon salt
1 teaspoon baking powder (optional)
2 cups water
¼ cup butter, bacon drippings, or vegetable oil

In a bowl, stir together the cornmeal, salt, baking powder (if using), and water and mix well.

In a cast-iron skillet over high heat, melt the butter and add the cornmeal mixture. Stir well and reduce the heat to medium-low. Cover and cook, stirring often, 20 minutes. When a crust has formed on the bottom, stir and serve. It will be very thick and clump together. Mash it down and then spoon it onto a plate. Serve hot.

"The sharecroppers worked hard and the diet was a roughage diet with vegetables and corn bread and couche couche and greens and cabbage and biscuits.

"Those foods scraped their intestine out. Everything was fresh from the garden or the fruit tree. If Mama canned fruit for winter, she canned with sugar and she boiled those jars and caps. She didn't use preservatives or chemical additives, and it's those things that are causing so much illness today."

Rebecca Henry of Opelousas, Louisiana

Yams Louisiane

Like scalloped potatoes, this old standby is layered and baked. Unlike scalloped potatoes, the natural sweetness of the gold-fleshed sweet potato is enhanced with a bit of sugar, a dash of cinnamon, and the crunch of chopped pecans. The combination is associated with holiday feasts, especially when served with salty hams.

The yams are boiled for this dish because the extra moisture gained in boiling helps activate the starch and hold the dish together. Leaving their jackets on while boiling helps retain their shape.

Serves 6–8

2 pounds garnet or red jewel yams or sweet potatoes
3 tablespoons butter, melted
1½ tablespoons sugar
2–3 tablespoons fresh lemon juice
salt and ground white pepper
1 teaspoon ground cinnamon (optional)
½ cup chopped pecans

Bring a large pot three-fourths full of water to a boil. Add the yams and boil until tender, 15–20 minutes, depending upon size. Drain. When cool enough to handle, peel and slice into rounds ¼ inch thick.

Preheat an oven to 325 degrees F. Butter a 2-quart baking dish with some of the melted butter. Place a layer of the yam rounds on the bottom of the dish. Brush with melted butter and sprinkle with a little sugar, lemon juice, salt, pepper, and cinnamon (if using). Continue layering in the same manner until all ingredients are used. Sprinkle with the chopped pecans.

Bake until the tops of the yams get a little crusty and the pecans are fragrant and toasted, 35–40 minutes. Serve hot.

The fertile and water-rich region of western Louisiana, where many people still speak a French dialect, feels like a foreign country. Cooks I interviewed grew up speaking the melodic patois at home. For many, it is the only language their parents knew.

Red Beans and Rice

More than a staple dish, red beans and rice are nutritional complements, each providing what the other is missing to make complete protein. This recipe is from Wilbert Guillory, a Creole who grew up on a farm near Opelousas, Louisiana. Wilbert was active in the civil rights movement in the 1960s and still works at community organizing, helping farmers get good prices, and introducing new crops and animals for farming.

For the best melding of flavors, make this dish a day in advance. See the glossary for information on other beans that would be delicious in this recipe.

Serves 6

2¹⁄₂ cups (1 pound) dried red beans or kidney beans, rinsed and picked over
8–10 cups water
2 tablespoons vegetable oil
2 bell peppers, seeded and chopped
3 celery stalks, chopped
1 bunch green onions, including tops, chopped
4 garlic cloves, chopped
1 large yellow onion, chopped
4–6 Creole or other spicy sausages, sliced into ¹⁄₂-inch rounds (optional)
salt and ground black pepper
about 1 cup chopped fresh parsley
Plain Rice (page 107)

Soak the beans overnight in water to cover by several inches. Drain.

Put the drained beans in a large, heavy pot with the water, adding enough water to cover by about 6 inches. Bring to a boil, reduce the heat to medium-low, cover partially, and cook until tender, 1¹⁄₂–2 hours.

Meanwhile, in a skillet over medium heat, warm the oil. Add the bell peppers, celery, green onions, 3 cloves of the garlic, and onion. Sauté over medium-low heat, stirring frequently, until soft, about 30 minutes.

When the beans are tender, stir in the celery mixture. If using the sausage, brown the slices in the skillet over medium heat and stir into the beans or serve the slices alongside them. Season the beans to taste with salt and pepper. Simmer over low heat 15 minutes longer to blend the flavors. About 5 minutes before serving, mince the remaining garlic clove, add to the beans, and stir well. Serve hot over the rice. Sprinkle with plenty of parsley.

Rice has been a Louisiana staple since the Africans and Europeans first arrived. It was introduced as a crop by the French in 1718, but commercial production didn't get going until 1884, when mechanized methods made cultivation viable in the broad prairie land of southwestern Louisiana. It had been said that a Louisianan eats as much rice in one year as any other American eats in five.

Hoppin' John

This nutritious and delicious combination of black-eyed peas and rice has been known as Hoppin' John for generations. It might have gotten its name from a lively waiter in South Carolina or in New Orleans, or because you feel so good from eating it you could just hop around. It's one way southerners eat black-eyed peas on New Year's Day, a custom believed to guarantee good luck the rest of the year.

This version is made without pork fat. For extra flavor, cook the beans and rice in chicken stock.

Serves 6

1¼ cups (½ pound) black-eyed peas, rinsed and picked over
1 tablespoon vegetable oil
½ yellow onion, chopped
1 celery stalk, including leaves finely chopped
5 cups water or chicken stock (see Glossary)
salt and ground black pepper to taste
½ cup long-grain white rice
Pepper Vinegar Sauce (page 105), Tabasco sauce, or other hot-pepper
    sauce
chopped fresh parsley

Soak the black-eyed peas overnight in water to cover by several inches. Drain.

In a heavy saucepan or dutch oven over high heat, warm the oil. Add the onion and celery and sauté briefly just to heat, about 1 minute. Stir in the water or stock and bring to a boil. Add the drained black-eyed peas, reduce the heat to medium-low, cover partially, and cook, stirring occasionally, until tender, 40–50 minutes. Season to taste with salt and pepper.

Stir in the rice and continue cooking until the rice is tender, about 15 minutes. Season with hot-pepper sauce to taste. Sprinkle with chopped parsley and serve a dish of good luck and great flavor.

Chicken and Shrimp Gumbo

If one dish deserves the distinction of being the quintessential African contribution to America's culinary legacy, gumbo is it. Created by African cooks in plantation kitchens, gumbo combines the Spanish custom of mixing seafood and meat with French andouille-type sausage, native American sassafras (from which comes file), and African okra.

Gumbo is a catchall soup with a little of this and a little of that, or an elegant main course with the finest seafood, poultry, and sausage. To be authentic gumbo, however, two things must be included in the peppery broth—okra and file. This recipe is a basic. It begins with a roux, includes water or stock and tomatoes, and finishes with file and okra. Whatever else goes in the pot is up to the cook: all chicken, chicken and shrimp, a mélange of seafood, a few rounds of sausages. Or it can be a vegetarian dish, as in Green Gumbo (page 181).

Serves 6–8

1/2 cup all-purpose flour
1 teaspoon paprika
1 teaspoon salt
1/2 teaspoon ground black pepper
1 teaspoon ground or dried thyme, crushed
1 teaspoon cayenne pepper, or to taste
1 chicken, about 3 pounds, cut into 8 serving pieces, skins removed
3 tablespoons vegetable oil
3 garlic cloves, minced
2 yellow onions, chopped
2 celery stalks, chopped
1 green or red bell pepper (or 1/2 of each), seeded and chopped
2 cups water, chicken stock (see Glossary), or fish stock
2 cups canned tomato sauce or crushed tomatoes
1/2 pound fresh or frozen okra, left whole
1/2 pound medium shrimp, peeled and deveined
2 tablespoons file powder
chopped fresh parsley or thyme
6 cups hot Plain Rice (page 107, double recipe)

In a brown paper bag, combine the flour, paprika, salt, pepper, dried thyme, and cayenne pepper. Shake well. One at a time, drop the chicken pieces

File powder *comes from the bushy sassafras trees that grow wild on the Gulf Coast. The dried leaves were used by Choctaw Indians, who introduced them to Africans and Europeans. When dried and ground, the grayish green powder, which resembles ground thyme, acts as a thickener for soups and stews. It must be added at the end of cooking and only simmered. Boiling will cause it to become stringy. It also adds the greenish tinge that characterizes the best gumbos.*

into the bag and shake to coat evenly with the flour mixture. Reserve any left-over flour for thickening the sauce.

In a deep, heavy pot or dutch oven over high heat, warm the oil. Brown the chicken, a few pieces at a time, until evenly colored. Remove to a plate. Add the garlic, onions, celery, and bell pepper to the same pot and sauté until just beginning to soften, 5–7 minutes. Add the reserved seasoned flour and cook over medium heat, stirring all the while, to toast the flour lightly. Slowly pour in the water or stock while stirring constantly, then continue to cook and stir until it thickens. Add the tomato sauce, raise the heat and bring to a boil. Return the chicken pieces to the pan, lower the heat to medium, and simmer, uncovered, until the chicken is tender, about 30 minutes. (The gumbo can be prepared up to this point a day or two ahead. It gets better if it sits for at least a few hours to allow all the flavors to blend together. Reheat before proceeding.)

Over medium heat, stir in the okra and simmer until almost done, about 3 minutes. Add the shrimp and cook until they turn pink, 3–4 minutes.

In a tiny bowl, stir together the file powder and enough of the hot broth to moisten and make a runny paste. Stir this mixture into the pot. Stir and cook a minute or so; don't overcook the file or it will get stringy. Taste for seasoning. Sprinkle with parsley or thyme and serve over the hot rice.

In the summer months when okra is abundant in the garden or at the markets, freezing a batch ensures there will be okra on hand to make gumbo anytime. To do this, wash as many pounds as you want of crisp, brightly colored, blemish-free okra and drain. In an enameled or stainless-steel kettle with a steaming rack, pour in water to just below the bottom of the rack. Bring to a boil. Place the okra pods in a single layer on the rack, cover, and steam for 1 minute. Discard any okra pods that discolor. Lay the pods in a single layer on a baking sheet. Place in the freezer until frozen solid. When frozen, pack into plastic freezer bags, label and place in the freezer for up to 6 months.

Green Gumbo

Similar to a creole classic known as gumbo z'herbes, which is "green gumbo" and includes as many leafy greens as possible, this gumbo is also reminiscent of the Caribbean Callaloo (page 34) and of West African one-pot stews. In this version the meat is left out completely. It can be enriched with chicken stock used in place of the water, or with the addition of chick-peas or black-eyed peas (see variation). Serve this steaming hot as a soup or over rice.

Serves 6–8

3 tablespoons vegetable oil
$^1/_3$ cup all-purpose flour
2 yellow onions, chopped
6 green onions, including tops, chopped
2 celery stalks, including leaves, finely chopped
1 green bell pepper, seeded and chopped
4 garlic cloves, minced
8 cups water or chicken stock (see Glossary)
1 dried red chile
1 bay leaf
1 teaspoon dried thyme, crushed
$1^1/_2$ teaspoons salt
$^1/_2$ teaspoon ground black pepper
4–6 cups shredded mixed greens such as collard, kale, mustard, turnip
    tops, chard, beet tops, cabbage, and/or spinach, in any combination
$^1/_4$ pound okra, left whole if small or sliced in half
2 tablespoons file powder
$^1/_2$ cup chopped fresh parsley
6 cups hot Plain Rice (page 107, double the recipe; optional)
Pepper Vinegar Sauce (page 105), Tabasco sauce, or other
    hot-pepper sauce

VARIATION: *Add $1^1/_2$ cups cooked garbanzo beans, black-eyed peas, or lentils just after the greens are wilted and continue as directed.*

In a large, heavy pot or dutch oven over medium-low heat, warm the oil and stir in the flour. Cook, stirring constantly, until thickened and lightly browned, about 5 minutes. Raise the heat to medium and add the yellow and green onions, celery, and bell pepper. Sauté until wilted, about 5 minutes. Stir in the garlic and cook, stirring all the while, about 30 seconds.

Raise the heat to high and slowly stir in the water. Add the dried chile, bay leaf, thyme, salt, and pepper. Bring to a boil, reduce heat to medium-high, and cook uncovered at a low boil, for 15 minutes. Then add the greens and cook until tender, 5–15 minutes (depending upon how crisp or soft you like them). Stir in the okra and cook another 5 minutes.

In a tiny bowl, stir together the file and enough of the broth to make a runny paste. Stir into the gumbo and bring just to a boil. Lower the heat immediately and stir in the chopped parsley. Taste for seasoning. Serve hot in soup bowls or ladled over rice. Pass the pepper sauce.

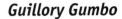

Guillory Gumbo

Wilbert Guillory spent his childhood on a farm in Louisiana where everything the family ate was grown or produced. For his gumbo, he likes to buy premade roux from a store called Savoir Roux in St. Landry Parish. But he makes his own file powder from a sassafras tree that grows in his yard. Wilbert also grows his own seasonings of onion, bell pepper, and parsley.

Serves 10

1 cup Roux (page 166)
2 yellow onions, chopped
2 green bell peppers, seeded and chopped
1 bunch celery, chopped
1/2 cup chopped fresh parsley
2 bay leaves
3 quarts water
1 turkey neck
1 "gumbo-sized" chicken, skinned and cut into serving pieces
1 teaspoon salt
1/2 teaspoon ground black pepper
1 pound fresh or frozen okra, left whole if small or sliced in half
1 1/2 pounds spicy creole or other Louisiana-style sausage, sliced
1 pound medium shrimp, peeled and deveined
1 or 2 small pieces catfish fillet, cut into bite-sized pieces
2–3 tablespoons file powder
9 cups hot Plain Rice (page 107, triple the recipe)

In large, heavy pot or dutch oven over medium heat, warm the roux. Stir in the onions, bell peppers, and celery and sauté until soft, 5–7 minutes. Add the parsley and bay leaves. Slowly stir in the water, incorporating it with the roux. Cook over medium heat, stirring regularly, until thickened, about 10 minutes. Add the turkey neck, chicken pieces, and salt and pepper to taste. Cook until the chicken is tender, about 45 minutes.

Add the okra and sausage and cook 5 minutes. Add the shrimp and catfish and cook another 5 minutes. In a tiny bowl, stir together the file and enough of the hot broth to moisten and make a runny paste. Stir this mixture into the pot and taste for seasoning. Serve hot in bowls over the rice.

Traditional Jambalaya

In a traditional jambalaya, like this one shared by Helen Comeaux, a seventy-year-old Creole from Lafayette, Louisiana, all the ingredients are cooked in one big pot. Some cooks, like Arthur Wardsworth, chef at the Southshore Restaurant in Kenner, Louisiana, never put rice in their jambalaya sauce. They serve jambalaya over rice. And others make a quick sauce and add leftover rice for a casserole that can be heated or reheated in the oven. These variations are what make jambalaya so appealing.

Helen Comeaux, who grew up on a farm in Maurice, Louisiana, where she began cooking at age eight, starts her jambalaya with pork ribs, cut into small pieces. And she washes the rice before adding it to the jambalaya, to minimize the starchiness and keep the grains separate.

Serves 6–8

5 tablespoons vegetable oil
1–2 pounds pork ribs, separated and each rib cut into thirds
1 chicken, about 3 pounds, cut into serving pieces and skinned, or
    8 favorite chicken parts such as thigh or breast, skinned
1/2 pound Cajun or other spicy link sausages, cut into 1/2-inch thick rounds
1 large yellow onion, finely chopped
1 green bell pepper, seeded and chopped
2 celery stalks, chopped
4 garlic cloves, finely chopped
1 or 2 dried red chiles, chopped, or 1–3 teaspoons red pepper flakes
2 tablespoons all-purpose flour
3 cups water or shrimp stock (see note)
2 teaspoons dried thyme, crushed
1/2 cup chopped fresh parsley
2 bay leaves
1 can (16 ounces) tomatoes, with their juice, chopped
2 tablespoons tomato paste
salt and ground black pepper
2 cups long-grain white rice, rinsed and drained
1/2 pound medium shrimp, peeled and deveined (optional)
Tabasco sauce or other Louisiana hot-pepper sauce

In a large, heavy cast-iron pot or dutch oven over high heat, warm 2 tablespoons of the oil. Add the pork ribs and brown well on all sides. Remove

The name jambalaya is pure Louisiana creole: jam comes from the French word for ham, ala is from French or Acadian and means "of" or "with," and ya is an African word for rice. The dish is rooted in Senegalese tiebes and has relatives in Caribbean and South Carolina pilaus and Spanish paella. According to folklorist Rebecca Henry, it has also been called long gravy because of its versatility in stretching any combination of ham, sausage, chicken, seafood, and vegetables into a satisfying rice-filling meal.

to a plate. Add the chicken pieces, brown in the same manner, and remove to a plate. Then brown the sausage slices and remove and reserve. Pour off the fat.

To the same pot over medium heat, add the remaining 3 tablespoons oil. Add the onion, bell pepper, and celery and sauté until softened, about 5 minutes. Stir in the garlic and chiles and sauté 30 seconds. Stir in the flour and cook, stirring continuously and scraping up browned bits from the bottom of the pot, for a minute or two. Return the pork ribs to the pot and stir.

Slowly stir in the water. Then add the thyme, parsley, bay leaves, tomatoes and juice, and tomato paste. Stir well and season to taste with salt and pepper. Bring to a boil. Cover and cook over medium heat to tenderize the pork ribs, about 20 minutes. Add the chicken and cook 5 minutes.

Add the rice and sausage. Stir, put the lid on, and reduce the heat to low. Cook, stirring a couple of times, until rice is almost done, about 20 minutes.

If using the shrimp, place them on top of the rice. Re-cover and cook 5 minutes longer. Stir and serve. Pass the hot sauce.

NOTE: To make shrimp stock, in a saucepan, combine the shrimp shells with ½ yellow onion, chopped; 1 celery stalk, chopped; 1 garlic clove, smashed; 1 bay leaf; 1 fresh parsley sprig; ¼ teaspoon dried thyme, crushed; 4 black peppercorns; and 1 cup white wine (optional). Bring to a boil, reduce the heat, cover partially, and simmer 20 minutes. Strain.

The importance of a garden plot, passed on from agrarian ancestors, continues for many African-Americans. In Bahia, cassavas grow in yards or pots on apartment balconies. In the Caribbean, coconut palms and tropical fruit trees line the front yard. In Louisiana, tomatoes and peppers ripen on the south side of the house. In Oklahoma, country fields sprout collard and mustard greens.

"A home garden does two things," says Wilbert Guillory of Opelousas, Louisiana. "First, it gives you food with a sense of responsiblity for raising that food. Second, the nature of growing, raising food from the ground, brings your neighbors around to converse about it. These are two qualities of life having a garden preserves."

Jambalaya over Rice

This is an elegant presentation Louisiana chef Arthur Wardsworth demonstrated at the New Orleans Jazz Festival. To him, "The best jambalaya is one in which the sauce is hazy red." Here's how to do it.

Although amounts are specified, the type of meats used and the addition of shrimp are up to you. It's great with pork, ham, and chicken. Creole sausage adds a nice piquancy. The dish could also be made with only shrimp.

Serves 8

3 tablespoons butter or vegetable oil
3 tablespoons all-purpose flour
1/2 pound pork loin or shoulder, cut into cubes
1/2 pound chicken breast or thigh meat, cut into cubes
6 ounces Cajun or other spicy link sausages, sliced
2 celery stalks, chopped
1 yellow onion, chopped
3 garlic cloves, minced
1 green bell pepper, seeded and chopped
1 red bell pepper, seeded and chopped
2 bay leaves
1 teaspoon dried sage, crushed
1 teaspoon dried thyme, crushed
2 tablespoons tomato paste
2 cups chicken stock (see Glossary) or water
salt and ground black pepper
1/4 pound ham, cubed
1/2 pound medium shrimp, shelled and deveined (optional)
4 large tomatoes, seeded and finely chopped
1/4 cup chopped fresh parsley
2 green onions, including tops, finely chopped (optional)
6 cups hot Plain Rice (page 107, double the recipe)

In a large cast-iron skillet over medium heat, melt the butter. Stir in the flour and cook, stirring, to make a light roux, about 4 minutes. Add the pork cubes first. "Adding the pork stops the cooking of the roux," notes Arthur. Brown the pork on all sides, 5–7 minutes. Then, add the chicken and sausage and brown lightly, about 5 minutes.

Raising hogs was traditionally a communal event in the rural South. In western Louisiana, on Saturdays in the winter months, the neighbors got together to butcher two or three of them and share the meat around. These boucheries were social events in which the whole family participated. They began at four o'clock in the morning when the water was put to boil so the hair could be scalded off the pig's hide.

The butchering took most of the day, as the various parts were prepared for immediate cooking and for salting and smoking. Hog head cheese came from boiling the head with the gelatinous feet until the meat fell off. It was combined with the cooked liver, onions, bell peppers, salt, and black and red pepper, formed into a loaf, and bound by the gelatinous stock. A meal-in-a-casing called boudin used the scraps, the same seasonings as the hog head cheese, and included cooked rice. The mixture was stuffed into the intestine casing. Sausages were also made without rice, using just meat, bread, and seasonings. They were hung to dry for a week or so, or smoked.

The layer of fat under the pig skin was rendered to use for cooking. Cracklings (page 148) were made from what was left and were eaten right away. The whitest of the fatty portions was salted to save as salt pork for seasoning throughout the winter. Old recipes

Stir in the celery, yellow onion, garlic, and bell peppers and sauté until softened, about 5 minutes. Add the bay leaves, sage, thyme, and tomato paste. Slowly add the chicken stock, stirring constantly, and cook, stirring, until it thickens slightly, about 5 minutes. Add salt and pepper to taste. Cook about 10 minutes to blend the flavors.

Stir in the ham and shrimp (if using). Bring to a boil and cook 5 minutes. Stir in the tomatoes, parsley, and green onions (if using). Cook 5–10 minutes longer. Adjust the seasonings.

For an elegant presentation, scoop hot cooked rice into a lightly greased cup, pat down, and invert onto individual plates or wide-rimmed bowls. Spoon the jambalaya around it. Serve at once.

NOTE: If making with all meat and chicken, the entire dish can be made a day in advance. If shrimp are included, wait and add them after the sauce is reheated, about 10 minutes before serving.

calling for white meat refer to salt pork. The salty portions with the most meat were smoked and sometimes called streaks of lean.

After the hogs were butchered, a big pot of backbone stew was started. In it went green and white onions, garlic, parsley, salt, and pepper. It was cooked all day and was served over rice. "We grew rice here, by the chance," says Wilbert Guillory. That means they threw rice into the bayous and hoped for enough rain to make it produce.

At the end of the day, after everyone had eaten some stew, each family took home some of the cracklings and salt pork, boudin and sausage, and a little roast. If neighbors couldn't come to the boucherie, their portion was delivered to them. Then, when the neighbors' hogs were ready, the meat would be paid back.

Dirty Rice

The specks of chicken or pork liver dotted throughout the rice account for the name of this fragrant dish, also called rice dressing. The recipe is adapted from one by T. J. Robinson, whose Gingerbread House Restaurant in Oakland, California, elevates creole cooking to a regal dining experience. T. J. grew up in Louisiana, where she learned to cook from her grandmother. Her favorite child-hood story about the gingerbread man inspired the theme and whimsical decor of her restaurant.

Serves 4

2 tablespoons vegetable oil
1/2 red onion, finely chopped
1/2 red bell pepper, seeded and finely chopped
1/2 green bell pepper, seeded and finely chopped
1 or 2 chicken livers, chopped
2 green onions, including tops, chopped
2 garlic cloves, minced
1 teaspoon dried thyme, crushed
1/2 teaspoon paprika
1/4 teaspoon ground allspice
1/4 teaspoon ground mace (optional)
1/8–1/2 teaspoon cayenne pepper
1/4 teaspoon sugar
1 bay leaf
1/4 cup water or chicken stock (see Glossary)
salt and ground black pepper
2 cups Plain Rice (page 107), hot or leftover

In a heavy 10-inch skillet over medium heat, warm the oil. Add the onion and bell peppers and sauté until soft, about 5 minutes. Stir in the chicken livers, green onions, and garlic and cook another minute. Add the thyme, paprika, allspice, mace (if using), cayenne pepper to taste, sugar, and bay leaf and continue cooking and stirring for 30 seconds.

Stir in the water or stock and season to taste with salt and black pepper. Add the rice, mix well, and heat to serving temperature. Adjust sea-soning if necessary and serve.

The fritters *African cooks are known for are called croquettes in creole cooking. The word comes from the French verb that means to crackle between the teeth. When cooked right, that's exactly what the crunchy little morsels are supposed to do. Creole frit-ters combine crawfish, shrimp, crab, rice, or corn with bread crumbs, onions, bell peppers, and cayenne pepper. The Shrimp-Potato Fritters (pages 46–47) in the Caribbean chapter are good examples.*

Crawfish Boil

Boiled crawfish should be spicy enough to leave a brilliant afterglow on your lips. The cooked potato helps soothe the burn. Although the whole crustacean is cooked, the tail is the edible part. To eat one, twist off the head, then pinch the very end of the tail to separate the meat from the shell, raise it to your lips, and suck out the delicious lobsterlike morsel.

Save the shells to make soup or to put in the compost or chicken coop.
Serves 4–6

For the boil seasoning:
2 garlic cloves, minced
2–3 teaspoons cayenne pepper
1 teaspoon ground dried sage
1 teaspoon ground dried thyme
1 tablespoon salt
1 teaspoon ground white pepper
6–8 quarts water
1 dried red chile
1 yellow onion, sliced
1 lemon, sliced

8 small red potatoes
12–20 pounds live crawfish

Place all the ingredients for the boil seasoning in a large stockpot (see note). Add the water, chile, onion, and lemon. Bring to a boil and boil for 5 minutes to blend the flavors. Add the potatoes and when the potatoes are almost cooked, after about 15 minutes, add the crawfish. Cook until the crawfish turn bright red and are firm to the touch, 15–20 minutes.

Drain the crawfish and potatoes and serve. In Lafayette, Louisiana, they are served in big plastic tubs. You eat them while bending over the tub; the juicy broth running down your arms. It's messy, but worth every napkin and chin stain.

NOTE: You can substitute 2–3 tablespoons of your favorite commercial crawfish boil seasoning in place of this one.

A clove of garlic is often referred to as a "toe" in the South.

Catching crawfish in the rice fields was a boyhood pastime of Wilbert Guillory. He remembers tying a chicken feather on a broom straw and putting it in the mud where the crawfish liked to hang out. "It took a lot of time to catch enough for dinner, but when we were kids we had the time," he laughed. Crawfish are plentiful in the spring months in Louisiana, but can also be obtained at other times by mail order from farms (see Resources).

Rebecca's Crawfish Étouffée

Rebecca Henry of Lionville has adapted this classic recipe classic. Instead of preparing the sauce with roux, stock, and tomato purée, she substitutes canned Golden Mushroom Sauce as the base.

Serves 4

1/4 cup butter or vegetable oil
1 pound crawfish tails, cooked and peeled
salt and ground black pepper
1 yellow onion, chopped
3 green onions, white part only, chopped, plus 1/4 cup chopped green
    onion tops for garnish
1/2 green bell pepper, seeded and chopped
2 garlic cloves, minced
3 tablespoons all-purpose flour
1 1/2 cups stock from cooking crawfish, strained, or shrimp stock (see note,
    page 185)
1 cup tomato purée
cayenne pepper
3 cups hot Plain Rice (page 107)
1 tablespoon chopped fresh parsley

In a nonstick, enameled, or stainless-steel skillet over medium heat, melt the butter. Add the crawfish tails and season generously with salt and black pepper. Sauté 3 minutes. Using a slotted spoon, remove the tails to a plate.

To the same skillet over medium heat, add the yellow onion, the white portion of the green onions, bell pepper, and garlic. Sauté until very soft, 8–10 minutes. Stir in the flour and continue cooking, stirring constantly, over medium heat until the flour is cooked and the mixture is gummy, at least 5 minutes.

Slowly add the stock, stirring constantly, and bring to a boil. Add the tomato purée and cayenne pepper to taste and stir well. Simmer uncovered, stirring occasionally, 15 minutes.

Return the crawfish tails to the skillet and stir well. Taste for seasoning. Heat to serving temperature. To serve, spoon over rice. Garnish with the chopped green onion tops and parsley.

NOTE: For this dish a nonstick, enameled, or stainless-steel skillet is preferable to cast iron, which has a tendency to darken crawfish.

VARIATION: Shrimp may be substituted for crawfish. They don't need to be cooked first, just peeled and sauteed.

Rebecca Henry, the daughter of a sharecropper, grew up in Lionville, in western Louisiana. She used to tie a piece of chicken on a string and leave it overnight in the swamps to attract what were called mud bugs and écrevisse. Her mom boiled them and everyone helped in the peeling to make a pile of crawfish tails to add to jambalaya or étouffée. The latter is the French word for "smothered," a popular African-American cooking technique.

Redfish Creole

Redfish has been a Louisiana staple for far longer than its current popularity, as this recipe adapted from a 1929 cookbook exemplifies. It is no longer in plentiful supply, but other Louisiana fish such as sheepshead, grouper, and gaspergou, as well as ling cod and red snapper, are good substitutes.

The whole fish is rubbed with olive oil, salt, and pepper and baked until done. Meanwhile, a highly seasoned sauce is prepared to serve with it. For a company or buffet presentation, place the fish on a serving platter and spoon the sauce around it.

Serves 6

1 whole redfish, red snapper, or sheepshead, 3–5 pounds, cleaned
5 tablespoons olive oil
1 tablespoon paprika
$1/2$ teaspoon cayenne pepper
salt and ground black or white pepper
juice of 1 lemon
Creole Sauce (page 167) or Rémoulade Sauce (page 168)

Preheat an oven to 350 degrees F.

Pat the fish dry with paper towels. Make several gashes through the skin into the flesh on both sides of the fish. In a small bowl, combine the olive oil, paprika, cayenne, salt and black pepper to taste, and lemon juice and mix well. Massage the mixture over the skin and into the gashes and cavity of the fish. Place it on a baking sheet or in a baking dish. Bake until done, about 30 minutes, turning once after 15 minutes. To check if it's done, look into one of the gashes; it should be milky white rather than opaque. Or you can lift the fish gently and check the center of the cavity; it should be steaming hot and the fish should be beginning to separate from the bones.

Transfer the fish to a heated serving platter and serve with one of the sauces.

Return the fish balls to the skillet and finish cooking them in the sauce, about 10 minutes. Serve hot with the rice.

Louisiana's waterways provide a wealth of fish, of which crawfish, shrimp, oysters, and redfish are the most widely known. Other varieties to look for include sheepshead, gaspergou, drum, garfish, and grouper. Sheepshead is lean, firm, and sweet tasting; it is available whole or filleted year-round but is particularly abundant January through April. Gaspergou is a freshwater relative of the drum and has a sweet mild flavor; sometimes called gou, it is sold whole or filleted and is in season March through August. Drum or black drum is a member of the same family as the redfish. Its flesh is soft and flaky and has a mild taste. It is sold whole and filleted during its peak season from April to August. Garfish are bony, ugly fish with a good flavor once you get past the bones. Grouper is a fine-textured firm fish with a divinely slightly sweet taste; it comes to market whole, headless (dressed), and filleted, and is best from April to October.

Garfish Boulettes with Herbed Tomato Sauce

Garfish are tough, ugly creatures that used to be known as "trash" fish. Mike Johnson, chef at The Landing in Lafayette, Louisiana, first cooks the fish a little to aid in removing the bones. Then he grinds the fish, forms it into small balls, and cooks them in tomato sauce with lots of garlic. Serve the balls with Plain Rice (page 107) or Oven Rice (page 109).

Serves 6

1½ pounds garfish, catfish, shark, or any rockfish fillets
3 green onions, including tops, chopped
½ yellow onion, finely chopped
1 teaspoon salt
½ teaspoon ground white or black pepper
¼ cup chopped fresh parsley
2 tablespoons olive oil or vegetable oil

For the sauce:
½ yellow onion, finely chopped
3 garlic cloves, minced
½ teaspoon dried sage, crushed
½ teaspoon dried oregano, crushed
½ teaspoon dried basil, crushed
2 cups canned tomato sauce
salt and ground black pepper

Check the garfish fillets for any errant bones. Place the fillets in a food processor with the green and yellow onions, salt, pepper, and parsley. Pulse to form a coarse paste. Alternatively, finely chop the fish fillets and place in a mixing bowl. Add the remaining ingredients and mix well. Form into small walnut-sized balls. Set aside.

In a skillet over medium-high heat, warm the oil. Add the fish balls and quickly brown on all sides. Using a slotted spoon, remove and reserve.

To make the sauce, place the same skillet over medium heat. Add the onion to the oil remaining in the skillet and sauté until soft, about 5 minutes. Stir in the garlic and sauté 30 seconds. Add all the remaining sauce ingredients, including salt and pepper to taste, and stir well. Cook to blend the flavors, about 15 minutes.

Creole Meat Loaf

This recipe is for a large meat loaf, which makes it good for company or to take to a potluck. Or plan on serving only part of the meat loaf the first day and make sandwiches with the leftovers the following day. Creole Sauce is spread on the meat after it is partially cooked, giving it a hot-tart accent.

Serves 12

1 yellow onion, chopped
1 celery stalk, finely diced
1 green bell pepper, seeded and finely diced
2 garlic cloves, minced, or 1 tablespoon garlic powder
1 cup canned tomato sauce
$^1/_2$ cup cracker meal, fine dried bread crumbs, or rolled oats
$1^1/_2$ teaspoons salt
1 teaspoon Worcestershire sauce
1 egg
3 pounds lean ground beef, or 2 pounds ground beef plus
    1 pound ground pork
Creole Sauce (page 167)

Preheat an oven to 375 degrees F.

In a large mixing bowl, combine all the ingredients except the Creole Sauce. Mix with your hands, kneading to mix well. Form into 1 or 2 loaves and place in a large roasting or baking pan.

Bake for 30 minutes. Remove from the oven and pour off the fat. Spread about half of the Creole Sauce over the top of the meat loaf (or loaves) and return to the oven. Bake until done, 35–45 minutes longer.

Remove from the oven and let stand 5 minutes, so the juices will set up and not run out when the loaf is cut. Meanwhile, heat the remaining Creole Sauce. Then slice the meat loaf and serve hot with the reheated sauce on the side.

During the seventeenth, eighteenth, and nineteenth centuries, thousands of head of cattle were slaughtered annually for leather. The leftover flesh, which was as tough as the leather, was given to the slaves for food. Preparing ground-meat dishes and smoking and drying thin meat strips were two ways to use the poor-quality beef, which was abundant.

Skillet-Baked Corn Bread

When Africans first started making corn bread in America, it was baked in cast-iron skillets over coals or on the hot hearth. This recipe, which uses whole-wheat flour and stone-ground cornmeal and is cooked in a cast-iron skillet in a hot oven, comes close to the authentic fresh corn flavor and crisp texture of those early breads.

Serves 6

1 cup stone-ground white or yellow cornmeal
1/2 cup whole-wheat flour
1/2 cup unbleached all-purpose flour
1/2 teaspoon salt
1 tablesoon sugar
2 teaspoons baking powder
1 egg, beaten
3/4 cup milk
2 tablespoons vegetable oil

Preheat an oven to 425 degrees F. Lightly butter or grease a well-seasoned 9-inch cast-iron skillet (see page 268) or an 8-inch square baking pan.

In a bowl, stir together the cornmeal, both flours, salt, sugar, and baking powder. In another bowl, beat together the egg, milk, and oil. Add the wet ingredients to the dry ingredients and mix until fully combined. Pour into the prepared skillet.

Bake until puffed and browned on the top, 25–30 minutes. Serve hot.

VARIATION: *To make muffins, grease 12 muffin-tin cups and divide the batter evenly among them. Bake in a 425 degree F oven until puffed and browned, 15–20 minutes.*

Spoon Bread

This eggy corn bread is baked in a cast-iron skillet. Originally it had no leavening and was baked in a "spider" directly over the coals. The eggs can be separated and the whites beaten until stiff for a lighter texture. Traditionally, this bread is made with white cornmeal, which has a finer texture than yellow.

Serves 6

3 cups milk
1 cup white or yellow cornmeal, preferably stone-ground
1 teaspoon salt
2 teaspoons baking powder
1 tablespoon butter
3 eggs

Preheat an oven to 350 degrees F. Lightly butter or grease a 9-inch cast-iron skillet or 8-inch square baking pan.

In a saucepan, heat 2 cups of the milk until small bubbles begin to form around the edges of the pan.

In a mixing bowl, stir together the cornmeal, salt, and baking powder. Slowly stir the hot milk into the cornmeal mixture. When it is incorporated, return the mixture to the saucepan and cook over medium heat, stirring constantly, until thickened, 6–8 minutes. Stir in the butter. Remove from the heat and let cool to lukewarm.

Beat in the remaining 1 cup milk. If using whole eggs, beat them together lightly and then beat them into the lukewarm cornmeal mixture. Alternatively, separate the eggs and beat the yolks into the cornmeal mixture. In a clean bowl, beat the egg whites until stiff peaks form and fold the whites into the cornmeal mixture. Pour into the prepared pan. Bake until puffed and browned, 30–40 minutes. Spoon out of the skillet and eat hot as a side dish or bread.

VARIATION: Instead of cooking the cornmeal mixture after it is combined with the hot milk, beat in the rest of the milk, the butter, and the whole eggs. Pour the mixture into the greased skillet and bake in a preheated 350 degree F oven until puffed and set, 45–55 minutes. A thin layer of egg will separate on top of the baked cornmeal, giving a delicious custardy texture on top of the corn bread crumb.

Bread Pudding

Born out of leftovers, bread puddings are an ingenious dessert, whether the stale bread is simply baked with eggs, sugar, and milk or elaborately embellished with raisins, rum, bourbon, nuts, or berries. The bread soaks up the milk and eggs and develops into a soft-textured custard. This is a basic recipe with suggestions for embellishments. Evaporated milk gives it an old-fashioned flavor from the days when refrigeration was rare and canned milk was the only option for many. Try this with canned jackfruit to give it a Caribbean flair. Drain the canned fruit before using.

Serves 8–10

1/2 cup butter, melted
3/4 cup sugar
4 eggs, beaten
1 tablespoon vanilla extract
3 cups milk, or 1 can (12 ounces) evaporated milk plus 1 cup water
1/2 teaspoon grated nutmeg, preferably freshly grated
1/2 teaspoon ground cinnamon
10 slices stale (several days old) Yeast-Risen Wheat Bread (page 241)
*   or any French bread, lightly toasted and cut into cubes (about*
*   6 cups cubes)*

OPTIONAL ADDITIONS:
3/4 cup golden raisins or dried currants; 1 or 2 cups blueberries;
2 apples, cored and grated; 1 can (8 ounces) crushed pineapple, drained;
1 can (8 ounces) fruit cocktail; 1 can (8 ounces) peaches, drained;
or 1 can (20 ounces) jackfruit, drained

Preheat an oven to 325 degrees F. Butter a 9-by-12-inch baking dish.

In a bowl, beat together the butter, sugar, eggs, vanilla, milk, nutmeg, and cinnamon until well mixed. Stir in the bread cubes and any of the fruits, if desired. Pour into the prepared baking dish.

Bake until a knife inserted in the center comes out clean, 40–50 minutes. Serve hot.

Creamy Pralines

According to Loretta Harrison, the proprietor of Loretta's Authentic Pralines in New Orleans, this most famous of creole desserts started out as a homemade confection, a special treat that was wrapped in waxed paper to give as a gift. Loretta's recipe comes from her grandmother. Her pralines, which are available by mail order (see Resources), were selected to be sold on the mall at President Clinton's Inauguration Reunion in January 1993. "Pralines are all different," says Loretta. "Some are real sweet, some chunky, some crystallized, and some, like the ones in Texas, are chewy. Mine are creamy."

The word *praline* comes from a French word that means "to burn with sugar." The following recipe is for a creamy-style praline. For a caramelized praline, make the Goober Brittle (page 151) and substitute pecans for the peanuts. Make these one batch at a time.

Makes ten 2-inch pralines

³/₄ cup firmly packed brown sugar
³/₄ cup granulated sugar
¹/₂ cup evaporated milk or heavy cream
1 tablespoon butter
¹/₂ teaspoon vanilla extract
2 cups pecans, lightly toasted and coarsely chopped (see note)

In a heavy pan, combine the sugars and milk. Bring to a boil and boil until it registers 234 degrees F (soft-ball stage) on a candy thermometer, or until a small bit dropped into a glass of ice water holds together and is quite soft when pressed between your fingertips. Remove from the heat.

Add the butter and vanilla and beat with a spoon or whisk until creamy and beginning to thicken. Stir in the pecans. Drop by spoonfuls, forming 2-inch disks onto a baking sheet lined with buttered waxed paper or parchment paper. Let cool. Store in an airtight container up to a week.

NOTE: To toast pecans, place them in a single layer on a baking sheet in a preheated 325 degree F oven until they begin to change color and their nutty fragrance comes up, 8–10 minutes.

When Helen Comeaux, who has been cooking in western Louisiana for over sixty years, was a child, sugarcane syrup and molasses, which were readily available, were used for making for pralines. The sugar syrup was heated until dark and caramelized and mixed with peanuts, pecans, benne (sesame) seeds, or sometimes cornflakes. A little butter might be added to make a creamy praline. The nutty confections were poured out onto corn husks to set up.

Granny Brown's Gingerbread Cookies

Lillie Brown learned this recipe from her mother when she was growing up in Louisiana. She passed it on to her own children and shared it in *County Fare Collector's Cookbook*. Traditionally made around Christmas, this recipe makes cookies and can also be formed into sheets to create gingerbread houses. The houses are stuck together with caramel glue and the recipe is below.

Makes about sixty 2-inch cookies

1 cup unsalted butter
³/₄ cup blackstrap molasses
³/₄ cup sugar
1 egg, beaten
grated zest of 2 oranges
5–6 cups all-purpose flour
3¹/₂ teaspoons baking soda
1 tablespoon ground ginger
1¹/₂ teaspoons ground cloves
¹/₂ teaspoon ground cardamom or ground nutmeg
Sugar Frosting (following; optional)
Caramel Glue (following; optional)

Preheat an oven to 375 degrees F. Lightly grease a baking sheet.

In a bowl, using an electric mixer, beat together the butter, molasses, and sugar. Beat in the butter and orange zest. In another bowl, combine the flour, baking soda, ginger, cloves, and cardamom and stir to mix. Beat into the butter mixture until creamy and smooth. Wrap in plastic wrap and chill until firm.

On a lightly floured surface, roll out the dough ¹/₄ inch thick. Using cookie cutters, cut out desired shapes: gingerbread people, stars, angels, and so on. Alternatively, roll the dough into similar-sized squares to make gingerbread houses, cutting out windows and doorways as desired. Place on the prepared baking sheets.

Bake until set and lightly browned, about 10 minutes. Let cool on pan. Decorate with Sugar Frosting, if desired, or assemble gingerbread house using Caramel Glue and then ice with the frosting. Store in an airtight container for up to 1 week.

SUGAR FROSTING: In a bowl, beat together 2 egg whites with approximately 2 cups powdered sugar. Beat well and keep adding powdered sugar until the mixture is stiff enough to put into a pastry tube for decorating. The frosting may be tinted with food coloring, if desired.

CARAMEL GLUE: In a heavy skillet melt 1 cup sugar over low heat. To help keep it from sticking to the sides of the skillet, stick a whole lemon on the end of a fork and use it to stir the sugar constantly so it melts evenly. When the sugar is melted and light golden, turn off the heat. Working quickly and carefully, dip the edges of the gingerbread "walls" and glue together to make houses. Decorate with sugar frosting.

Brown Sugar Cookies

In a time when no one went to the store to buy sweets, cookies like these were baked at home. The dough is made, shaped into a log, and refrigerated to make uniform-sized cookies the kids won't fight over. Before the advent of refrigeration this dough would have been dropped by spoonfuls onto a hot griddle, or placed on a baking sheet and baked in the hot coals. Brown sugar, sold in cone-shaped solids, had to be grated for use. Add the sesame seeds for an authentic African flavor.

Makes about 60

1 cup butter, at room temperature
2½ cups firmly packed brown sugar
2 eggs
3½ cups all-purpose flour
½ teaspoon salt
1 teaspoon baking soda
1 teaspoon vanilla extract
1 cup finely chopped nuts (pecans, walnuts, almonds, or peanuts) or
   whole sesame seeds

In a bowl beat together the butter and sugar until light and fluffy. Beat in the eggs. In another bowl, stir together the flour, salt, and baking soda. Beat the flour mixture, one third at a time, into the butter mixture. Stir in the vanilla and nuts. Divide the mixture into fourths. On a lightly floured surface, working with one-fourth of the dough at a time, roll the mixture into a log, about 1½ inches in diameter. Repeat with the remaining dough portions. Wrap the cylinders in plastic wrap, place on baking sheets, and refrigerate overnight.

Preheat an oven to 325 degrees F. Lightly grease a baking sheet.

Cut each log into slices ¼ inch thick. Place on the prepared baking sheet, about 1 inch apart. Bake until lightly browned, 8–10 minutes. Remove to wire racks and let cool. Store in an airtight container up to a week.

Pecan Pie

Louisiana pecans are combined with sweet corn syrup, butter, and eggs to make one of the South's best desserts. Lightly toasting the pecans that go in the filling gives them a rich flavor.

Serves 8

Pie Crust (page 152)
¹/₃ cup butter
³/₄ cup sugar
1 cup light corn syrup
3 eggs
dash of salt
1 teaspoon vanilla extract
1 cup toasted pecans (see note page 197), coarsely chopped, plus 1 cup
*   pecan halves*

Preheat an oven to 400 degrees F. Make the crust as directed and put it in the freezer for 15 minutes.

Line the crust with a piece of aluminum foil and spread a layer of dried beans over the foil. Bake the crust for 10 minutes to set it and keep it from getting soggy. Remove from the oven and remove the beans and foil. Let cool. Reduce the oven temperature to 325 degrees F.

In a saucepan, combine the butter, sugar, and corn syrup. Cook over low heat, stirring, until thickened and the butter is melted, 4–5 minutes. Let cool.

In a bowl, beat the eggs with the salt and then beat in the cooled syrup. Stir in the vanilla and chopped pecans. Pour into the cooled crust.

Arrange the pecan halves over the top. Bake until the filling is set and the crust is brown, about 50 minutes. Serve hot or at room temperature.

The thirty-thousand-year-old practice of cooking over an open fire continues to be an integral part of Africa's culinary heritage. In Togo today, street vendors cook *michui*, spicy skewered fish and meat, over charcoal. In Mali, whole goats are still ceremoniously roasted for weddings and other special occasions.

Coming to America in the seventeenth and eighteenth centuries, African cooks were obliged and then encouraged to continue this age-old technique. In Bahia, street vendors carry portable charcoal braziers to char cheese sticks and whole fish. Jamaican barbecued jerked meats, cooked over beach and roadside grills, are legendary.

In the United States, as nowhere else, barbecue has evolved into a popular form of entertaining. With the same kind of resourcefulness that created a cuisine out of scraps, African-Americans took one of their hardships and turned it from cooking in fireplace ashes to smoking in custom-built brick-framed pits.

Originally, the "pit" was a hole dug in the ground and lined with rocks. The fire was built inside the pit and the meat, fish, or vegetables went on grates over the fire, or were set on the coals and covered with dirt. Hickory and oak logs and chips burned for hours to infuse smoky tenderness into tough, economical cuts of pork and beef.

Commercial African-American barbecue got started after the Civil War. When segregation forced the creation of parallel businesses and services in black communities, enterprising cooks who made great barbecue rented storefronts from which to sell meats smoked in brick or oil-drum "pits" in the back. Mobile pits were built to set up at fairs and picnics and to take into the cotton fields to feed the laborers.

After the world wars, in the 1920s and 1940s, when a steady migration of southern blacks moved north, west, and east to the cities, barbecue joints opened in Kansas City, Chicago, New York, Los Angeles, and Oakland.

Barbecue is the only African-American cooking style where meat gets star billing. Even at that, it is always served with salad, beans, and bread, which balance the meal, fill you up, and cool the fiery sauces. When seasoned properly, a little meat, of which spareribs are a prime example, goes a long way.

There are a few mandatory elements for successful African-American barbecuing. First, you need a "pit," whether it's a hole in the ground, a used oil drum cut sideways and hinged, or a factory-made brazier with a cover. The sauce and seasoning are important. So are the type of firewood and the ability to close down the grill. These are details that must be attended to, but there is one more.

Every cook I talked to emphasized the secret to success is time. It takes hours to smoke typically tough cuts of pork, beef and mutton to melt-in-your-mouth tenderness. And that is what sets good barbecue apart. It is also why barbecue joints continue to be successful today.

A day or two before the actual cooking, hunks of pork or beef, ribs, links, chickens, or game are marinated in spices, garlic, and herbs. On The Day, the fire is built with hickory or oak and allowed to burn down to coal-perfection. The meat goes on the grill, the cover comes down, and the smoking begins.

What comes out of that barbecue depends on where you were raised or how you learned to like your 'cue. Next to chili, no other food raises the heat in a discussion like who makes the best barbecue. Geography plays a part in regional preferences.

Pork, which wasn't surpassed by beef as America's favorite meat until long after the Civil War, is the predominant choice for barbecue, just as it is the favored meat for other African-American cooking. (See the Glossary for information on different cuts of pork.)

Ribs and links are on most menus, but other cuts are found in different regions. From South Carolina to Tennessee, pork shoulders and Boston butts are slow roasted and "shredded" to put on bread and buns. Kentucky is known for its tender mutton and Arkansas for whole pigs cooked in a pit. Texas barbecue is best known for the hunks of beef brisket marinated for days and smoked for hours in converted oil drums over hickory-fueled fires. Whole chickens, as well as quarters, legs, and wings, are increasingly popular in cities from coast to coast. Goat and lamb, which harken back to African roots, are additional selections in Texas and Tennessee.

Generally speaking, sauces include the basic ingredients of tomato (often from ketchup), mustard, onions, vinegar, garlic, salt, and the all-important powdered, fresh, dried, or puréed chiles. What makes one sauce different from another is which ingredient gets top billing: the tomato, the vinegar, the mustard, or the chile. Some regional classifications can be made.

South Carolina sauces fall into four regional variations. From Charleston to the center of the state, the sauce is a tart-tangy yellow mustard base. Eastern South Carolinians like a vinegar and pepper sauce. The southwestern wedge next to Georgia opts for a sweet-and-mild tomato ketchup base, while next to North Carolina a wide variety of mustard-ketchup combinations, from hot to sweet, are found.

North Carolina sauce is vinegar-based, thin, and more like a marinade. In Georgia, most sauces are ketchup-based, with flavors varying from sweet to sour to spicy. They are served with spareribs on the bone and with sliced smoked pork loaded on white bread and toasted over charcoal. Tennessee pork shoulders are marinated overnight, barbecued, and then chopped and served with a spicy tomato-based sauce on rolls. Oklahoma sauce is sweet, tomato-based, and smoky. Kansas City style is very tomatoey—good enough to put on spaghetti! In Texas a thin, tart vinegar and cayenne sauce is served alongside brisket slices.

What follows are recipes that represent sauce, marinade, and smoking styles, developed from interviews with professional and home barbecuers. Variations based on how much onion, garlic, chile, or whatever are endless and subject to the cook's whim and what's on the shelf.

Many commercial sauces are excellent, and a whole lot easier than a couple of the recipes here. Some barbecue joints opt for them and then personalize them with garlic, chiles, and vinegar, or secret ingredients like beer, orange juice, hog's blood, or the liquid from spiced peaches. Even if a store-bought sauce is used, the meat still needs its prior seasoning. Once again, this seasoning is what epitomizes African-American cooking.

Although side dishes are secondary, a bite of sliced white or corn bread, a little slaw or potato salad, and a forkful of baked beans are just right to freshen the palate before that next ribald bite. Salads, slaws, breads, baked beans, pickles, and other picnic-type sides are included in this chapter. So are Bahian, Caribbean, and African recipes.

Also included are recipes for oven barbecue. This is the "barbecue" listed on menus of soul food restaurants. Oven barbecuing is meat cooked slowly in the oven the same way it would be done over the coals, and with the same seasoning and sauces. It's great in winter when the barbecue is covered up.

For generations, African-Americans have celebrated holidays, hog butcherings, and family reunions around the barbecue. In the southern and western United States, it continues to be the favorite way to entertain. An authentic American culinary phenomenon, barbecue is an excuse to invite your friends over and enjoy one another's company while the smoky puffs billow about teasingly in anticipation. Try one of the following sauce recipes, then personalize it with your own favorite spice.

Building the Perfect Barbecue Fire

As every barbecue cook I talked to emphasized, one of the most important elements of great barbecue is the fire. The best fires are built with hickory or oak. Hardwood charcoal like mesquite is an acceptable substitute for home grills, but petroleum-based briquettes and fire starters should be skipped.

Here's how to build a great fire in the home barbecue pit, whether a steel drum, a round portable, a heavy-duty covered steel pit, or a home-built brick-framed grill. A cover is important. If your grill doesn't have a cover, aluminum foil can be used.

newspaper
1 pound hickory or oak wood for every pound of food to be cooked
kindling such as small pieces of hickory, oak, alder, or madrone or
    fruit tree prunings
matches
hickory, alder, or fruit wood chips or shavings; grapevines; or apple-tree
    prunings, soaking in water

Pile plenty of crumpled newspaper on the bottom of the barbecue pit. Take 2–4 large pieces of hardwood—preferably hickory or oak, but alder, madrone, or walnut are okay, too—and place them several inches apart on the newspaper.

Add small pieces of charcoal from the previous fire, commercial mesquite from a package, or chunks of oak, hickory, or other hardwood. Then pile on smaller pieces of wood. Fruit wood such as apple or pear tree prunings are great. Strike a match and light the paper.

Once lit, the fire burns furiously for 10–20 minutes, depending upon the size of the pile, and reduces to a crackly sizzle on its way to grill-perfect heat. If it seems to be fizzling out before the wood catches, pour a little cooking oil over the wood. Stoke the fire periodically and move the hot coals next to the retainer logs to start them burning or, more accurately, smoldering.

The ideal temperature for grilling is attained by keeping a layer of ash in the center and pushing the hot coals against the larger logs, which get very smoky from the coals. Moving the coals is a better way to maintain the heat than dousing them with water, which reduces the temperature.

When there are no more flames and the coals are a smoldering bed of heat, they are ready for the food. Keep a bucketful of wood chips soaking in water to throw on every half hour or so throughout the cooking to keep the fire smoky. Plan on 1 cup of wood chips for every 30 minutes of barbecuing.

NOTES: If you want to catch drippings for a sauce or gravy, place a small pan under the meat.

For long slow cooking, build the fire on one side of the barbecue and place the food on the other. Cover.

If you have an electric or gas grill, hickory chips or fruit-tree twigs can be added on top of the heating element or rocks during the last few minutes of cooking to impart a significant amount of flavor.

Pit cooking *originally meant cooking in the ground. Now it describes any kind of barbecue where a wood fire is used, or at least one with real wood charcoal. In the South, the barbecue grill is known as the pit whether it is a stone-lined hole in the ground or an elaborate brick or iron custom fabrication. It doesn't refer to a grill fired by electricity, by briquettes, or by gas.*

Sam Mayes, *proprietor of Sam's in Austin, Texas, recommends the following time for slow cooking over a home-style barbecue: Chicken, 45 minutes, tops; sausage and ribs, 2 hours; and a small brisket, 3–4 hours. He agrees the best barbecue is over oak wood, never charcoal briquettes.*

Ribs

Short for spareribs, ribs prove the best meat is next to the bone, however spare it may be. An argument might spring up about whether or not to parboil or pre-bake ribs before barbecuing them. Every professional barbecue cook I talked with said never. Home cooks, however, differ. Without the time to tend ribs for as long they'd need on the grill, and without the even heat a brick pit provides, precooking is acceptable.

Buy ¾–1 pound ribs per person

Parboiling: Drop the ribs in boiling water for 5 minutes. Remove and rub with All-Purpose Seasoning Rub (page 210) or cover with favorite sauce. Marinate in the refrigerator overnight. Grill over hot coals in a covered barbecue, turning once or twice, 30–40 minutes.

Prebaking: Rub the ribs with All-Purpose Seasoning Rub. Arrange in a single layer in a shallow baking pan. Place in 325 degree F oven for 20 minutes. Remove and chill until ready to barbecue. Grill over hot coals in a covered bar-becue, turning once or twice, 25–30 minutes.

Dry ribs: Rub the ribs with All-Purpose Seasoning Rub. Marinate, refrig-erated, overnight and then barbecue. Extra cayenne, salt, and pepper can be added to the rub. Serve with or without sauce.

Wet ribs: Precook by one of the methods above. While still hot, slather with your favorite sauce. Cover and refrigerate overnight. Cook over or next to hot coals. The sauce will tend to burn faster than ribs cooked dry, so adjust their situation on the grill to compensate. Brush with sauce several times while cooking. Finish with a baste of sauce.

In 1985, Jean McWashington returned to her home state of Mississippi after twenty years in California. She bought ten acres in the eastern part of the state and opened Jean's Red Door BBQ, a smoky treasure that draws barbecue lovers from all over the area. Jean cooks over hickory wood in a style she learned when she was going to high school in Texas. Ribs, sausage, chicken, Boston butt, and beef brisket are dry-cooked and served with her sweet, mild sauce.

Leon Finney, Sr., is one of the acclaimed barbecue kings of Chicago. He moved from Mississippi in 1940, and started working with his aunt at a barbecue place where she was first a cook and then the owner. He eventually took it over and renamed it after himself. Leon's continues to attract barbecue lovers who go to Chicago. Thousands of conventioneers, as well as a devoted local clientele, are responsible for consuming the three hundred thousand pounds of glorious ribs that are sold each year by Leon.

Sauces

Seasoning is indispensable in African-American barbecuing. Professional and home barbecue cooks love to talk about their art and how much their particular flavor is appreciated, but they guard their personal recipes. "Some even take them with them when they die," says Vernell Davis, Jr., whose family owns K. C. Barbecue in Berkeley, California.

Between the secrecy of barbecuers, the lack of written recipes, and the fact that most sauces are variations on the theme of ketchup, sugar, and vinegar with spices and other provocative ingredients, most homemade sauces are reinvented each time they are made, depending on what is in the pantry. Here are sauces representative of the various styles found all over the country. They have received blessings from barbecue cooks and testings from barbecue lovers and are a dynamite sampling.

First, coat whatever is being barbecued with All-Purpose Seasoning Rub (page 210), then try different sauces until you find the one you like best. And don't forget to personalize it with your own extra spice.

In all the barbecue joints I visited, the sauce is cooked separately from the meat. Then it may be basted on the meat at the end of cooking, or it is ladled over the smoky ribs or chicken or served next to them. Hot, medium, and mild variations are often on the menu. The heat comes from fresh chiles, dried chiles, or ground chile powders (like cayenne), from hot pepper sauces like Tabasco, or from purées of *habanero* (Scotch Bonnet) chiles.

All of the sauces get better when aged for a week or so before using. Any of the following sauces can also be frozen or be canned. To can, bring the sauce to a boil and ladle into hot, sterilized half-pint or pint jars. Seal with lids and rings according to the manufacturer's directions and process in a hot-water bath for 15 minutes. Store in a cool, dark place up to 1 year.

Whether the term comes from barbe à queue, French for from "beard to tail," or from barbacoa, the Spanish adaptation of an Arawak Indian word for the grate used when cooking over coals, this once primitive method of cooking infuses food with the most divine smoky flavor no matter how it is spelled—barbecue, barbeque, bar-b-que, or bbq.

All-Purpose Seasoning Rub

Use this on chicken, pork, beef, or fish. Everything but fish can, and should, be done the day before. Fish needs only 30–60 minutes in the seasoning. The dry ingredients can be mixed and saved in a jar for a couple of months. Add the oil when ready to use.

Makes enough for 3 pounds meat

1 teaspoon salt
1 teaspoon ground black pepper
2 cloves garlic, minced, or 1 tablespoon garlic powder
1 teaspoon paprika
1 teaspoon cayenne pepper
1/4 cup vegetable oil

Combine all the ingredients in a bowl. Place the meat in a shallow pan or dish. Using a pastry brush or hands, cover the meat on all sides with the seasoning. Cover with plastic wrap. Refrigerate at least 8 hours, or overnight.

Vinegar Marinade

This adaptation of a mixture recommended by Jesse Thomas of Thomas Bar-B-Q in Houston, Texas, is for tough cuts of beef, pork, or goat. The vinegar and lemon juice help tenderize. Jesse cooks his barbecue over Texas mesquite.

Makes 1 1/2 cups; enough for 5–6 pounds meat

1 cup distilled white, cider, or red wine vinegar
1/2 cup water
1 lemon, sliced
1 or 2 tablespoons sugar
1 yellow onion, chopped or sliced
1/4 cup Tabasco or other hot-pepper sauce
ground black pepper
1 tablespoon dried sage, crushed
3 tablespoons tomato paste

Combine all the ingredients in a saucepan. Bring to a boil over medium heat. Reduce the heat to low and simmer 10–15 minutes. Let cool and pour over meat in a nonreactive shallow pan or dish. Cover and refrigerate overnight before grilling.

Jerk Seasoning

Jamaicans who sell jerked meats from huts along the road make up their own seasoning or buy bottled jerk seasoning. Like curry mixtures, each jerk seasoning has its own special flavor. Here is a lively combination to make and keep on hand. Personalize it with your own additions.

Make this in quantity, combining only the dry spices and storing in an airtight container. Add the fresh garlic, oil, and liquid just before using.

Makes about ⅓ cup; enough for 3–4 pounds meat

1 tablespoon granulated dried onion
1 tablespoon ground allspice
1 tablespoon ground ginger
1 tablespoon ground thyme
1 teaspoon salt
1–3 teaspoons cayenne pepper
½ teaspoon ground black pepper
1 teaspoon sugar
dash of ground cinnamon
3 tablespoons garlic powder, or 3 garlic cloves, minced
2–3 tablespoons vegetable oil
¼ cup fresh lime juice, rum, coconut milk, or water

Combine all the dry ingredients and mix well. Store in an airtight container. When ready to use, take a couple of tablespoons out for each pound of meat, chicken, or fish and mix with the oil and the liquid of choice. Marinate fish 1 hour and anything else overnight.

Red or Green Chile Relish

This sauce pops up in Togo, Bahia, and in the Caribbean. It is an everyday condiment, kept on the table like Mexican salsa, and used for seasoning everything from grilled meat and fish to greens and beans.

Makes about 1 cup

2–4 fresh red or green chiles, finely chopped (see Glossary)
4 firm, ripe tomatoes, chopped
1 yellow onion, finely chopped
1 garlic clove, minced
1 teaspoon salt
1/4 teaspoon ground black pepper
juice of 2 lemons or limes

Combine all the ingredients in a bowl and stir to mix.

Tomato-Onion Relish

A West African condiment, this simple salsalike mixture is great with Spicy Meat Sticks (page 228) or *Yassa* (page 263). Its citric tang refreshes the hottest of chile-seasoned meat, chicken, or fish.

Makes about 1 1/2 cups

4 firm tomatoes, chopped
1 yellow onion, finely chopped
1 garlic clove, minced
1 teaspoon salt
1/4 teaspoon ground black pepper
juice of 2 limes or lemons

In a bowl, stir together all of the ingredients and mix well. Let stand 1 hour to blend the flavors. Store, covered, in the refrigerator up to 3 days.

In Togo, anything barbecued, from whole fish to little skewered tidbits, is called michui. The fish and meats are highly seasoned with spices and herbs before being grilled. Corn is a popular barbecue item in Togo as well.

Basic Red Barbecue Sauce

This sauce combines all of the most commonly used ingredients for home barbecue. Adjust the amounts to suit your own taste. Add the onions if you want an extra oniony sweetness and the texture.

Makes about 1¼ cups; enough for 3 pounds meat

1 cup ketchup
¼ cup cider or red wine vinegar
3 tablespoons firmly packed brown sugar
2 garlic cloves, minced
1 tablespoon dry or prepared mustard
1 teaspoon Worcestershire sauce
½ teaspoon cayenne pepper or Tabasco sauce or other hot-pepper sauce
½ yellow onion, finely chopped (optional)

Combine all the ingredients in a small saucepan. Bring to a boil, reduce the heat to low, and cook until thickened and flavors are blended, about 5 minutes. Adjust the vinegar, sugar, and hot pepper to suit your taste. For best results make up to a week in advance. Store, covered tightly, in the refrigerator for up to a month.

Leon's Basic Barbecue Sauce

Leon McHenry is proprietor of Leon's Restaurants in San Francisco, where he serves great barbecue and equally good creole dishes. Leon's signature rich hot barbecue sauce is on the market, but as a cooking teacher he's always developing new recipes. This is his basic sauce, with the optional embellishment of sweet peach preserves.

Makes about 2 cups

2 tablespoons vegetable oil
1 yellow onion, chopped
1 celery stalk, chopped
2 tablespoons distilled white or cider vinegar
1/4 cup fresh lemon juice
1 cup ketchup
3 tablespoons Worcestershire sauce
1/2 teaspoon dry mustard
1/2 cup water
1/2 cup firmly packed dark brown sugar
1/4 teaspoon Tabasco sauce, or to taste
1 cup peach preserves (optional)

In a saucepan over medium heat, warm the oil. Add the onion and celery and sauté until soft, about 6 minutes. Add all the remaining ingredients and bring to a boil, stirring constantly. Reduce the heat to low and simmer 5–15 minutes, depending upon how much texture you want in it. For best results make the sauce up to a week before using. Store, covered tightly, in the refrigerator for up to a month.

Leon McHenry grew up in Tulsa, Oklahoma, and has lived and owned restaurants in San Francisco for over thirty years. He recommends seasoning ribs for a few hours in a seasoning blend, then basting while cooking with a marinade. "The long, slow cooking and basting gives the flavor all the way to the bone," he says. Just before taking it off the grill, the meat should be slathered with sauce.

Bronze Barbecue Sauce

This reddish brown sauce is the hottest one here. It hits the palate with sweetness and finishes with a long, pleasant afterburn. It is reminiscent of the sauce at E & L's (for Eddie and Lola's) Bar-B-Que in Jackson, Mississippi. Ed Hilliard is planning to put his sauce on the market and I recommend being on the lookout for it. For ribs, cover with a dry marinade and refrigerate overnight, then smoke for 2 hours. Spoon on the sauce when serving. Try this with Oven-Barbecued Ribs (page 233) or for any meat barbecue.

Makes about 2 cups; enough for 4 pounds meat

2 tablespoons vegetable oil
1 large red onion, chopped
1/2 cup sugar
2 teaspoons paprika
1/2 cup cider vinegar or red wine vinegar
1 cup molasses
1 tablespoon Worcestershire sauce
1 can (28 ounces) crushed tomatoes in purée
3 tablespoons mustard
2 bay leaves, crushed
1/4 cup Tabasco sauce or other hot-pepper sauce
1/2 cup ketchup
salt

In a heavy saucepan over low heat, warm the oil. Add the onion and sauté over low heat until very soft, 15–20 minutes. Raise the heat to medium and add the sugar. Cook until the sugar melts and begins to caramelize, stirring frequently. Stir in the paprika. Now add the vinegar, stir, and stand back to avoid inhaling the fumes. Stir well and add all the remaining ingredients, including salt to taste. Bring to a boil. Reduce the heat to low and cook until thickened, 30–40 minutes.

If you wish a smoother sauce, purée it in a blender or food processor. Taste and adjust the seasonings. For best results make sauce up to a week before using. Store, tightly covered, in the refrigerator for up to a month.

Mahogany Sauce

A quickly prepared sauce to brush on at the last minute or to serve with ribs, steaks, or chicken. Its dark richness makes it a natural with Texas Brisket (pages 224–225) or any beef barbecue. It can even be used for marinating the brisket or chuck.

Equal amounts of ketchup, water, sugar, and vinegar are combined here. Make it once, then vary the amounts to suit your own taste, depending upon whether you prefer your barbecue sweeter (more sugar), tarter (more vinegar), saltier (more Worcestershire), hotter (more chile powder or cayenne pepper), thinner (more water), or tomatoey (more ketchup or tomato paste). Minced garlic and onions can also be added.

Makes about 1¼ cups; enough for 3 pounds meat

¹/₃ cup ketchup
¹/₃ cup water
¹/₃ cup brown sugar
¹/₃ cup cider vinegar or red wine vinegar
1 heaping tablespoon chile powder
¹/₄ teaspoon cayenne pepper
2 tablespoons Worcestershire sauce

Combine all the ingredients in a small saucepan. Bring to a boil and cook until thickened, 10–15 minutes. Taste and adjust the seasonings. Cook for another couple of minutes. Let cool before serving. For best results make up to a week in advance. Store, tightly covered, in the refrigerator for up to a month.

Yellow Sauce

Mustardy and tart, this sauce from South Carolina goes with chicken and fish (see variation), but its natural affinity for grilled hot dogs makes everyone beg for more. It will keep in the refrigerator several months, at least through the summer barbecue season. It's also good on boiled hot dogs and makes a great spread on ham or cheese sandwiches.

Makes about 8 cups unstrained, 6 cups strained

4 cups mustard
1 cup ketchup
2 tablespoons mustard seeds
2 tablespoons dried oregano, crushed
2 tablespoons dried basil, crushed
1 cup sugar
³/₄ cup cider vinegar
2 yellow onions, finely chopped
4 cloves garlic, minced
1 tablespoon white peppercorns
1 cup water

Combine all the ingredients in a large stainless-steel or other nonreactive saucepan. Bring to a boil, stirring frequently. Reduce the heat to low and simmer, stirring frequently, until the onions are very soft and the mixture is thickened, about 45 minutes. Let cool and store tightly covered in the refrigerator for 1-2 months.

VARIATION: *For a smooth texture, strain. I like to strain half to use as a baste on barbecued or baked chicken and save the rest for sandwiches.*

K. C.'s Homemade Barbecue Sauce

Vernell Davis, Jr., is one of the first people I talked to about African-American barbecue. His enthusiasm helped fan the fire for writing this book. Talking with Vern in the restaurant his family has operated on San Pablo Avenue in Berkeley, California, for over twenty-five years, is like taking a short history course in the movement of African-Americans from the South to the West.

His dad, Vernell, Sr., came to Berkeley from Arkansas in the forties and hooked up with his brother, who arrived from Kansas City where he'd been working in a barbecue restaurant. They started K. C. Barbeque, named because the sauce is thick and tomatoey.

This is Vern's home version of the house sauce and a good one to make in summer when tomatoes are plentiful and ripe. It has a very lemony tang the first day, which mellows out after a week or so. The sweet tomato richness makes it ideal for any meat from chicken to ribs, links to beefsteak. I've added a little liquid smoke, which adds a nice dimension, especially when used on oven-barbecued meat.

Makes about 4 cups

4 pounds ripe tomatoes, diced
1 yellow onion, chopped
2 garlic cloves, chopped
1/2 teaspoon dried thyme, crushed
1 teaspoon dried basil, crushed
1 cup fresh lemon juice
1 cup cider vinegar
2 tablespoons tomato paste
3/4 cup firmly packed brown sugar
4 teaspoons paprika
2 teaspoons salt
1–2 teaspoons cayenne pepper
3/4 teaspoon natural liquid smoke
2 tablespoons vegetable oil

In a stainless-steel or other nonreactive saucepan, combine the tomatoes, onion, garlic, thyme, and basil and cook over medium heat, stirring frequently, until thickened and fragrant, 25–30 minutes. If you want a smooth texture, pass the mixture through a food mill or rub it through a sieve set over a bowl, then return it to the saucepan. Add all the remaining ingredients,

A brisket done at home Kansas City style by Addie Echols, proprietor of the famed Arthur Bryant's, is marinated overnight in thousand island dressing to which extra onions and garlic are added. Then he smokes it twelve to fifteen hours or overnight in a barrel smoker fired with hickory or oak. The meat goes on the grate next to the fire, "never directly over it." Every three hours he gets up and turns the meat. "The slower the cooking, the better the flavor and more tender the meat," says Addie.

except the oil, and bring to a boil. Reduce the heat to low and cook to thicken and blend the flavors, 10–15 minutes.

Stir in the oil and continue simmering over low heat to reduce the mixture to a puréelike consistency, 20–30 minutes longer. Let cool and use to baste on or serve with barbecued meat or fowl.

Red Yellow Sauce

Here is a fiery-hot sauce courtesy of South Carolina cook Dye Rhodan.

Makes about 1¼ cups

1 green bell pepper, seeded and minced
6 green onions, including tops, chopped
2 garlic cloves, minced
1 tablespoon sugar
¼ cup mustard
¾ cup ketchup
½ cup water
Tabasco Sauce or habanero *(Scotch Bonnet) hot-pepper sauce*

In a stainless-steel or other nonreactive saucepan, combine all the ingredients. Be warned that the *habanero* sauce comes from the hottest chile in the world, so add it by drops and taste until the desired heat is reached. Bring to a boil, reduce the heat to low, and simmer until thickened and the flavors are blended, about 20 minutes. For a smooth texture, purée the sauce in a blender or food processor. Let cool before using on any barbecued meats. For best results make a week in advance. Store tightly covered in the refrigerator for 1–2 months.

Chili Sauce

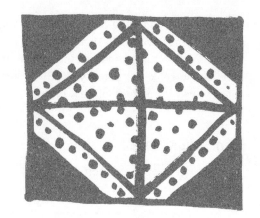

This versatile condiment is similar to sauces found in Georgia. Make it when the garden is overrun with tomatoes and bell peppers are at their peak. Its sweet-tart essence is great with grilled links and on barbecued meat sandwiches. Add it to other barbecue sauces such as the Louisiana Creole Sauce on page 167. Or stir a little into stews or spoon it over eggs. Adjust the amount of sugar depending on sweetness of tomatoes and personal taste.

Makes about 2 quarts

8 pounds ripe tomatoes, coarsely chopped, or 4 cans (28 ounces each) tomatoes with their juices, coarsely chopped
2 yellow onions, finely chopped
4 green or red bell peppers, seeded and finely chopped
$1^1/_2$ cups distilled white vinegar or cider vinegar
1 tablespoon salt
$^1/_2$–$^3/_4$ cup sugar
2 teaspoons dry mustard
1 teaspoon ground allspice
1 teaspoon ground cloves
1 teaspoon ground mace
3 or 4 fresh red or green chiles (see Glossary), 2 teaspoons red pepper flakes, or cayenne pepper to taste

In a large, heavy stainless-steel or other nonreactive pot, combine all the ingredients and bring to a boil. Reduce the heat to medium and cook, stirring occasionally, until thickened, about 1 hour. After 30 minutes, taste and adjust the seasonings. Continue cooking to thicken and blend the flavors.

Place the mixture, one-third at a time, in a blender or food processor and purée. Let cool, cover, and store in the refrigerator at least a week before using. It will keep up to 4 weeks in the refrigerator. The sauce can also be frozen up to 6 months, or canned and stored in a cool, dark place for up to a year. To can, ladle into hot $^1/_2$-pint canning jars and seal according to manufacturer's directions. Process in a hot-water bath for 10 minutes. Let stand at least a week before using.

The Original Clewis Barbecue Sauce

This is the barbecue sauce from Benny Clewis's family in Palestine, Texas. Originally it was "used to barbecue goats and later was passed on for beef and pork." Then, Benny's grandfather bottled the sauce in old Town Hall soda-water bottles and sold it in Dallas in the 1940s. The hickory flavoring comes from cooking all the ingredients together with real hickory chips.

Makes about 2 gallons

1 pound hickory chips, commerically packaged or homemade by shaving a piece of hickory with a knife
4 teaspoons fresh lemon juice
6 celery stalks, chopped
6 heads garlic, chopped
4 baseball-sized yellow onions, finely chopped
1 green bell pepper, seeded and chopped
1 cup firmly packed brown sugar
1/4 cup distilled white vinegar or cider vinegar
4 quarts tomato purée
6 bay leaves
3 teaspoons salt
1 1/4 cups mustard
1 cup pork drippings or lard (see note)
4 teaspoons cayenne pepper
3 cups water

In a large, heavy pot or dutch oven, combine all of the ingredients and bring to a boil. Reduce the heat to low and simmer uncovered, stirring occasionally, until thickened and flavors are blended, about 1½ hours.

Set a colander over a bowl and strain the sauce. After straining the sauce you won't have quite 2 gallons. To make it 2 gallons, just run hot water over the remainder in the colander, which will be the herbs and spices. The run-off is used to build up the barbecue sauce to make 2 gallons.

NOTE: I've made this without the lard; it loses the sheen and that extra dimension of flavor, but otherwise is still a great sauce.

Spicy Meat Sauce

Serve this on Pig's Ear Sandwiches (page 227), or by itself on bread for a fiery sloppy joe.

Makes 6 servings

1 pound finely ground bulk pork sausage
2 tablespoons vegetable oil or lard
3 fresh red chiles, seeded and minced (see Glossary)
2 green bell peppers, seeded and finely chopped
3 garlic cloves, minced
2 teaspoons sugar
2 teaspoons dry mustard
1 teaspoon ground allspice
1/8 teaspoon ground cloves
1/4 teaspoon ground mace
pinch of cayenne pepper, or more to taste
1/4 cup distilled white vinegar or cider vinegar
1 cup (8 ounces) canned tomato sauce
1 can (16 ounces) tomatoes, with their juice, chopped
salt

If the sausage meat comes coarsely ground, put it in a food processor and process until fine. In a heavy skillet over high heat, brown the sausage. Using a slotted spoon, remove to paper towels to drain. Pour off the fat.

In the same skillet, warm the oil over medium heat. Add the chiles, bell peppers, and garlic and sauté until just beginning to brown, about 6 minutes. Return the meat to the skillet and stir in the sugar, mustard, allspice, cloves, mace, and cayenne. Cook a minute or so, stirring all the while.

Stir in the vinegar, tomato sauce, and chopped tomatoes and their juice. Add salt to taste. Bring to a boil, reduce the heat to low, and simmer until thickened, 20–30 minutes. Taste for seasoning and add more cayenne, if desired.

Hecky's, one of the Chicago area's foremost barbecues, is where proprietor Hecky Powell carries on the tradition of the wood-fired pit barbecue originated by Chicago's old barbecue kings. Although related to the hole in the ground over which meat was once roasted, the pit now refers to custom-built brick-lined ovens that hold huge chunks of hickory and oak and can be closed down to maximize the amount of smoke. At Hecky's, a heavy creole influence comes from his Louisiana-born mother who is responsible for all the recipes, including the red beans and rice served with the ribs and the sweet potato pie for dessert.

Barbecued Chicken

Chicken is one of the best meats in the world to cook over coals. To cook it the African-American way, season it first with All-Purpose Seasoning Rub, cover, refrigerate overnight, and barbecue the next day. Serve it straight from the grill or with your favorite barbecue sauce. It will be the best barbecued chicken you have ever eaten.

Serves 4

1 chicken, about 3 pounds, cut into serving pieces, or 3 pounds
favorite chicken parts
All-Purpose Seasoning Rub (page 210)
favorite barbecue sauce (optional)

Remove the skin from the chicken and cut off the extra fat. Rub or brush the seasoning or sauce all over the chicken pieces. Place in a glass or ceramic dish, cover, and refrigerate at least 4 hours or up to overnight.

Prepare a charcoal fire on one side of the barbecue. Place the chicken pieces on the hot side of the grill briefly to brown on each side. Move the chicken pieces to the opposite side of the grill, next to (not over) the coals. Cover the grill, and cook, turning occasionally until tender, 30–40 minutes.

If desired, brush the chicken with your favorite sauce just before removing from the grill, or serve the sauce on the side.

Commercial Texas barbecue started out in smokers behind German butcher shops in the twenties and thirties. The butchers smoked their sausages in old oil drums laid on their sides, cut in half, and hinged. Itinerant blacks who came to work the cotton fields were not allowed inside the butcher shop and had to buy their sausages and meat at the back door where the smokers were. Seeing this set-up was an inspiration to enterprising cooks, who made their own smokers and put them along the roads or next to the cotton fields. To this day, black-owned portable barbecue pits are still operating along roadsides in rural Texas on the weekends.

Texts Brisket

Long, slow cooking of beef brisket in old oil drums are what the legendary Texas barbecue is all about. These big sooty masterpieces turn out the most incredible hunks of beef, fork tender and provocatively seasoned. Here's how to do it at home. Serve it with Mahogany Sauce (page 216) on the side.

Serves 10–12

1 beef brisket or chuck roast, about 5 pounds and 2 inches thick
salt and ground black pepper
2 tablespoons vegetable oil
2 teaspoons dry mustard
2 teaspoons dried sage, crushed
2 teaspoons dried oregano, crushed
4 garlic cloves, minced
2 teaspoons ground ginger
1/2 teaspoon ground allspice
1 teaspoon red pepper flakes
1/4 cup molasses
1/4 cup cider vinegar or red wine vinegar
2 tablespoons tomato paste
1/2 cup ketchup
1 cup water
cayenne pepper
Mahogany Sauce (page 216; optional)

One or two days before barbecuing, place the roast in a deep glass or ceramic dish or stainless-steel roasting pan. Sprinkle all over with salt and black pepper.

In a saucepan over medium heat, warm the oil. Add the mustard, sage, oregano, garlic, ginger, allspice, and red pepper flakes and sauté 3–4 minutes. Stir in all the remaining ingredients, excepting the sauce and including cayenne pepper to taste. Simmer, uncovered, until thickened and the flavors have blended, 10–15 minutes. Pour the hot sauce over the meat. Cover and refrigerate 1–2 days, turning occasionally.

You will need about 5 pounds hickory or other hardwood coals and a pound or two of hickory chips to cook the meat. Prepare the coals about 5 hours before you want to serve the meat. When they are hot, move the coals to one side or spread in a circle around the bottom of the grill. Remove the meat from

You can tell if meat has been cooked for a long time over a wood fire if, when you cut it, there is a red rim just under the crispy seared crust. Gas-fired grills won't leave this.

the marinade, reserving the marinade, and place the meat in the center or side, not over the coals. Put a drip pan under it. Cover and cook 3½–4 hours, replenishing the coals and hickory chips as needed. Using a meat thermometer check the internal temperature occasionally; don't let it rise above 180 degrees F. This will help ensure tenderness. Turn the meat occasionally and baste frequently with the reserved marinade as it cooks. The meat is done when it gives easily when pressed with fingers or sliced with a knife.

Remove from the grill and let stand about 10 minutes to keep the juices intact. Slice thinly and serving with Mahogany Sauce, if desired.

Tennessee-Style Chopped Pork Shoulder

One of the finest examples of this smoke-infused sandwich meat, found in many southern states but renowned in Tennessee, is served at Payne's BBQ in Memphis. Although a big brick pit and someone to tend the fire and meat for hours is the professional way to produce this kind of barbecue, a good home grill with a tight lid and enough room to build a fire on one side and smoke the meat on the other will accomplish a fine version as well.

At Payne's, the meat is chopped and served on buns in a light, hot aromatic sauce, which is similar to Basic Red Barbecue Sauce, but with an extra dose of cayenne. Crisp coleslaw is also piled on the sandwich.

Serves 8–10

1 pork shoulder, 3–4 pounds, butterflied
All-Purpose Seasoning Rub (page 210)
Basic Red Barbecue Sauce (page 213) or other favorite barbecue sauce

Rub the pork with the All-Purpose Seasoning Rub and place in a glass or ceramic dish, cover, and refrigerate overnight.

Prepare a charcoal fire on one side of the barbecue. Lay the pork out on the hot side and brown it quickly on each side. Move it to the opposite side of the grill, next to (not over) the coals. Cover the barbecue and smoke 3–3½ hours, turning occasionally and adding more coals or wood chips as needed.

When done, remove the pork and let stand 10 minutes. Using a thin, sharp carving knife, slice across the grain as thinly as possible. Serve with barbecue sauce.

K. C.'s Barbecued Goat Marinade

Vernell Davis, Jr., shares this tart, spicy mixture that complements the strong flavor and breaks down the dense texture of goat. He feels this marinade is enough to tenderize goat without parboiling it. Check Resources for mail-order goat, if it isn't readily available where you live.

Makes about 4 cups; enough for 5–6 pounds goat

2 cups cider vinegar
1 teaspoon finely grated lemon zest
1 cup fresh lemon juice
1 cup vegetable oil
2 bay leaves
1 tablespoon dried thyme, crushed
1 tablespoon whole cloves
1 tablespoon whole allspice
1 tablespoon crushed black peppercorns
1 tablespoon sugar
2 garlic cloves, crushed
1 teaspoon salt
5–6 pounds goat shoulder or leg
All-Purpose Seasoning Rub (page 210)
K. C.'s Homemade Barbecue Sauce (pages 218–219)

In a saucepan, combine all the ingredients, except the goat, sauce, and seasoning rub. Bring to a boil over medium heat. Reduce the heat to low, cover partially, and simmer, stirring occasionally, to blend the flavors, about 1 hour. Strain and let cool.

Place the goat in a glass or ceramic dish and pour the marinade over it. Cover and marinate in the refrigerator for 24 hours. Turn frequently if not fully covered by the marinade.

After 24 hours, remove the goat, wipe dry, and season with All-Purpose Seasoning Rub. Prepare the coals. When they burn down to embers, place the goat on the grill. Cook 30 minutes per pound, turning every 15 minutes. Frequently baste with K. C.'s Homemade Barbecue Sauce during the last half of cooking.

African-Americans from the Caribbean to Texas savor strong-flavored goat, a holdover from the mother country where hearty goats are numerous and have provided protein for centuries. Sarah Greenberg, a math teacher in Charleston, South Carolina, recommends boiling the meat before barbecuing to make it tender. Benny Clewis of Rosharon, Texas, boils his in vinegar to "pull out the wildness." And, Vern Davis, from K. C. Barbeque in Berkeley, California, feels a twenty-four-hour marinade will do the trick.

Pig's Ear Sandwiches

The best place to have these is at the Big Apple Inn on Farish Street in Jackson, Mississippi. They aren't really barbecued, but the sauce is so spicy it gives the feeling of barbecue, and that's why they are in this chapter. Gene Lee is the proprietor of this thriving little take-out his grandfather, Juan Mora, started in 1939 as a storefront stand. Pig's ear sandwiches, smoked sausage sandwiches, and homemade tamales are the specialties. If you have even the slightest affection for pork fat, the ears are for you. They aren't very big and you can't eat them every day, but they are an incredible treat and they won't kill you.

This is how they are cooked at the Big Apple; the sauce is from another source. They are best served on small, soft white bread rolls. Shredded cabbage is added to help cool the heat of the sauce.

Serves 6

> 6 pig's ears, cleaned
> Spicy Meat Sauce (page 222)
> mustard
> 6 small soft rolls
> 1/4 head green cabbage, shredded

If the ears are not clean when you get them, they will need to be singed to remove hair and then scrubbed.

In a saucepan, combine the ears with salted water to cover. Bring to a boil, cover, and cook at a medium boil until tender when pierced with a fork, about 1 hour. Alternatively, in a pressure cooker, add water to a depth of 2 inches and the ears and cook at a gentle rock for 25 minutes. Keep the ears warm in the hot water while preparing the sauce.

Spread a little mustard on the cut side of the rolls, top each with a pig's ear, some sauce, and a little cabbage. Serve at once.

Spicy Meat Sticks

All over the African continent snacks are sold by roadside vendors. Grilled meats and fried pastries and fritters are cooked over charcoal fires in small portable drums. This tradition continued in the New World, especially in Bahia and in the Caribbean where the tropical climate accommodates the custom. In Togo, grilled meat tidbits are called *michui*, in Cameroon they are *sawyer*, in Ghana they are *chichinga,* and in Somalia they are *moushkaki*. Here, the most common seasonings are combined with beef cubes and skewered. Eat these with Tomato-Onion Relish.

Makes about 12 skewers

1¹/₂ pounds beef round steak or London broil, cut into 1-inch cubes
1 onion, quartered and then cut into 1-inch squares
1 teaspoon cayenne pepper
1 teaspoon salt
2 garlic cloves, minced, or 1 tablespoon garlic powder
1 tablespoon minced fresh ginger, or 1 tablespoon ground ginger
1 teaspoon dried basil or other favorite herb, crushed (optional)
juice of 2 lemons
3 tablespoons olive, peanut, or vegetable oil
Tomato-Onion Relish (page 212)

Place the meat and onion in a shallow baking dish. In a small mixing bowl combine all the rest of the ingredients except the relish. Pour over the meat and onions and stir well. Cover and refrigerate at least 6 hours or overnight.

Prepare a charcoal fire. Soak twelve 6-inch bamboo skewers in water to cover 30 minutes.

Drain the skewers. Alternately thread the meat cubes and onions onto the skewers. Grill over hot coals until browned and cooked through, 3–5 minutes on each side. Serve hot with the relish.

The Jamaican method of marinating meat in a highly spiced seasoning for a day or two and then barbecuing it started in the mid-seventeenth century when runaway slaves escaped to the mountains. These runaways were called Maroons and they learned about the spices and chiles growing wild from the native Arawaks. The Maroons hunted wild boars. To preserve the meat for as long as possible, they slathered it in peppery mixtures made from the indigenous spices mixed with salt stolen from the planters or traded with slaves. Then they grilled the meat over open fire pits. This method of seasoning and grilling continued, but it has only been in the last two decades, since independence from Britain, that the popularity of Jamaican jerked meats has become widespread. Today, jerk huts all over Jamaican beaches and street corners offer the tasty lip-burning snacks to locals and tourists.

Jerked Pork

This may be the best way in the world to barbecue pork. The overnight marination in jerk seasoning with lime juice allows the spices to soak into the meat, which complements the smokiness from the fire. At the Pork Pit in Montego Bay, Jamaica, a fifteen-foot brick-lined grill smolders all day infusing pork like this. Slice it thinly and serve with Mango Relish (page 25) or Papaya-Chayote Hot Sauce (page 24) from the Caribbean chapter or Red or Green Chile Relish (page 212) from this chapter.

> Serves 6–8

Jerk Seasoning (page 211)
1 boned pork loin or shoulder, 3–4 pounds

Prepare the Jerk Seasoning as directed, using fresh garlic and lime juice.

Place the pork in a baking dish and rub well all over with the seasoning. Cover and refrigerate overnight.

Prepare a charcoal fire on one side of the barbecue. When the coals have burned to glowing, place the meat over them and quickly sear to brown. Move the meat to the side of the coals, cover the barbecue, and smoke until tender, turning several times, about 1 hour. Remove from the grill and let stand 5 minutes before slicing thinly. Serve with a sauce (see recipe introduction).

Before the Spanish arrived in the West Indies, the diets of the Arawak and Carib Indians were based on fish, fruits, and vegetables. Their method of preserving food by smoke-drying over a pit fire was adopted by runaway slaves and shipwrecked sailors, who hunted the wild progeny of domesticated pigs brought to the islands by the Spanish. After digging the pit and building a fire from the bones and hides of the pig, a grate of green wood for holding the meat was placed over the fire. The grate allowed the smoke to encircle and permeate the meat while the hot sun contributed to drying. The French word for this process of smoking is boucan. Some of these displaced men, after banding together, went on to raid and harass the Spanish coastal colonies. Consequently, their smoky lifestyle contributed to their becoming known as buccaneers.

Jerked Chicken Drumettes

This is how Icy Vincent, owner of Geva's, a contemporary Caribbean restaurant in San Francisco, makes her spicy appetizers. Use the jerk seasoning recipe in this chapter or find a commercial blend you like at a Caribbean or specialty-food store (see Resources).

Drumettes are the two meaty wing portions. The wing tips are cut off and saved for stock. The other two joints are trimmed of as much skin as possible, rubbed with jerk seasoning, and marinated. According to Icy, the word jerk came from the motion used when pulling the meat from your teeth after biting into it.

Serves 6 as an appetizer

Jerk Seasoning (page 211)
2 1/2 pounds chicken drumettes (see recipe introduction)

Prepare the Jerk Seasoning as directed, adding fresh garlic, oil, and liquid of choice.

In a bowl toss together the chicken drumettes and seasoning. Cover and refrigerate for at least 4 hours or overnight.

Prepare a charcoal fire. Grill the drumettes over hot coals 5–6 minutes on each side. Serve hot or at room temperature.

VARIATION: Erica Gillette, while a student at Piney Woods Country School in Mississippi and a member of the school's International Culinary Club, shared her method for cooking jerk chicken in the oven. Take 3 pounds of your favorite chicken parts and 1/3 cup of your favorite jerk seasoning. Pat dry the chicken with paper towels. Rub vegetable oil over the chicken. Then rub the jerk seasoning all over the chicken. Bake in a preheated 350 F degree oven for 1 1/4 hours, basting occasionally. Serve with rice and salad.

Sidewalk vendors in Bahia carry small lighted charcoal-filled drums with grates on top for cooking skewers of Brazil's fresh mozzarella-type cheese. The vendors weave in and out of the sidewalk cafes until a customer beckons. Putting down the tin, they fan the coals until a crackly heat is resparked. A skewer of cheese is retrieved from a tray and place on the hot grate, turned frequently, and served slightly charred on the outside, a delicious contrast to the creamy, salty interior.

Jerked Fish

Whole fish or boneless fillets become cooling, fresh contrasts to the spike and heat of jerk seasoning. Multiply the ingredients to accommodate the number of diners.

Serves 1

1/2 pound whole fish or 1 fish fillet, 4–5 ounces
1 tablespoon Jerk Seasoning (page 211; dry mixture only)
1 teaspoon vegetable oil
1 tablespoon fresh lime juice, coconut milk, or rum

Lay the fish in a dish. In a tiny bowl, stir together the seasoning, oil, and lime juice. Brush over both sides of fish. Cover and refrigerate 1 hour.

Prepare a charcoal fire or preheat a broiler. Cook the fish over the hot coals or under the broiler, 2–5 minutes on each side, depending upon the thickness of the fish (see note). Serve hot.

NOTE: The rule for perfectly done fish is to cook it 10 minutes per inch of thickness. If it is 1/2 inch thick, cook it 2 1/2 minutes on each side. It should feel firm to the touch when done.

Smoked Turkey

If the turkey is frozen, defrost it in the refrigerator for 1–2 days. Coat it with All-Purpose Seasoning Rub (page 210) or Jerk Seasoning (page 211) and marinate in the refrigerate for several hours or overnight. Truss the bird by tying the wings and legs to the body; tie the tail tight against the body to form a compact package. The trussing helps keep the meat moist.

In a large covered grill, build a fire as directed on pages 206–207. When it has burned down to coal-perfect stage, after 20–30 minutes, move the coals to one side, oil the opposite side of the grate, and place the trussed bird on the oiled grate. Cover with the lid. Place a drip pan under the turkey. Smoke it for 1–2 hours, adding small bits of wood or soaked alder or fruit-wood chips if needed to keep the fire hot and smoky. Turn the turkey occasionally so it browns evenly. If it browns too much, cover it with foil.

After 2 hours, the turkey can be finished in the oven. Place it in a roasting pan and cook at 325 degrees F until it reaches an internal temperature of 180 degrees F on a meat thermometer. Let cool before slicing.

The country smokehouse was an integral institution for African-Americans. Benny Clewis's grandmother, who lived in Palestine, Texas, had two of them. One was used to store the salted meat while it was curing and to hang the meat after it was smoked. The floor and sides of the smokehouse were made of hardwood. Tin covered the roof and exterior walls. In the back was a room for the fire that fed smoke into the house. A chimney poked out the top to allow the smoke to circulate and permeate the hams and sausages. "We hand-ground the meat and seasoned it with bell pepper, onions, and chiles," recalls Benny. "Sometimes the sausage meat was precooked. Like when we made boudin with rice in it."

Skillet-Barbecued Shrimp

At his Showcase Eatery in Atlanta, Georgia, Samuel Simmons creates a menu blending his heritage with his classic training and his travels through the South and the Caribbean. Here is a quick recipe using a commercial barbecue sauce. He recommends using a stainless-steel skillet and getting it very hot before sautéing the shrimp.

Serves 4

1¼ cups Kraft brand regular or other favorite barbecue sauce
2 tablespoons white wine vinegar or lemon juice
2 tablespoons dry white wine
1 tablespoon olive oil
1¼ pounds medium shrimp, peeled and deveined
1 garlic clove, minced
1 teaspoon chopped fresh rosemary, or ½ teaspoon dried rosemary, crushed
1 teaspoon chopped fresh thyme, or ½ teaspoon dried thyme, crushed
Plain Rice (page 107)

In a bowl stir together the barbecue sauce, vinegar, and white wine.

In a stainless-steel skillet, heat the olive oil until almost smoking. Carefully drop in the shrimp and sprinkle them with the garlic and herbs. Sauté until the shrimp turn pink, about 2 minutes.

Then pour the barbecue sauce mixture over the shrimp. Cook another minute until bubbly. Serve over hot rice.

Catfish, trout, shrimp, oysters, and other freshwater fish and seafood have always found a place on barbecues. Quick grilling, as opposed to the long, slow cooking of meat, is the right method. A simple marinade or rub is left on the whole fish or fillet for an hour or less. Then the fish is quickly seared over hot coals.

Oven-Barbecued Ribs

This is the method of cooking ribs in the oven shared by Anthony Bundy, a chef at Rita's Olde French Quarter Restaurant in New Orleans. They come out melt-in-your-mouth tender with the most incredible flavor, perfect for spicing up a wintertime dinner.

Serves 4

4 pounds spareribs
1 yellow onion, sliced
1 green bell pepper, seeded and sliced
1 red bell pepper, seeded and sliced (optional)
3 garlic cloves, minced
salt and ground black pepper
natural liquid smoke (optional)
1 1/2 cups Bronze Barbecue Sauce (page 215) or your
    favorite barbecue sauce

Preheat an oven to 300 degrees F.

Lay the ribs in single layer in a shallow roasting pan. Top with the onion, bell peppers, garlic, and salt and pepper to taste. Sprinkle with a little smoke (if using). Cover securely with aluminum foil. Bake 1 1/2 hours.

Raise the oven temperature to 325 degrees F. Remove the ribs from the pan. Discard the vegetables or chop them finely or purée them and use to embellish the barbecue sauce. Return the ribs to the pan and coat them with the sauce. Return the pan to the oven and bake, uncovered, until the ribs are tender, 45–60 minutes.

Barbecued Corn on the Cob

Cooking corn over coals was learned from Native Americans in the Caribbean and in the United States. For each person, take 1 or 2 ears of corn still in the husks. Soak the corn in a pot of water for at least 10 minutes to moisten the husks. Place the corn on the grill, next to or over the hot coals. Or put the corn into the hot coals if the fire is in an open pit in the ground or at the beach. Cook, turning occasionally, 15–20 minutes. Remove from the fire, peel back the husks, and eat.

In a typical barbecue joint in the United States, side dishes don't vary much. A salad of potatoes or cabbage, a slice or hunk of white or corn bread, and in some places a scoop of red, baked, or chili beans are the common accompaniments. These serve as palate refreshers for the fiery sauces. At home barbecues, pickles—chow chow, beets, and watermelon rind—are also on the menu. In addition to meat, other ingredients are being added to the grill. In Bahia, street vendors grill skewered cheese over portable barbecues. Plantains, corn, and pineapple find their way onto Caribbean barbecues. And, in kitchens of young African-American chefs, like Samuel Simmons in College Park, Georgia, seasonal vegetables are put on the grill.

Grilled Plantains

Sidewalk vendors from West Africa to the Caribbean grill plantains to eat as a snack or with spicy grilled meats or stews.

Serves 2

1 ripe yellow plantain
1 tablespoon vegetable oil
salt

Prepare a charcoal fire or preheat a broiler.

Cut the plantain in half lengthwise. Do not peel. Brush the cut side with the oil. Place the plantain halves over the hot coals or under a broiler, skin side toward the heat, and grill or broil until softened and heated through, about 5 minutes. Turn over and grill another 2–3 minutes to impart a little smoky flavor. Serve hot.

Although it is sometimes spelled *"cold" slaw, the word* cole *comes from* colis, *Latin for "cabbage," and* slaw *comes from the Dutch* sla, *meaning "salad."*

Cool Coleslaw

This is a sweet-tart version of the coleslaw typically served with barbecue. It reminds me of one at Doug's Bar-B-Que, a twenty-five-year-old establishment on San Pablo Avenue in Emeryville, California. In the Tennessee tradition, put a couple of spoonfuls of the slaw on a sandwich laden with smoked chopped pork shoulder (page 225).

Serves 6–8

1/2 cup pickle relish
3 green onions, including tops, or 1/2 yellow onion, finely chopped
1 teaspoon sugar (optional)
1 tablespoon mustard
2/3 cup mayonnaise
1 tablespoon red wine vinegar
1 small head green cabbage, shredded (about 8 cups)
1 carrot, peeled and grated
salt and ground black pepper

In a big bowl, stir together all the ingredients. Add salt and pepper to taste and mix well. Cover and refrigerate at least 1 hour to mellow the flavors before serving.

Potato Salad

Potato salad is a cool counterpoint to spicy barbecue. Optional ingredients are used by barbecue chefs to personalize their potato salads. Always combine the potatoes while they are still hot with some kind of seasoning—garlic, onions, vinegar, white wine. The heat helps them to absorb more flavor. Save the mayonnaise until they are lukewarm so it doesn't melt.

White Rose or red new potatoes tend to keep their texture better than russets, which can get mushy. If a mashed potato consistency is desired, use a combination of potatoes for combination of textures.

Serves 6

4 large White Rose or 6 red new potatoes, unpeeled and scrubbed well
3 green onions, including tops, minced
3/4 cup white wine vinegar or cider vinegar
2 garlic cloves, minced
salt and ground black pepper
2 celery stalks, finely chopped
3/4 cup mayonnaise
2 tablespoons prepared mustard, or 2 teaspoons dry mustard
1/4 cup milk
1/4 cup chopped fresh parsley
optional: 1 carrot, grated; 1 hard-cooked egg, chopped; 1/3 cup pickle
    relish; 1 dill or sweet pickle, chopped; chopped black or green olives;
    1/2 red or green bell pepper, seeded and chopped

Place the potatoes in a single layer in a wide saucepan. Add water to cover by 1 inch. Bring to a boil and boil until tender, about 20 minutes. Test by inserting a bamboo skewer in the center of a potato; if it goes in easily, the potato is cooked. Drain the potatoes in a colander and let cool slightly. They should be hot but not so hot they burn you. Peel, if desired, or leave some or all of the skins on. Cut the potatoes into cubes and put into large bowl. Immediately add the green onions, 1/2 cup of the vinegar, and 1 clove of the garlic. Sprinkle with salt and pepper. Let cool to room temperature.

In a small bowl, stir together the celery, mayonnaise, mustard, milk, parsley, and the remaining minced garlic clove; mix well. Add to the potatoes and stir to combine thoroughly. Add any of the optional ingredients, if desired, and stir once again to mix well. Taste for seasoning. Serve at room temperature.

Molasses Baked Beans

The slight sweetness of the sauce makes these beans a perfect complement to salty hot ribs. They can be made with Great Northern, pinto, red, or navy beans, or with any of the more exotic varieties mentioned in the Glossary. Because acidity inhibits the softening of beans, be sure the beans are tender before adding the tomatoes. Traditionally, baked beans were slowly cooked in cast-iron pots hanging over the fire. They had to be stirred frequently to keep them from burning. Cooking them in the oven at a low temperature for a long time is a less worrisome method. A crockpot is also a great way to cook these. Adjust the amount of molasses, also known as burnt sugar, to your taste.

There is no meat in these beans. If you like, add a few ounces of chopped salt pork or bacon as in the recipe for Pot of Beans (pages 124–125).

Serves 8–10

2¹/₂ cups (1 pound) dried beans, rinsed and picked over
2 tablespoons vegetable oil
1 yellow onion, chopped
3 garlic cloves, minced
2 tablespoons dry mustard
1 cup ketchup
1 teaspoon salt
2 tablespoons Worcestershire sauce
¹/₂–³/₄ cup molasses, cane syrup, or sorghum syrup
1 cup canned tomato sauce
2–3 tablespoons cider vinegar or red wine vinegar
freshly ground black pepper

Soak the beans overnight in water to cover by several inches. Drain.

Place the drained beans in a heavy pot and add water to cover by 3–4 inches. Bring to a boil, cover partially, reduce the heat to medium-low, and simmer until tender, 1–1¹/₂ hours; the timing will depend upon the bean variety. Check after 30 minutes.

Meanwhile, in a skillet over medium-high heat, warm the oil. Add the onion and garlic and sauté until softened, about 5 minutes. Stir in the mustard and sauté briefly. Stir in all the remaining ingredients, including pepper to taste. Cook a couple of minutes.

Other beans to serve with barbecue include Pot of Beans (pages 124–125) and Red Beans and Rice (page 178).

Add the onion mixture to the beans and stir well. Add water if necessary to make sure the beans are covered by a couple of inches of liquid.

Preheat an oven to 250 degrees F. Pour the beans into an ovenproof casserole. Cover and bake until thickened and syrupy, about 4 hours. Check occasionally to see if more liquid is needed. Taste for seasoning about halfway through. Add more molasses, pepper, vinegar, or salt as you like.

VARIATION: When time is short, these may be made with canned beans. Prepare the sauce and combine it with canned beans that have been drained and rinsed to rid them of some salt. Bake as directed above.

Pickled Beets

A sweet-tart marinade gives beets a perky boost, making them a good side dish or salad to accompany any dinner and an especially welcome palate-cleansing tidbit between bites of barbecue. Fresh beets must be cooked and peeled. Canned beets are easily substituted and take only an hour in the marinade to start soaking up the flavor. These will keep in the refrigerator up to a month.

Serves 10–12

2 pounds fresh beets, or 2 cans (16 ounces each) sliced beets
3/4 cup red wine vinegar
2/3 cup firmly packed brown sugar or granulated sugar
1 whole clove

If using fresh beets, cut off the root, leaving 1/4 inch intact, and trim the stem but do not cut it off or the beets will bleed. Place the beets in a single layer in a large wide saucepan. Cover with water by 1 inch. Bring to a boil and cook until tender, about 20 minutes. Test by inserting a bamboo skewer into the center. Drain in a colander and when cool enough to handle, slip off the skins. Slice into 1/4-inch-thick rounds.

If using canned beets, drain well, reserving the liquid.

Place the beets in a bowl or a jar. In a small bowl, stir together the vinegar and sugar. Pour over the beets and stir gently to mix. Add water or canned beet juice to cover the beets completely. Drop in the clove. Refrigerate at least 1 hour for the canned beets and 6 hours for the fresh before serving.

Watermelon Rind Pickle

Here's a great use for something frequently thrown away. These spiced pickles are great at picnic barbecues and for lunch in the dead of the winter. Scoop out the sweet red melon and eat it right away. Then peel off the tough green skin and cut the white rind into squares, cubes, or other serving-sized pieces. These will keep in the refrigerator for up to 6 months. As is true when making any pickle, the flavor improves with age. Make these at least a week before serving. Directions are also given for canning.

Makes about 4 pints

1 watermelon rind, from a 4–5 pound watermelon
2 quarts water
1/4 cup pickling salt or iodized salt
4 cups cider vinegar
5 cups sugar
1 piece fresh ginger, about 2 inches long
3 cinnamon sticks, broken
1 tablespoon whole cloves
1 tablespoon whole allspice

Prepare the rind by scooping out (and eating) the red part of the watermelon. Using a knife or vegetable peeler, peel off the green rind. Cut the white rind into squares, cubes, or sticks. You should have about 8 cups. Combine the water and salt in a nonreactive container and stir in the rind pieces. Soak 8 hours or overnight.

Drain, but do not rinse. Place the watermelon in a heavy, nonreactive pot and add cold water to cover. Bring to a boil. Reduce the heat to medium and cook until the rinds are just tender, about 15 minutes. Drain.

In a large nonreactive pot, stir together the vinegar and sugar. Place the ginger, cinnamon, cloves, and allspice on a piece of cheesecloth, gather together the corners, and tie securely with kitchen string. Add to the pot. Bring to a boil over high heat, and boil, stirring frequently, until the sugar is dissolved and forms a syrup, about 5 minutes. Stir in the watermelon rinds, reduce the heat to medium-low, and simmer, uncovered, until the rinds turn clear, about 1 hour.

Using a slotted spoon, transfer the rinds to sterilized canning jars. Ladle in the syrup to cover the rinds completely. Seal with lids and rings. Store in the refrigerator up to 6 months.

Watermelons are originally from Africa, where they once served as canteens. To choose a perfectly ripe melon, look for an opaque skin and an overall green appearance, except the area where it lay on the ground, which should be yellowish, not white. It should feel heavy and firm.

If canning, fill jars with syrup to within $1/2$ inch of the rim. Wipe the rim with a clean, damp cloth and seal with lids and rings according to the manufacturer's directions. Process in a hot-water bath for 15 minutes.

Check for proper seals, then store in a cool, dark place for up to 1 year. (Store any jars that did not seal properly in the refrigerator for up to 6 months.)

Basic Corn Bread

Cook this corn bread in a cast-iron skillet to give it a crisp, crusty surface. Some cooks prefer white cornmeal and some prefer yellow. Some never add sugar and some always do. Experiment and decide how you like it best. Buttermilk gives it a slightly sourdough flavor. Use this to make Corn Bread Dressing (page 121).

Makes one 10-inch round, or ten 3-inch muffins

1 1/2 cups white or yellow cornmeal
1 1/2 cups unbleached flour
1 tablespoon sugar (optional)
1 tablespoon baking powder
1/2 teaspoon salt
1 egg
1/2 cup safflower, corn, or canola oil
1 1/2 cups milk or buttermilk

Preheat an oven to 400 degrees F. Grease a 10-inch oven-proof skillet, 8-inch square baking pan, 10-inch cake pan, or 10 muffin-tin cups.

In a bowl, stir together the cornmeal, flour, sugar, baking powder, and salt. In another bowl, beat the egg. Stir in the oil and milk. Stir the wet ingredients into the dry ingredients until moistened; do not overbeat. Pour into the prepared skillet, pan, or muffin tin.

Bake until risen and just beginning to brown on top, 40–50 minutes for 1 loaf or 20–25 minutes for muffins. Serve hot.

Chow Chow

Like barbecue sauce, chow chow can be made hot, medium, or mild. It goes with hamburgers and other barbecue and is a great accompaniment with boiled mustard and turnip greens. This started out as one way to preserve some of the harvest when all the vegetables ripened at once.

Makes about 12 pints

at least 20 green tomatoes or unripe winter tomatoes
4 white onions
6–8 green and/or red bell peppers, seeded
6 cucumbers, or 1 large bottle sour gherkins
2 gallons chopped fresh vegetables (see sidebar)
small fresh chiles, to taste (see Glossary)
$1/2$ cup salt

For the syrup:
8 cups distilled white vinegar
2 tablespoons ground turmeric
2 tablespoons mustard seeds
$1^1/2$ cups sugar
1 tablespoon celery seeds

Finely or coarsely chop the tomatoes, white onions, bell peppers, and cucumbers. Select whatever vegetables appeal to you and finely or coarsely chop them as well. Mince the chiles. Place all the vegetables in a large nonreactive container and sprinkle with the salt. Let stand overnight. Drain in a colander.

In a large stainless-steel or other nonreactive pot, stir together all the syrup ingredients and bring to a boil, stirring to dissolve the sugar. Add the vegetables and boil, stirring occasionally, for 10 minutes. Ladle into sterilized jars and screw on the lids. Let stand in the refrigerator at least a week or more before serving to allow the flavors to mellow. Store in the refrigerator for up to 6 months.

To can, ladle the chow chow into hot, sterilized canning jars and fill to within $1/2$ inch of the rim. Wipe rims with a clean, damp cloth and seal with lids and rings according to the manufacturer's directions. Process in a hot-water bath for 15 minutes. Check for proper seals, then store in a cool, dark place for up to 1 year. (Store any jars that did not seal properly in the refrigerator for up to 6 months.)

Green tomatoes are called for in this recipe, but the hard tomatoes in most supermarkets in the winter months make fine substitutes. This means that chow chow can be made any time of the year, using whatever vegetables are available. Green tomatoes, onions, bell peppers, chiles, and cucumbers or bottled gherkins are frequently included. So are celery, cauliflower, green beans, and tiny white onions. Benny Clewis of Rosharon, Texas, remembers his grandmother making chow chow and putting it up in old-style Ball jars with glass tops. She would top the hot relish with a spoonful of olive oil before clamping down the top and putting it in a hot-water bath rigged in a roasting pan.

Yeast-Risen Wheat Bread

Slices of white or whole-wheat bread accompany barbecue when cornbread doesn't. They cool the incendiary chiles and mop up leftover sauce.

This recipe is for a large moist loaf that can be baked in a loaf pan, a coffee can, or in a large free-form round on a baking sheet. It is enriched with a little shortening and milk. Leftovers can be used to make Bread Pudding (page 196).

Makes 1 large loaf

1 envelope active dry yeast (scant 1 tablespoon)
1 tablespoon sugar
1/2 cup lukewarm water
2 cups milk
2 tablespoons shortening
6–7 cups unbleached white flour, or 2 cups whole-wheat flour and
*   4–5 cups unbleached white flour*
2 teaspoons salt

In a large bowl, dissolve the yeast and sugar in the lukewarm water. Let stand until bubbly, about 5 minutes. Meanwhile, combine the milk and shortening in a saucepan and place over medium heat until the shortening melts. Cool to lukewarm.

Pour the lukewarm milk into the bubbly yeast mixture and mix. In another bowl, stir together the flour and salt. A cup at time, stir the flour mixture into the milk-yeast mixture until a firm dough forms. Using an electric mixer fitted with a dough hook, knead the dough on medium speed until smooth and elastic, about 6 minutes. Alternatively, turn the dough out onto a lightly floured surface and knead until smooth and elastic, about 10 minutes.

Shape the dough into a ball and place in an oiled bowl. Turn the ball to coat the surface with oil. Cover the bowl with plastic wrap. Set in a warm, draft-free place and let the dough rise until doubled, 2–3 hours.

Punch down the dough. Knead lightly on a floured surface. Form into a loaf and place in a greased standard loaf pan or a greased 2-pound coffee can. Or form into a large round loaf and set on a greased baking sheet. Let rise in a warm place until almost doubled, about 45 minutes.

Meanwhile, preheat an oven to 350 degrees F. Bake until nicely risen and golden brown, about 1 hour. Tap the bottom; if it sounds hollow it is done. Let cool on a wire rack at least 15 minutes before slicing.

recent
african immignants

Africans who recently immigrated to the United States bring interpretations of native cuisines straight from the mother countries. Although Africa is vast and the geography varied, ingredients and cooking methods in the sub-Saharan regions of the continent tend to be similar. This is because drought and famine historically forced the people to be on the move, carrying what beans and greens would grow in such dire conditions with them.

The Muslim movement from the Middle East that swept and controlled most of eastern, central, and west Africa until the sixteenth century contributed to a reliance on grains and greens. In addition, the Muslim proscription of pork kept that meat out of traditional African cooking. Seafood, goat, chicken, and a little beef added to the millet-, sorghum-, rice-, bean-, lentil-, and vegetable-based dishes.

A look at recipes that come directly from the source illustrates the antecedents of many of the dishes in this book. For example, a fish-and-okra stew in Senegal is translated to *caruru* in Bahia. It becomes *poisson et gombo* in Martinique and gumbo in Louisiana.

Another example is grain or vegetable mush, a dish that is prevalent in Africa and commonplace in America. Typically, it is the main starch served with soups and stews. *Fufu* from Togo, *foutou* in Martinique, and *foofoo* in Cuba are made of mashed yams, plantain, or cassava. In Bahia, *farofa* is a loose translation made with dried and toasted cassava (manioc) meal. When made of cornmeal, a mush in Senegal is called *menue*, in Gambia it's mealie-meal, in Louisiana it's couche couche, and in Martinique it's *couscous de mais*, or *cou-cou* for short. When okra is added to the corn, it becomes *coo-coo* on Trinidad, Tobago, and other Caribbean islands.

Fritters, made of grains, fish, and vegetables, are another typical dish found in African cooking. Whether fried in palm or olive oil in West Africa and the Caribbean, in lard or peanut oil in the American South, or in *dendê* oil in Bahia, crisp fried morsels are snacks, breads, and main courses on African-inspired menus.

Akara is a black-eyed pea or bean paste fritter in Togo and other West African countries. In Bahia the same fritter is called *acarajé*. In Jamaica it is *accra* and in Martinique *acra pois*.

In the early 1500s, many New World foods were introduced to Africa and acclimated readily to the soil and diet. This means corn, tomatoes, chiles, cassava, and peanuts are found in African cooking on both sides of the Atlantic.

Chiles, from a New World plant, were adapted in every African cuisine. The indigenous peppery African *melegueta* had forged a taste for spicy food even before Columbus made his world-opening voyage in the fifteenth century. The spicy herb called *aframomum melegueta* comes from a small berry grown on a wild tree and is also referred to as *atare* or as African or Guinea pepper. When the slaves arrived in Brazil, they called the hot little capsicum chiles they found there *malagueta*, in honor of their spice from home.

Peanuts, known as groundnuts, form the base for many characteristic West African sauces and stews. Peanuts proved resistant to such above-ground blights as locusts that regularly decimated crops. Their high protein content makes them a boon to the diet.

Some ingredients, such as the palm used for making red palm oil and certain greens, did not easily transplant to the New World soil. Others, like okra, sesame, and watermelon, acclimated to the new growing conditions.

The African yam transplanted well in the Caribbean next to the native American sweet potato. In the United States, the sweet potato, of which some varieties are called yams, superseded the African yam, creating a confusion in the use of the name. The African yam is coarser textured than the sweet potato, but they are often used interchangeably.

Dasheen, or taro, another African staple used for both its starchy root and leafy greens, took to the tropical heat of the Caribbean, where the greens are known as callaloo. The greens used for stewing in West Africa are coarser and thicker than the chard, collards, mustard, beet, or turnip tops that go into a pot of greens in the American South. In Togo, short, thick green leaves are called *gboma* and go into a dish called *gboma dezi*, where they are combined with chiles, seafood, beef, and chicken.

Okra, an elongated green pod whose transplanted North American size is about half that of the ones found in the tropics, grows wild in West Africa and adapted well to southern soil. Known as gumbo in several languages in West Africa, okra is the ingredient that gives creole gumbo its name.

The recipes that follow are a sampling of East and West African dishes. They were chosen to show the similarities in methods and combinations they share with their counterparts in the Americas.

Bajia · *Red Chile Sauce*

A table condiment for spiking any dish, this fermented version of chile sauce is from Kenyan Raymond Thoya. Raymond, a member of the Griama tribe, grew up in the bush, near the town of Malindi. In Kenya, this sauce is made with coconut alcohol. Raymond substitutes Miller Lite beer in the United States.

Makes about 1½ cups

1 can or bottle (12 ounces) Miller Lite beer
4–6 fresh red chiles, minced (see Glossary)
10 tomatoes, chopped
1 cup coconut milk

Open the beer and pour it into a glass. Let stand 2 hours until warm and flat.

In a saucepan, combine the beer with all the remaining ingredients and bring to a boil. Stand back so as not to inhale the chile fumes. Cook over high heat until reduced by half.

Let cool and store in a covered jar in the refrigerator or a cool, dark place for a couple of weeks.

Achari · *Green Chile Sauce*

This is Raymond Thoya's Kenyan version of the fresh green chile sauce used to season dishes at the table. The sweet-tart fruit complements the chiles, the coconut adds cool texture, and the cilantro brings up the green in this uncooked sauce that is most often used with vegetarian dishes. It can also be stirred into sauces and stews.

Makes about 1 cup

6 fresh green chiles, minced (see Glossary)
1 green (unripe) mango, peeled, pitted, and puréed
1 cup fresh cilantro leaves, chopped
1 cup unsweetened finely shredded dried coconut

In a bowl, combine all the ingredients and mix well. Store in a covered jar in the refrigerator up to a week.

Berberé · *East African Spice Mixture*

In Ethiopia and Eritrea, the Middle Eastern influence is felt in this combination of spices that, as with curry blends, is personalized by each cook. Adjust the heat by adjusting the amount of cayenne pepper.

Makes about 1/4 cup

1 tablespoon paprika
1–3 teaspoons cayenne pepper
1 teaspoon garlic powder
3 teaspoons ground ginger
1 teaspoon dried savory, crushed
1 teaspoon dried basil, crushed
1 1/2 teaspoons ground cumin
1/2 teaspoon ground turmeric
1/2 teaspoon ground allspice
1/4 teaspoon ground cinnamon
1 teaspoon dry mustard
1 1/2 teaspoons ground coriander
1/2 teaspoon ground cloves
1/2 teaspoon salt

In a bowl, combine all the ingredients and mix well. Store in a jar with a tight-fitting lid up to 2 months in the pantry.

Piri piri, a word for chile in East Africa, is also the name of a hot chile sauce and marinade from Mozambique that resembles Bahian Môlho de Pimenta e Limão (page 75).

Baloumbum · *Senegalese Peanut Sauce*

Peanuts are a major crop in Senegal, where they are used as snacks, in sauces and stews, and for their oil, which goes into marinades for lean cuts of beef, lamb, and goat. This is a recipe from Senegalese-born Moussa Dieme, who says its name comes from southern Senegal. It is reminiscent of *vatapá* in Bahia, which combines peanuts and dried shrimp in coconut milk. The sauce is for rice, but it would be good on grilled or sautéed fish as well.

> Makes about 2 cups

> *2 1/2 cups water*
> *3/4 cup creamy peanut butter*
> *1 ounce dried salted fish, or 1 tablespoon dried shrimp*
> *2 garlic cloves, minced*
> *1/4 cup tomato purée*
> *1/2 yellow onion, finely chopped*
> *1/4 teaspoon ground cumin*
> *1/2 teaspoon ground coriander*
> *1/4–1/2 teaspoon cayenne pepper or other ground red chile pepper*
> *salt*

In a saucepan, bring the water to a boil. Stir in the peanut butter and boil 5 minutes. Add all the remaining ingredients, including salt to taste, and stir to mix. Reduce the heat to low and simmer, stirring frequently, to blend the ingredients and thicken the sauce, about 1 hour.

The sauce will be thick and hot. Taste for seasoning and serve.

The importance of yams in the African diet is based on the yam's reliable yield, resistance to pests, and versatility in cooking. Boiled, baked, cooked in ashes, fresh, dried, and powdered yams have been dietary staples for hundreds of years. The yam is one of the few foods to have originated in Africa. It came to America with the slaves, where it has been used interchangeably with the American sweet potato, a plant of a different family.

Rice is known to have been cultivated in A.D. 50 at Jeno Jeno, the oldest known Iron Age City in sub-Saharan Africa.

Fufu · *Mashed Yams*

Starchy thick mushes are standard accompaniments to one-pot soups and stews in African cooking. They are typically made from African yams, plantains, cassava, and other root vegetables. American couche-couche and Caribbean *coo-coo,* made from corn, are relatives. This recipe, shared by Evangeline Fogam from Cameroon, uses powdered yams. The powdered version produces a creamy texture and the aromatic essence of the fresh yams. *Fufu* is cooked, stirring all the while, until very smooth, thick, and sticky, "like Cream of Wheat," says Evangeline. It is eaten by spoonfuls or fingerfuls with Okra Soup (page 257), *Efo* (page 258), or any other soup or stew. To substitute fresh yams, peel them, boil until soft, and mash them well with a little salt.

Serves 4

3 cups water
1 cup powdered yam (see Resources)
salt

Pour the water into a heavy saucepan and bring to a boil. Slowly stir in the powdered yam, a little at a time, stirring constantly to keep it from lumping. Add salt to taste. Reduce the heat to medium and continue cooking and stirring until very thick like a pudding, about 6 minutes. Serve hot.

Whether it's called agidi, ugali, bidia, menue, *or mealie-meal, the ubiquitous cornmeal mush on African tables is compared to bread in the European cultures. Even though corn is a New World ingredient, it was embraced early in African countries because of its vitality and versatility. In the Americas, every culture with an African heritage has some form of this mush. For recipes see Couche-Couche (page 176) in the Louisiana Creole chapter and Cornmeal with Okra (page 38) in the Caribbean chapter. Its Bahian name is* angu.

When corn first arrived in Africa in the sixteenth century, it rapidly replaced sorghum, millet, and sorgo as the staple grain. At first the dependence on corn caused people to conract pellagra, a disease brought on by a diet deficient in niacin and protein. When they learned about eating corn with peppers, tomatoes, and fish, which are rich in the missing elements, the condition vanished.

Fufu Nyame · *Yam Balls*

In Sierra Leone little savory balls of puréed yam, cassava, and plantains are also called *fufu*. These are sautéed or deep-fried and eaten like bread. When the balls are made of cornmeal, wrapped in banana leaves or aluminum foil, and steamed in the Ivory Coast, they are called *foutout*. Here is a version made from African yams or fresh cassava. If neither is available, substitute sweet potatoes. Egg and evaporated milk are the binders.

In Kenya these mashes are called *kimanga* and are most commonly made from pumpkin and cassava and sometimes bananas or plantains.

Makes about twelve 1½-inch balls

> 1 large African yam or cassava, about 2 pounds, peeled and cut into
>   1-inch chunks
> ½ yellow onion, coarsely chopped
> 1 teaspoon salt
> 1 egg, beaten
> ¼ cup evaporated milk
> all-purpose flour, if needed
> ¼ cup vegetable oil

In a saucepan combine the yam with water to cover. Bring to a boil and boil until very tender, about 10 minutes. Drain.

Place the yam in a blender or food processor and add the onion. Purée until smooth. Transfer to a bowl and let cool until lukewarm. Stir in the salt, egg, and milk. Form the mixture into 1½-inch balls. If it is too wet and sticky, stir in a little flour to make a firm dough. Dropping by spoonfuls into a little flour will aid in rolling them.

In a nonstick skillet over medium-high heat, warm the oil. Add the balls and sauté, turning, until browned and heated through, about 5 minutes. Serve hot.

Injera *is* a flat, slightly sour crêpelike bread used like a utensil to pick up spicy stews and other dishes in Eritrea and Ethiopia. "It's like a big plate," says Eritrean Akberet Keleta, "and it can be made with all-purpose flour, whole wheat flour, or corn flour." The flour, either self-rising or yeast-risen, is mixed with water and left to stand for a day to start fermenting, which gives it the sour flavor. Another Eritrean, Maaza Haile, who lives in Sunnyvale, California, makes injera for big events or parties. She fills the big flat pancakes with spiced lentils (Shiro Wot, page 252), vegetables, or meat, rolls them up, and cuts them into bite-sized pieces. Look in an African cookbook for a recipe for injera, or buy fresh injera from an Eritrean or Ethiopian restaurant.

Moyinmoyin · *Bean Pudding*

Moimoi is the shortened Nigerian name for this steamed black-eyed pea dish that is like the *abará* of Bahia. Traditionally, the thin outer covering with the namesake black spot on it is skinned from each pea. This is done for both this steamed pudding and the fried version known as *akkra* in Nigeria and *acarajé* in Bahia (pages 76–77). To do this, soak the peas overnight in cold water, then rub them together until the skins pop off—a tedious but fairly easy task. If the black spots and fibrous texture of the skins don't bother you, the peas can be puréed as they are. According to Edith Ezigbo, who owns the African King Restaurant in Atlanta, Georgia, the pudding is steamed in leaves in her native Nigeria; here aluminum foil is substituted.

> Serves 4

> 1¼ cups (½ pound) dried black-eyed peas
> ½ yellow onion, coarsely chopped
> 1 garlic clove
> 2 tablespoons (1 ounce) dried shrimp
> ½ teaspoon cayenne pepper or other ground red chile pepper
> 2 or 3 tablespoons of red palm (dendê) oil or vegetable oil
> salt
> Red Chile Sauce (page 246) and/or Green Chile Sauce (page 246)

Soak the beans overnight in water to cover by 4 inches. Drain. Add fresh water to cover and remove each bean skin by rubbing the beans under the water. Discard the skins. Drain the beans and transfer them to a blender or food processor. Add the onion, garlic, dried shrimp, and cayenne. Purée until very smooth. Add oil and salt to taste and blend again.

Cut six 12-inch squares of aluminum foil and lightly oil them. Divide the bean mixture among them, placing it in the center and smoothing to make an even thickness about 4 inches square. Fold the foil over, wrapping the edges around to enclose the beans securely. Pour water to a depth of 2 inches in the bottom of a steamer pan and bring to a boil. Set the packets on the rack, cover, reduce the heat to medium, and steam until firm, about 1 hour. Check after 30 minutes. When done, the beans will be pudding soft and won't have a raw bean taste or aroma.

Serve hot with one or both of the chile sauces.

Shiro Wot · *Lentil Stew*

Typically eaten with *injera* (page 250), the national bread of Ethiopia and Eritrea, this is a classic dish of Ethiopia. Prolific and high in protein, lentils have been a major food around the Mediterranean and eastern Africa for eight thousand years. This may be served as a side dish or as an appetizer with crackers.

Serves 6–8

2 cups dried lentils (1 pound), rinsed and picked over
2 tablespoons vegetable oil
1 yellow onion, finely chopped
2 garlic cloves, minced
1 or 2 small fresh red chiles, minced (see Glossary)
1 teaspoon salt
ground black pepper

In a heavy saucepan, combine the lentils with water to cover by 2 inches. Bring to a boil, reduce the heat to medium-low and simmer until tender, 30–45 minutes. Mash with a fork.

In a skillet over medium heat, warm the oil. Add the onion, garlic, and chiles and sauté until soft, about 5 minutes. Add the mashed lentils and salt and pepper to taste. Cook until the flavors are blended and the mixture is heated through, 8–10 minutes. Taste for seasoning and serve.

Kelewele · *Spicy Fried Plantains*

These spicy little appetizers are found in Ghana, where they are eaten for breakfast or for snacks.

Serves 4

2 teaspoons ground ginger
1/2 teaspoon salt
1/4 teaspoon cayenne pepper or other ground red chile pepper
1 tablespoon water
1 plantain, peeled (see Glossary) and sliced 1/2 inch thick
1/4 cup peanut oil

On a plate, stir together the ginger, salt, pepper, and water to form a paste. Dredge the plantain slices in the paste.

In a nonstick skillet, heat the oil until almost smoking. Add the plantain slices, a few at a time, and fry, turning once, until golden brown, about 2 minutes on each side. Drain on a rack or on paper towels. Serve hot.

Fried plantains have been cooling fiery stews in Africa for centuries. At the Bennachin, a West-African restaurant in Metarie, Louisiana, plantains are served as appetizers or as a side dish with the restaurant's namesake, which is jambalaya in Gambia. In West Africa, the plantains, are fried in red palm oil, known as dendê *in Bahia. Here they are fried in peanut oil. They are also popular in the Caribbean; see the recipe on page 29.*

Matoke · *Mashed Bananas*

Bowls of seasoned mashed bananas are eaten to cool fiery stews from Basse to Mombasa. In East Africa, *matoke* is made differently by each cook. This is how Raymond Thoya of Kenya prepares this delicious starchy dish, which he compares with mashed potatoes.

Makes about 2½ cups

4 or 5 green bananas, peeled and finely chopped or mashed (if difficult
to peel, see Glossary on peeling plantains)
dash of cayenne pepper
dash of ground nutmeg
½ teaspoooon ground cardamom
¼ teaspoon ground ginger
1½ cups coconut milk

In a saucepan, stir together the bananas, cayenne, nutmeg, and cardamom. Mix in the coconut milk and place over medium-low heat. Cook, stirring, until the bananas are very soft and the mixture is thick, about 20 minutes. Taste for seasoning. Serve hot as a vegetable.

Raymond Thoya's grandmother pickled limes and mangoes when he was growing up in the bush in Kenya. He is a professional cook in Mendocino, California, at the Cafe Beaujolais, and has guest-chefed at various restaurants, where he shares the traditional cooking of his home. The traditional way of making pickles was to slice the fruits, sprinkle them with salt and ground red pepper, and lay them in the sun to dry for a couple of days. Then they were cooked in water until very tender and stored in crocks for at least a month before eating. Watermelon rinds and pineapple slices were also pickled this way.

What makes African cooking unique? "It's naturally flavored. It's also spicy hot and healthy for the body," says Bennet Yohannes of Ethiopia, a high-school student at Piney Woods Country Life School in Mississippi.

Jamma Jamma · *Spiced Greens*

This wonderful dish of spicy greens comes from Cameroon. The Bennachin restaurant in Metairie, Louisiana, served a similar version at the annual New Orleans Jazz Festival, an event that is worth going to for the food as well as the music. Serve it with Fried Plantains (page 29) and *Efo* (page 258), Jollof Rice (page 259), or any of the stews in this book.

Serves 4–6

2 tablespoons vegetable oil
1/4 cup minced red onion
1/2 teaspoon cayenne pepper
1 bunch (about 1 pound) greens such as collard, mustard, chard, or
    spinach, chopped
1/2 cup water
salt and ground black pepper

In a nonstick skillet over medium heat, warm the oil. Add the onion and sauté until softened, about 5 minutes. Stir in the cayenne and cook 20 seconds. Add the greens, stir, and cook over medium heat until wilted, about 3 minutes.

Add the water and salt and pepper to taste. Cover and cook until tender, depending on the variety of green, 8–15 minutes. Serve hot.

"Nothing is more impressive in viewing the social institutions of Africa than the cohesive influence of the family. The immediate family, the clan, and the tribe underguide every aspect of life."
John Hope Franklin and Alfred Moss, Jr.,
in From Slavery to Freedom

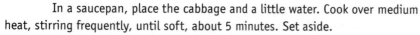

Atakelte · *Ethiopian Cabbage*

Benmett Johannes, a student at Piney Woods Country Life School in Mississippi, shared this straightforward cabbage dish with the most wonderful flavors, which she suggests eating with *injera* (page 250) or inauthentic pita bread. Benmett came to Mississippi from Ethiopia and was in the International Food Club at the school.

Serves 6

½ head green cabbage, shredded
1 yellow onion, chopped
few spoonfuls water, plus ½ cup water
2–3 tablespoons vegetable oil
1 cup canned tomato sauce
2 carrots, peeled and chopped
2 potatoes, peeled and chopped (optional)
salt
cayenne pepper or other ground red chile pepper (optional)

In a saucepan, place the cabbage and a little water. Cook over medium heat, stirring frequently, until soft, about 5 minutes. Set aside.

In a skillet, combine the onion with a little water. Cook over medium–high heat until the water evaporates, about 5 minutes. Reduce the heat to medium, stir in the oil, and cook until just beginning to brown, 4–5 minutes longer. Then put in the carrots and potatoes (if using), the tomatoe sauce, and the ½ cup water. Simmer to blend the flavors, 10–15 minutes. Add the steamed cabbage. Sprinkle with salt and cayenne to taste. Mix well, cover, and simmer to blend all the flavors together, about 10 minutes. Serve hot.

Okra Soup

Okra's prominence on the African table is exemplified by soups like this, which are mainstays in the mother countries and comfort food abroad. Related to gumbos and pepperpots, they are traditionally flavored with a piece of smoked or dried fish, according to Togo-born Yao Afantchao, who lives in Baltimore, Maryland. "We have always smoked and dried fish to carry it to the hinterlands for seasoning," he says. It adds a richness and slightly smoky flavor to the light tomato base. Yao formed a company, Deku Enterprises, Inc., to market the many varieties of fish he smokes. Whiting, although bony, is one of his favorites, and so is blue fish. Dried shrimp can also be used. Other meats like beef or chicken can also be added to the soup. Serve this with Corn Dumplings (page 146), known as *banku* in Ghana, or *Fufu* (page 249) and Plain Rice (page 107).

Serves 4

1 yellow onion, finely chopped
4 tomatoes, seeded and chopped
1 fresh red or green chile, finely chopped (see Glossary)
1/4 pound dried smoked fish or dried shrimp
6 cups water
1/2 teaspoon aniseeds
1 tablespoon minced, peeled fresh ginger
salt and ground black pepper
1/2 globe eggplant or 2 Japanese eggplants, cut into 1/2-inch cubes
1/2 pound crab meat, picked over for shells (optional)
1/2 pound okra, cut into 1/2-inch-thick rounds
2 tablespoons red palm (dendê) *oil (optional)*

In a heavy saucepan, combine the onion, tomatoes, chile, dried fish, water, aniseeds, ginger, and salt and black pepper to taste. Bring to a boil and stir. Reduce the heat to medium and simmer, uncovered, to blend the flavors, about 10 minutes.

Stir in the eggplant and cook until tender, 6–8 minutes. Add the crab meat, if using, and the okra and cook until the okra is tender, another 5 minutes or so. Stir in the palm oil, if using. Taste and adjust the seasonings.

Efo · *Nigerian Stew*

Efo refers to greens in Nigeria, and this combination of meat or fish with shrimp and greens is the ancestor of Caribbean Callaloo (page 34) and Louisiana's Green Gumbo (pages 181–182). In Nigeria, *efo* is served with *agidi*, which is like Creole Cornmeal Mush (page 176). It could also be served with *Fufu* (page 249) and rice.

Serves 6

1 yellow onion, finely chopped
4 tomatoes, diced
2 garlic cloves, minced
1 teaspoon ground thyme
1/2 teaspoon red pepper flakes
3 tablespoons red palm (dendê) oil or vegetable oil
salt
3 cups water
1 1/2 pounds firm white fish fillets, cut into 1-inch pieces; chicken parts; or beef round, cut into 1-inch cubes
1 bunch (about 1 pound) collard greens, chard, or spinach, finely shredded
1/2 pound medium shrimp, peeled and deveined

In a heavy pot or dutch oven, combine the onion, tomatoes, garlic, thyme, red pepper flakes, palm oil, salt, and water. Bring to a boil over high heat.

If including fish, first reduce the liquid to 1 cup and then add the fish. If including chicken, reduce the liquid to 2 cups, and then add the chicken. If including beef, add it now.

Cook until the fish or meat is tender and the liquid has almost evaporated, about 5 minutes for the fish, 30 minutes for the chicken, and 1 hour for the beef. Stir in the greens and cook 10 minutes. Add the shrimp, cover, and cook until they turn pink, 3–4 minutes.

Taste for seasoning. Serve hot.

New World foods that had immediate acceptance in Africa include corn, tomatoes, cassava, chiles, peanuts, guavas, papayas, and avocados. Cassava has become a major starch in the diet. The tuber is cooked and mashed to make the all-important fufu to eat with spicy stews. The Amerindian method of drying ground cassava (manioc) meal has been adapted along the West African coast where it is called gari. In Ghana, gari foto is similar to Bahian farofa (page 73), but embellished with vegetables and cooked in stock to serve with stews.

Jollof Rice

Jollof rice, jambalaya's ancestor, is reputed to have originated in Senegal, where the Wolof-speaking inhabitants lived in the kingdom of Jollof. This recipe is similar to the one Adelaide Wilson from Sierra Leone served at the Africa in Mississippi Festival, an event held on Farish Street in Jackson each April. The optional ham is an American addition.

Serves 4–6

3 tablespoons vegetable oil
1 chicken, about 3 pounds, skinned and cut into serving pieces, or
    8 chicken pieces, skinned
1 tablespoon paprika
1–2 ounces cooked ham, finely chopped (optional)
2 yellow onions, chopped
2 garlic cloves, minced
1 small fresh red chile, minced (see Glossary); 1/2 to 1 teaspoon red
    pepper flakes; or 1 teaspoon cayenne pepper
1/2 teaspoon ground allspice
1/2 teaspoon ground turmeric
1 cup long-grain white rice, rinsed and drained
1 can (16 ounces) tomatoes with their juice, chopped
2 cups chicken stock (see Glossary) or water
1 carrot, peeled and sliced
salt and ground black pepper
1/2 cup fresh, frozen, or drained canned peas

In a heavy pot or dutch oven over high heat, warm the oil. Add the chicken, a few pieces at a time, and brown well on all sides. Dust with the paprika to aid in browning. Remove from the pan to a plate. To the same skillet, add the ham, if using, and the onions. Reduce the heat to medium and cook until the onions are wilted, just a few minutes. Add the garlic and chile and cook a minute or so. Stir in the allspice, turmeric, and rice and cook another minute.

Add the tomatoes and stock. Stir well and return the chicken to the pan. Stir in the carrot and season to taste with salt and pepper. Bring to a boil, stir well, reduce the heat to low, cover, and simmer for 25 minutes. Lift the lid, spoon the peas over the top, re-cover, and cook until the rice is tender and most of the liquid is absorbed, about 5 minutes longer. It will be a little soupy.

Stir to mix all the ingredients and serve hot.

To approximate the color of the red palm oil she was raised on in Cameroon, Evangeline Fogam, of Alameda, California, combines a less saturated oil such as canola or safflower with a litttle tomato sauce. She stirs it well and then waits for the solids to drop before ladling it out to use for dishes like koki, a steamed black-eyed pea pudding. Another substitute is annatto oil (see Glossary).

Millet is one of the oldest cereal crops grown in Africa and was a primary staple before corn was introduced. The tiny grains that puff when cooked are best known in the United States as birdseed, but their nutty flavor and aroma are being rediscovered for eating as cereal and in breads.

Tiebe Dienn · *Fish Stew*

Senegal's national dish is a direct ancestor to America's gumbo. It's an everyday dish like other West African one-pot stews, which combine whatever vegetables and fish or meat are available. It is also like jambalaya in that the sauce can be made and served over rice or the rice can be cooked in the sauce. This recipe, shared by Moussa Dieme, who was raised in Thionck-Sessyl, a Senegalese coastal town south of Dakar, is similar to Gambia's *bennachin*.

Serves 6–8

3 tablespoons peanut oil or vegetable oil
1¹/₂–2 pounds firm white fish fillets, cut into 2-inch pieces
salt and ground black pepper
1 large yellow onion, sliced or chopped
3 carrots, peeled and sliced or cut into 2-inch-long sticks
¹/₂ head green cabbage, shredded
1 green bell pepper, seeded and chopped
1 or 2 small fresh chiles, seeded and minced (see Glossary),
    or 1 teaspoon red pepper flakes
1 or 2 turnips, peeled and sliced or cut into ³/₄-inch cubes
1 or 2 sweet potatoes, peeled and cut into ³/₄-inch cubes
1 small eggplant, cut into ³/₄-inch cubes
10 Roma tomatoes, chopped, or 1 cup canned tomato sauce
2 garlic cloves, minced
3 cups water
1 cup raw long-grain white rice, or 1 recipe hot Plain Rice (page 107)
¹/₄ pound okra, sliced

In a heavy pot or dutch oven, heat the oil until almost smoking. Slip in the fish and sprinkle with salt and pepper. Brown quickly on both sides and remove to a platter.

In Ghana and Togo eggplants are called garden eggs.

Reduce the heat to medium, add the onion to the oil remaining in the pot, and sauté until soft, about 5 minutes. Stir in the carrots, cabbage, bell pepper, chiles, turnips, sweet potatoes, eggplant, tomatoes, and garlic and sauté a couple minutes. Sprinkle with salt and pepper to taste. Add the water, stir, and bring to a boil. Reduce the heat to medium-low and simmer until the vegetables are tender, 10–15 minutes.

Stir in the raw rice, if using, cover, and cook until the rice is tender, 15–20 minutes. Alternatively, cook the sauce at least 30 minutes to blend the flavors before adding the okra.

Add the okra and cook 5 minutes. Return the fish to the pot, adjust the seasoning, heat to serving temperature, and serve. If serving Plain Rice, spoon the stew over the rice.

VARIATION: *When tiebe is made with meat, it is called* tiebe yape *and is similar to Bahian* Cozido *(pages 86–87). With chicken it is like West Indian Pepperpot (pages 40–41). To make* tiebe yape, *substitute 1½ pounds chicken pieces, or beef, lamb, or goat cubes for the fish. Leave the meat in the pot after browning and cook it along with the vege-tables until it is tender, about 30 minutes for the chicken, 1 hour for the beef and lamb, and 1½ hours for the goat. If adding rice, add it the last 25 minutes of cooking; add the okra the last 5 minutes of cooking.*

Lamb or Chicken Peanut Stew

Lamb or chicken is combined with peanuts all over West Africa into rich tantalizing stews with names like *dommo dah* in Gambia and *maafe* in Mali. It is also related to the Brazilian *Xinxim de Galinha* (pages 88–89). Here is a recipe like one I had at the New Orleans Jazz Festival. It was served by Fanta, a native of Gambia, who cooks at the Bennachin Restaurant in Metarie, Louisiana. Try the Senegalese Peanut Sauce instead of plain peanut butter for extra flavor and depth.

Serves 8

3–4 pounds lamb shoulder, trimmed of fat and cut into 1-inch cubes, or
    2 chickens, about 3 pounds each, cut into serving pieces
1 tablespoon paprika
salt and ground black pepper
1½ teaspoons cayenne pepper or other ground red chile pepper
3 tablespoons peanut or vegetable oil
2 yellow onions, chopped
4 garlic cloves, minced
1 teaspoon dried oregano, crushed
1 teaspoon ground ginger
2 cans (16 ounces each) tomatoes with their juice, chopped
3–4 tablespoons tomato paste or sauce
2 cups lamb or chicken stock (see Glossary) or water
3–4 tablespoons creamy peanut butter or ⅓–½ cup Baloumbum
    (page 248)
salt and ground black pepper
1–2 tablespoons red palm oil (dendê) *(optional)*
6 cups hot Plain Rice (page 107, double the recipe)

Place the meat or chicken in a bowl. In a small bowl, stir together the paprika, salt and pepper to taste, and ½ teaspoon of the cayenne pepper. Sprinkle over the meat and stir to coat evenly.

In a large, heavy pot or dutch oven over high heat, heat the oil to almost smoking. Add the meat, a few pieces at a time, and brown well on all sides. Remove to a plate as each batch is browned. When all of the meat is browned, return it to the pot. Add the onions and garlic and sauté until browned, then continue cooking until all the meat juices evaporate, about 10 minutes.

Stir in the oregano, ginger, and remaining 1 teaspoon cayenne pepper and cook, stirring constantly, 30 seconds. Add the tomatoes and juice, tomato paste, and stock and bring to a boil. Put the peanut butter in a small bowl and stir in enough of the hot pot liquid to thin it. Add to the pot. If using the *Baloumbum,* just stir it in. Stir well, add salt and black pepper to taste, reduce the heat to medium-low, and simmer, covered partially, until the meat is tender, about 30 minutes for chicken and 45–60 minutes for lamb.

Taste for seasoning and stir in the palm oil, if using. Serve over the rice.

Yassa · *Grilled Fish, Chicken, or Meat*

Yassa is citrus-marinated chicken, beef, or fish that is traditionally chargrilled. Here is the version of one shared by Moussa Dieme, from Senegal, who now lives in Mendocino, California. Firm fish or chicken cubes can be substuted for the beef.

Serves 4 or 5

1¹⁄₂ pounds lean beef, cut into 1-inch cubes
1 yellow onion, cut into 1-inch squares
1 fresh red or green chile, minced (see Glossary)
2 cloves garlic, minced
¹⁄₂ cup fresh lemon or lime juice
2 tablespoons vegetable oil
salt and ground black pepper
Tomato-Onion relish (page 212)

Combine the meat cubes and onion squares in a single layer in a ceramic or glass dish. In a small bowl, stir together the chile, garlic, lemon juice, oil, and salt and pepper to taste. Pour over the meat and mix well. Let stand at least 1 hour at room temperature, or cover and refrigerate overnight.

Soak bamboo skewers in water to cover. Prepare a charcoal fire. Remove the meat from the marinade and reserve the marinade. Drain the skewers and alternately thread the meat and onions onto the skewers. Grill, turning occasionally, over the hot coals until done, 6–8 minutes.

Meanwhile, in a small saucepan, heat the reserved marinade and boil for 2 minutes. Serve with the cooked meat. Pass the relish.

Sorghum, a cornlike stalk used for cereal and sweetener, is native to Africa, where it has been grown in the sub-Saharan savannah since Neolithic times. It came to the New World first to Jamaica, where it was called little millet or Guinea corn. A staple on African-American farms, the stalks were used for animal feed and were boiled to produce an economical, molasseslike table syrup. Sorghum and cane syrup were common sweeteners in rural America until after the Civil War, when sugar became more affordable.

Groundnut Toffee

Although similar to the Goober Brittle (page 151) and Pralines (page 197) of the American South and the *pé-de-moleque* of Bahia, these peanut candies are enriched with butter and rolled into small balls, rather than formed into flat disks. Groundnut is the common English word in West Africa for peanuts.

Makes about ten 1½-inch balls

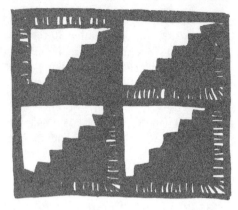

1½ cups sugar
1 lemon, or 2 teaspoons fresh lemon juice
1 tablespoon butter
2 cups roasted peanuts

Line a baking sheet with parchment paper and lightly oil it.

Put the sugar in a heavy saucepan and melt it over medium heat. To keep it from sticking to the pan sides and caramelizing too fast, put the whole lemon on the end of a fork and stir the sugar with the lemon. Alternatively, add the lemon juice to the sugar. Stir constantly so the sugar doesn't burn and melts evenly.

When it has become a thin, golden syrup, remove from the heat and stir in the butter and nuts. Pour the mixture onto a pastry board that has been lighlty dampened with a sponge. When cool enough to handle, quickly roll the peanut mixture into walnut-sized balls. Store in an airtight container up to 1 week.

Kinolo · *Steamed Banana Pudding*

Here is a steamed banana pudding recipe from Raymond Thoya of Kenya. The mixture of bananas and cornmeal is wrapped in banana leaves to steam until hot and fragrant. He serves the opened packets with a purée of golden mangoes. Banana leaves may be found at Latin American markets, or see Resources. Alternatively, substitute soaked corn husks.

Makes four 6-inch packets

1 cup water
1/2 cup cornmeal
6 ripe bananas, mashed
4 banana leaves
1 mango, peeled, pitted, and puréed

Combine the water, cornmeal, and banana purée in a bowl. Separate the banana leaves. Take 1 leaf and place one fourth of the banana mixture in the center. Wrap it up into a tidy, flat packet and tuck the ends underneath. Repeat with the remaining ingredients.

Bring water in a steamer pan to a simmer. Place the packets on the steamer rack, cover, and steam for 30 minutes. Let stand at room temperature 30 minutes.

Unwrap each packet and cut each portion into 4 slices. Serve the puréed mango on the side.

NOTE: If using corn husks, soak them in water to cover for 10 minutes.

Glossary

Here are techniques and ingredients used throughout the book. If a particular ingredient isn't here, check the index and read about it in one of the chapters.

Achiote/annatto: Small bright red seeds that grow on shrubs in the Caribbean, where they are used mainly to add color to pastries and other foods. When ground with other spices and formed into a brick the paste is used to rub on meats and season stews. For more information see the Caribbean chapter.

Annatto Oil: Heat 1 cup vegetable oil until very hot. *Do not boil.* Add 1/2 cup annatto seeds (see page 42) and stir. Let stand until the oil turns orange, about 1 hour. Strain. Store in the refrigerator for up to a month.

Bananas: The prolific fruit of the tropics is boiled and eaten as a starch when it is green and as a fruit or vegetable when ripe. It is sautéed, baked, fried, grilled, and boiled to make both sweet and savory dishes. In addition, the leaves are used for wrapping foods for steaming and for thatching roofs. If a green banana is difficult to peel, follow the directions for peeling plantains.

Beans: Black-eyed peas, pigeon peas, lentils, and chick-peas (garbanzos) came with the Africans to the New World, where varieties of red, black, and white beans were already growing. Black beans are most popular in Cuba and in Bahia, red beans in other islands of the Caribbean and the American South. Black-eyed peas are still mainstays in African diets everywhere. There are, however, hundreds of varieties of beans in a multitude of colors and shapes with names like calypso, pinquito, trout, scarlet emperor, prince, snow cap, rattlesnake, and painted pony that can be used in these recipes (see Resources).

Before using beans, soak them overnight in water to cover by several inches. Or give them a quick soak by placing the beans in a heavy saucepan with water to cover by several inches, bring to a boil, turn off the heat, cover, and let stand for 1 hour. Drain.

The length of time it takes to cook a pot of beans varies from bean to bean, depending upon their size, age, and innate tenderness. If you are going to combine different types of beans in one pot, cook the beans separately and then combine them with the seasonings. Never add tomato or other acidic ingredients until the beans are as tender as you want them. The acid tends to stop the cooking and the beans will remain hard if the acid goes in too soon.

Although pork is a traditional addition to a pot of beans, and ham hocks, salt pork, or bacon adds a rich saltiness, the meat can be omitted. Any beans can be substituted in any recipe.

Cassava: Native to Brazil, its Bahian name, *mandioca*, comes from the Tupi word for "root." In the Caribbean islands, cassava comes from the Taino (Arawak) *kasabi*, which the Spanish translated to *casabe*. To confuse matters even more, this long dark tuber with the white versatile flesh is also known as yuca. It was taken to Africa in the sixteenth century, where it is now a staple starch. This starch of the tropics comes in bitter and sweet varieties. Bitter cassava must have its liquid, which is poisonous until cooked, extracted. The liquid from cassava is saved to use for laundry starch or boiled down to make a thick dark syrup called cassareep and used for meat preservation. In Trinidad, cassareep flavors the pepperpot. Grated bitter cassava is made into Jamaican bammies. Sweet cassava is used like a potato. The pearls that are strained out of the boiled sweet cassava are tapioca, famous for the pudding of the same name and used for thickening soups.

For consistency in the recipes here, cassava is the primary name. When the peeled root is dried and ground into coarse flour, it is called cassava meal or manioc. Toasted and used like bread, it is known as *farofa* (page 73) in Bahia and *gari* in West Africa. The fine cornstarch-like flour is called cassava flour or tapioca. It is stickier to work with than all-purpose wheat flour, but adds a nice sheen when used to thicken stews.

Cast-iron skillets: An indispensable accessory to African-American cooking. In many families they were passed on from one generation to the next. "If someone's house burned down, the iron pot always survived," says Vernell Davis, Jr., a professional cook in Oakland, California. The thick, heavy surface of cast iron evenly distributes heat for everything from fried chicken to spicy sauces, from browning meat to baking corn bread. Some foods, however, are sensitive to the iron content; okra turns black, for instance.

A new skillet has to be seasoned before its first use, and an old one must be taken care of to preserve its stick-free surface. To season a new skillet, spray or rub oil all over the interior. Place it in a 300 degree F oven 1½ hours. Using a thick hot pad to prevent burned fingers, remove it from the oven and let cool.

To keep up the care of the skillet, never wash it in hot soapy water. Instead, rinse it out immediately after use and wipe dry or dry it over a low burner, then rub a little oil in the pan before putting it away.

Chicken: Chicken is economical to raise and has always been an important food in Africa, where its all-dark meat relative, the guinea fowl, originated. Both birds came to the New World with the slaves.

For the recipes here and for economy, I recommend buying whole chickens. Skinning is recommended to remove excess fat. The backs, necks, and wing tips can be saved, wrapped in plastic wrap, and frozen until there are enough to make chicken stock.

The Caribbean practice of cutting the chicken into uniform-sized pieces is also recommended. To do this, cut each breast in half or in thirds with the heavy hit of a cleaver. Cut the thighs and drumsticks in half if they are large. Cut the wing tips off and remove as much skin as possible.

Chicken stock: This is a basic stock recipe. The amounts and kinds of ingredients are not absolute. Any variation or amount will produce a great stock. Just use what is on hand or save odds and ends in your stockpile.

To make chicken stock, in a large, heavy stockpot, place 1 or 2 onions, quartered; 3 celery stalks with leaves, coarsely chopped; 2 carrots, peeled and coarsely chopped; 6 green onions or 1 leek, chopped, or use tops only; 1 bay leaf, crushed; 1 tablespoon vinegar (helps extract flavor from the bones); 3 fresh parsley sprigs; 2 garlic cloves, smashed; 6 black peppercorns; optional herbs of choice such as basil, thyme, marjoram, or sage; and 4 pounds chicken bones, especially legs and thighs, neck bones, and carcasses. Add water to cover generously (about 4 quarts).

Bring to a boil. With a slotted spoon, skim off any foam. Bring to a boil again, reduce the heat to low, cover partially, and simmer for 1½–2 hours, skimming as necessary. Strain and let cool. Cover tightly and refrigerate up to 5 days. Remove the fat that solidifies on top just before using. To freeze, remove the fat and freeze for up to 6 months.

This will yield about 3½ quarts.

Chiles: Any chile may be used when fresh chiles are called for in these recipes. They vary in hotness and flavor from one to the other, however. The lantern-shaped *habanero* (Scotch Bonnet), which is the world's hottest chile (use the green ones for soup and the yellow for sauces is the common admonishment), will lend the most authentic flavor to many of the Caribbean recipes, just as the *malagueta* chile will to the Bahian recipes. But bird, cayenne, and serrano chiles are also fine. If fresh chiles aren't available, purchase a jar of pickled small whole chiles, preferably the red bird, and store in the refrigerator. Unless specifically directed, seeding the chiles is optional. The seeds do add extra heat, so use according to personal taste.

The most common ground chile is cayenne, but look in African and Latin American markets for other ground chiles with different flavors. Pepper sauces include those made with vinegar and salt such as Tabasco and Louisiana hot sauce, but also try the red and green *habanero* (Scotch Bonnet) sauces from Jamaica (see Resources). In soups and sauces, ground chile pepper will season the entire pot uniformly. Red pepper flakes and minced chiles tend to give a fiesty bite here and there.

The oils in chiles can burn your hands or any cuts or abrasions you may have. If you have sensitive skin, wear rubber gloves. To take the seeds out of chiles, which reduces their potency, cut the pods in half and scrape out the seeds under cold running water. When you are done preparing the chiles, immediately wash your hands with warm soapy water. Wait several hours before getting your hands near your eyes.

I recommend tasting a minute fleck of the chile you are about to add to a dish to see what its possibilities are before deciding how much to add.

Coconut: When green, coconuts are ready for a machete to lop off the top and a straw for slurping their refreshing coconut water. The soft meat inside is for gouging out and eating with a spoon or knife. When brown and hairy, coconuts are really hard. After opening, the flesh is good for grating and for making coconut milk. Most of the coconuts found in the United States are brown and must be opened carefully. Here is the way to do it.

First, find the three "eyes" at one end. With a hammer and nail, punch them out. Pour out the liquid and drink it as it is.

Place the coconut in a preheated 325 degree F oven for about 40 minutes. Remove and place it on a secure surface. Using a hammer, hit it to break it open. It will fall apart in several pieces and the white meat should separate easily from the shell. It may be eaten right away, grated and dried, or frozen. Or it may be used to make coconut milk.

Coconut milk is made by grating the white coconut meat and placing it in a food processor or blender. Add 2 cups boiling water and pulse several times for several seconds to help extract all the flavor. Let it stand 15–20 minutes, then strain it through cheesecloth set over a bowl. You should have about 2 cups. Canned coconut milk is a convenient substitute and has a richer, thicker consistency than home squeezed. Look for it in Asian or Latin American stores or in well-stocked supermarkets or check Resources.

The leftover coconut meat can be combined with a little sugar and used in recipes, but it won't have as much flavor as before it is squeezed. Or the meat may be combined with another cup of hot water, pulsed in the processor or blender, left to stand another 15 minutes, and strained again. This will yield about 1 cup thin coconut milk, which may be blended with the thicker milk from the first pressing.

Store coconut milk in a covered container in the refrigerator for up to 4 days, and in the freezer for 1–2 months.

Corn: First cultivated somewhere in Central America between 6000 and 5000 B.C., this versatile grain has gone on to sustain populations all over the globe. The Native Americans who cultivated and ate it with beans must have had innate knowledge about the protein complement each provided the other. Corn dries well, becoming whole kernels of hominy or cracked into grits. It can be ground into coarse or fine flour. Look for stone-ground cornmeal for the best flavor when making the breads and other recipes in this book.

To freeze corn, leave the kernels on the cob or cut them off. Drop the whole ears or kernels into boiling water and blanch for 2 minutes. Drain and let cool. Pack in plastic bags or tubs, label, and freeze. It will keep for about 4 months.

Dendê oil: This is the distinctive orange oil from the red palm tree native to Africa and widely used in Bahian cooking. It is called red palm oil in West Africa. See Resources for mail-order information. Substitutions include adding a little paprika or turmeric to vegetable oil or annatto oil.

File: Pronounced fee-lay, the gray-green powder comes from grinding dried sassafrass leaves and was introduced to Africans and Europeans by the Native Americans. It is used to thicken soups and stews and is a signature ingredient of Louisiana gumbo.

Fish stock: Fish stock gives a great flavor to many of these rice and vegetable-based dishes. To make it, in a saucepan, combine 1–3 pounds fish bones, heads, tails and/or shrimp or crab shells; celery leaves from 2 or 3 celery stalks; 1 yellow onion, chopped; 1 carrot, peeled and chopped; ¼ cup fresh lemon juice or 1 cup dry white wine; 3 fresh parsley sprigs; 1 teaspoon dried thyme, crushed; and 2 quarts water. Stir well and bring just to a boil. Reduce the heat to low, cover partially, and simmer to extract the flavors, 30–60 minutes. Strain and use immediately. Or let cool, pour into a tightly covered container, and freeze up to 1 month. This will yield about 2 quarts.

Nonreactive pots or bowls: Made of stainless steel, porcelain, or glass, nonreactive pots or bowls are called for in some recipes because acidic ingredients such as tomatoes and citrus juices tend to discolor when placed in some materials, such as aluminum.

Okra: A pod with an attitude, okra has been prized in Africa since prehistoric times. It is found wherever people of African descent live. Seeds were reputedly smuggled in the ears of slaves on their long journey across the Atlantic. In the more temperate climates, the elongated green vegetables, with the viscous seedy interior that some people find objectionable, grow only to 3 or 4 inches long. In Brazil and the Caribbean, it can be up to 9 inches long. Okra is typically stewed, often with dried fish as in Bahia and West Africa, or with tomatoes as in Louisiana, where its West African name is the same as the dish gumbo.

Plantain: A relative of bananas, this starchy fruit is a common ingredient in the Caribbean, Bahia, and West Africa. Of Asian origin, plantains have been known in Africa since the tenth century. When the skin is green and unripe, the flesh is starchy and bland and it can be fried or baked. When the skin is blackened but the fruit is still firm, it has a soft, almost banana texture and aroma but it still must be cooked to be eaten.

To peel a plantain, cut it in half crosswise and slice off the ends. With a sharp, thin knife, cut lengthwise slits just through the skin and peel back the skin. Proceed with the recipe.

Pork: Africans had little experience with pork at home where the Muslim influence forbids it to be eaten. In the New World, however, they became quickly acquainted with pork, which came with Portuguese and Spanish settlers. Next to rabbits, pigs are the most prolific of all domestic animals. Here is a list of the most common cuts of pork used in African-American cooking.

Chops are individually portioned cuts from the lean center loin. Those from the blade end have T-shaped rib bones and those from the center of the loin have a C-shaped portion of the backbone. These can be panfried, broiled, braised, or smothered.

Shoulder steaks, which come from the pork shoulder, are cut across the blade bone and several muscles. Not as tender as chops from the loin, these lend themselves to braising and long, slow panfrying or smothering.

Boston butt, the top portion of the shoulder, falls where the shoulders and front legs "butt" up against the torso. It is lean but lightly marbled with intermuscular fat, which lends to its preferred flavor, low shrinkage, and desirability for long, slow barbecuing.

Hocks and shanks come from the lower leg bone, cut from the picnic shoulder or the pork leg. Usually smoked, the shanks are skinless and the hocks still have their skin on. These tasty morsels add fabulous flavor to a pot of beans or greens. And they are delicious cooked with onions and garlic as in Brazilian Feijoada Completa (pages 84–85).

Ham comes from the large hind pork leg. Fresh hams have a bone running through the center and the meat is covered with fat and skin. Fresh hams can be roasted, smoked, or braised in liquids. Smoked hams are cured and must be roasted or baked before eating. Country hams are heavily salted and must be soaked before cooking.

Links are sausages made from odds and ends and fat stuffed into intestine casings. Herbs, spices, onions, and chiles are added for flavor. When rice is added they are called *boudin.*

Ribs come from the long rib bones, which have the curved end cut off so they are straight and easy to cook. Spareribs deserve their name because of the little bit of meat in proportion to the amount of bone, exemplifying the notion that the best meat is next to the bone. Back or loin ribs carry a layer of meat on them that comes from the loin rather than the bottom side of the rib or brisket. Rib tips are the meaty portions on the smaller bones that run between the bacon and the loin. Chicago's famous rib tips are the meaty portions.

Slab bacon, or streak of lean, is cut from the side of the pork and comes in 1- to 2-inch-wide slabs, interspersed with lean and fat. Slab bacon is often sold with the skin still on. Most is smoked. Keeping a slab in the freezer is convenient for slicing off an ounce or two with a cleaver to season beans and greens.

Salt pork, sometimes referred to as white bacon, is pure pork fat, usually sold in 6-inch squares, liberally salted, brined, and cured for 3 weeks or so. It is used for seasoning beans and greens. Before using it is best to blanch it to remove some of the salt. To do this, place the whole piece or recipe-sized pieces in a small saucepan with water to cover. Bring to a boil and boil 3–10 minutes, depending upon the size of the pieces.

Rice: All the rice recipes in this book call for long-grain white rice and require the rice to be rinsed before cooking. This step helps to wash away some of the glutinous starch so that the grains are fluffy and separate. To do this, place the rice in a colander and run water through it, tossing the grains with your hands, until the water runs clear. Alternatively, place the rice in a bowl with water to cover and let it soak for a minute or so, then drain in a colander and rinse quickly. If short-grain rice is substituted, reduce the cooking time by about 5 minutes. If brown rice is substituted, use slightly less than white, and increase the cooking time by 15–20 minutes.

Sweet potato: A starchy tuber native to tropical America whose family includes a few members that, in the North American vernacular, are confusingly called yams but are not related to African yams. In the recipes, garnet and red jewel yams refer to the American sweet potatoes with skins that range from creamy brown to maroon and flesh from pale yellow to brilliant orange. Their flavor is sweeter and moister than the lighter-skinned and lighter-fleshed sweet potatoes. All American sweet potatoes are moister and sweeter than the dark-skinned, white- to yellow-fleshed African yam. All of these tubers can be used interchangeably.

Tapioca: See Cassava.

Tomato: Indigenous to the Americas, the tomato still grows wild in Brazil. Using the seeds of the tomato adds body to a sauce; the skins add texture. Some recipes call for seeding them. To do this, cut the tomato in half horizontally and squeeze the seeds out. Do this through a piece of cheesecloth or a strainer to save the juice that comes with the seeds. The seeds can be saved for the stockpot. Canned tomatoes can be seeded this same way. To skin a tomato, either peel off the skin with a vegetable peeler, or drop the tomato in boiling water for 10 seconds, remove it, and pop off the skin. Keep a tube of imported tomato paste in the refrigerator to use when small amounts of tomato paste are called for in recipes.

Yam: Not to be confused with the American sweet potato (see Sweet Potato), the African yam is also a tuber but the flesh is usually white and sometimes yellow to orange. It has a mealy texture and intense potato-rich flavor and is best served simply boiled and cut into wedges or mashed. The word is derived from *nyame,* Wolof for "to taste." Its ability to withstand droughts and other blights made it a dietary staple in West Africa. Tons were carried to feed the slaves enroute to the New World, where they are still a staple in the Caribbean. Fresh yams are found in Latin American groceries and they are also available powdered for making *Fufu* (page 249). See Resources.

Resources

The best places to look for fresh chiles, yams, and greens, and imported oils, condiments, and sauces are in neighborhood Hispanic and Asian markets.

Mail Order Sources:

Adams Milling Company
Route 6, Box 148 A
Dothan, Alabama 36303
800-239-4233, 205-983-4233
Stone-ground cornmeal, stone-ground grits, cane and sorghum syrups, hush-puppy mix

Aidell's Sausages
1575 Minnesota Street
San Francisco, California 94107
800-541-2233, 415-285-6660
Creole hot sausages, 25 different poultry sausages, and more

A & W Island Food Store
2634 San Pablo Ave.
Berkeley, California 94702
510-649-9195
Several varieties of fresh African yams, plantains, sorrel, salted mackerel and other fish, pigeon peas, Caribbean spices and condiments, canned ackee, canned jackfruit, plantain chips, bammies, frozen goat meat

Battistella's Seafood, Inc.
910 Touro Street
New Orleans, Louisiana 70166
504-949-2724, fax 504-949-2799
Crawfish shipped live; distributor of catfish, crab products, shrimp, drum, snappers and more

Beans and Beyond
Bean Bag Bulk Foods, Inc.
818 Jefferson Street
Oakland, California 94607
510-839-8988, 800-845-BEAN (2326)
Over 85 different bean varieties, including pigeon peas; habanero *(Scotch Bonnet) pepper*
powder, Louisiana dried shrimp, powdered yams, red palm (dendê) *oil, cassava meal (manioc,*
gari); specialty rices, and other African ingredients; located in the Housewives Market

Byrd Cookie Company
P.O. Box 13086
2233 Norwood Avenue
Savannah, Georgia 31406
912-355-1716
Benne cookies, creole spices, Caribbean curry spices, barbecue spices and rubs

Casa Hispania, International
P.O. Box 587
73 Poningo Street
Port Chester, New York 10578
914-939-9333
Cassava meal (manioc, farofa), red palm (dendê) *oil annato seeds and achiote paste;*
specializing in Central and South American ingredients

Char-Broil
P.O. Box 1300
Columbus, Georgia 31993
800-241-8981
Hickory and mesquite chips and chunks; apples, peach, and pecan chips; smoker for a gas grill;
barbecue sauces

Charleston Catalog Company
139 Market Street
Charleston, South Carolina 29401
800-533-6629, 803-577-7462
Benne cookies, South Carolina rice, dried bulk beans, red rice and rice and bean packets,
southern seasoning spice mixtures

Coisa Nossa
41 West 46th Street
New York, New York
212-719-4779
Bahian ingredients: dendê *oil, coconut milk,* malagueta *chiles, cassava meal, carne seca, pig's ears, and other specialty meats; call for catalog*

DeKalb World Farmer's Market
3000 East Ponce de Leon
Decatur, Georgia 30034
404-377-6401
Wide variety of fresh produce in season plus Caribbean seasonings and dried shrimp (will ship this to order)

Deku Enterprises
510 Parksley Avenue
Baltimore, Maryland 21223
410-945-6929
Dried smoked whole catfish, whiting, blue fish, ling cod, swordfish, salmon, red snapper, dried smoked ground shrimp, plus a wide variety of fresh greens and chiles in season

The Everyday Gourmet
2905 Old Canton Road
Jackson, Mississippi 39216
601-362-0723
Specializing in Mississippi food products, seasoning blends, biscuit mixes, stone-ground cornmeal, creole seasonings, southern cookbooks, and cooking classes

Frieda's Finest Produce Specialties
P.O. Box 58488
Los Angeles, California 90058
800-241-1771, 213-627-2981
Fresh plantains, jackfruit, many kinds of bananas; call for list of what's in season

Hoppin' John's Culinary Bookstore and Emporium
30 Pinckney Street
Charleston, South Carolina, 29401
803-577-6404, fax 803-577-6932
Stone-ground cornmeal and grits, new and out-of-print cookbooks

International Market
365 Somerville Avenue
Somerville, Massachusetts 02143
800-455-1880, 617-776-1880
Caters to Brazilian clientele: dendê *oil, cassava meal* (mandioca de farinha)*, coconut milk*

Jamaica Groceries and Spices
9628 South West 160th Street
Miami, Florida 33157
305-252-1197
Red palm (dendê) *oil, habanero* (Scotch bonnet) *peppers and sauces, jerk seasonings, Caribbean curry powders, and fresh African yams and other produce in season, also does mail order*

Jones & Bones
621 Capitola Avenue
Capitola, CA 95010
408-462-0521
Creole seasonings, Caribbean seasonings and condiments

Konriko Company Store
Box 10640
307 Ann Street
New Iberia, Louisiana 70562
800-551-3245
Lousiana rice, creole seasonings, bases for gumbo, jambalaya, crawfish boil

Loretta's Authentic Pralines
1101 N. Peters, Stalls 17-23
New Orleans, Louisiana 70116
504-529-4170
Creamy pecan pralines

Louisiana Seafood Exchange
428 Jefferson Highway
Jefferson, Louisiana 70121
504-834-9395, fax 504-834-5633
*Crawfish shipped live, dried shrimp, distributor of grouper, pompano, drum, mackerel,
red snapper, and more*

New Orleans School of Cooking
620 Decatur Street
New Orleans, Louisiana 70130
800-237-4841, 504-525-2665
Creole seasonings, crawfish boil, habanero *(Scotch bonnet) sauces, creole sausages,
cast-iron skillets, dutch ovens, and ribbed skillets*

Oriental Lucky Market
809 Clay Street
Oakland, California 94607
510-452-1556, fax 510-452-0321
Fresh yams, collards, habanero *(Scotch bonnet) chiles, dried fish, powdered yams, canned ackee,
large selection of African and Caribbean seasonings and condiments; will respond to mail-order
requests*

Park Seed Company
Cokesbury Road
Greenwood, South Carolina 29647-0001
800-845-3369
Seeds for okra, collards, beets, turnips, kales, pinto beans, habanero *(Scotch bonnet) and
cayenne chiles, watermelons*

Prince Neville's
505 A Divisadero Street
San Francisco, California
415-922-9037, 415-567-1294
Jamaican and other Caribbean condiments and seasonings

G.B. Ratto & Company
821 Washington Street
Oakland, California 94607
510-832-6503, fax 510-836-2250
Red palm (dendê) *oil, cassava meal (manioc,* gari*), habanero (Scotch bonnet) chile paste,*
malagueta *chile powder, powdered African yams, annato seeds, and achiote paste, many*
Brazilian, creole, and African condiments

Shepherd's Garden Seeds
30 Irene Street
Torrington, Connecticut 06790
203-482-3638
Seeds for cabbage, chard, kale, black beans, beets, corn, watermelon, habanero *(Scotch bonnet)*
and cayenne chiles, bell peppers, eggplants (garden eggs), squash

Spiceland
3206 North Major Avenue
Chicago, Illinois 60634
800-352-8671, 312-736-1217
Sesame seed (benne)*, whole nutmeg, ginger, various dried ground and crushed chiles, paprika,*
hundreds of dried herbs and spices; cheap prices!

Sunny Caribbe
216 King Street
Charleston, South Carolina 29401
803-723-6957
Jerk seasonings, Caribbean hot sauces, spice mixtures, and curry blends, ginger syrup,
sorrel syrup

Bibliography

Amado, Jorge. *Dona Flor and Her Two Husbands*. Translated by Harrit de Onis. New York: Avon Books, 1969.

Birnbaum, Alexandra Mayes. *Birnbaum's Caribbean 1993*. New York: Harper Perennial,1993.

Brown, Cora; Brown, Rose; and Brown, Bob. *The South American Cookbook*. New York: Dover Publications, 1971.

Bullock, Helen Duprey. *Recipes of Ante Bellum America*. New York: Heirloom Publishing Co., 1967.

Burn, Billie. *Stirrin' the Pots on Daufuskie*. Spartanburg, South Carolina: Billie Burn Book, The Reprint Co., 1992.

Butler, Cleora. *Cleora's Kitchens: The Memoir of a Cook and Eight Decades of Great American Food*. Tulsa, Oklahoma: Council Oak Books, Ltd., 1985.

Cobb, Thomas R. R. *Historical Sketch of Slavery from Earliest Periods*. Philadelphia: T. & J. W. Johnson, & Co., 1858.

Colquitt, Harriet Ross. *The Savannah Cookbook*. Charleston, South Carolina: Colonial Publishers, 1933.

Conde, Maryse. *Tree of Life*. New York: Ballantine Books, Random House, 1992.

———. *Segu*. Translated by Barbara Bray. New York: Ballantine/Viking Penguin, 1984.

Daise, Ronald. *Reminiscences of Sea Island Heritage*. Orangeburg, South Carolina: Sandpiper Publishing, Inc., 1986.

Da Mathilde. *325 Recettes de Cuisine Creole*. Martinique/Guadeloupe: Jacques Grancher, Vangirard, 1975.

DeKnight, Freda. *The Ebony Cookbook*. Chicago: Johnson Publishing Co., Inc., 1962.

Elgin Community Senior Citizens. *Country Cookin' Then and Now*. Elgin, Alabama.

Foster, Cecil. *No Man in the House*. New York: Ballantine Books, 1991.

Franklin, John Hope, and Moss, Alfred A.,Jr. *From Slavery to Freedom: A History of Negro Americans*. New York: McGraw Hill, 1988.

Freyre, Gilberto. *The Masters and the Slaves: Study in the Development of Brazilian Civilization*. Berkeley: University of California Press, 1986.

Frost, David. *David Frost Introduces Trinidad and Tobago*. London: Andre Deutsch, 1975.

Gadsen, Robert W. *The Education of the Negro: An NAACP Lecture on the History of the Negro in Savannah, Georgia*. Savannah, Georgia: Library copy, January 20, 1967.

Gaston, Felicia. *Gaston's Guide, The Authoritative Ethnic Guide, 1986/87: Exotic Cuisine in Northern California*. San Francisco: Migrations Limited, 1986.

Genovese, Eugene D. *Roll, Jordan, Roll: The World the Slaves Made*. New York: Vintage Books, Random House, 1976.

Gullick, Mary. *Country Cooking in St. Vincent*. Publisher unknown, 1975.

Harris, Dunstan. *Island Cooking: Recipes from the Caribbean*. Freedom, California: The Crossing Press, 1988.

Holder, Geoffrey. *Caribbean Cookbook*. New York: Viking Press, 1973.

Johnson, Charles. *Middle Passage*. New York: Penguin/Plume, 1991.

Junior League of Charleston. *Charleston Receipts*. Memphis, Dallas: Wimmer Brothers, 1950.

Killion, Ronald, and Waller, Charles. *Slavery Time: Interviews With Georgia Slaves*. Savannah, Georgia: Beehive Press, 1973.

Leonard, Jonathan. *Latin American Cooking*. New York: Time-Life Books, 1968.

Leroux, Guy. *Brazilian Cooking*. Translated by Pauline Manguel and Ana Butzelaar. Singapore: Times Editions, 1980.

Lustig, Lillie; Sondheim, Claire; and Rensel, Sarah. *The Southern Cookbook of Fine Old Recipes*. Reading, Pennsylvania: Culinary Arts Press, 1935.

Mackie, Cristine. *Life and Food in the Caribbean*. New York: New Amsterdam Books, 1991.

Meade, Martha. *Recipes from the Old South*. New York: Holt, Rinehart & Winston, 1961.

Moliterno, Irene Becker. *The Brazilian Cookbook*. Translated and adapted by Charles Frank & Assoc. New York: Charles Frank Publications, 1963.

Morrison, Toni. *Beloved*. New York: Penguin, 1988.

Nabwine, Constance, and Montgomery, Bertha Vining. *Cooking the African Way*. Minneapolis: Lerner Publications, 1988.

No Restaurante Senac do Pelourinho. *A Cozinha Baiana*. Salvador, Bahia, Brazil: Departamento Regional da Bahia, 1991.

Odaatey, Bli. *A Safari of African Cooking*. Detroit, Michigan: Broadside Press, 1971.

Ortiz, Elizabeth Lambert. *The Complete Book of Caribbean Cooking*. New York: M. Evans & Co., Inc., 1973.

Perdue, Robert E. *The Negro in Savannah, 1865–1900*. New York: Exposition Press, 1973.

Princess Pamela. *Princess Pamela's Soul Food Cookbook*. New York: Signet Book, 1969.

Puckett, Susan. *A Cook's Tour of Mississippi*. Jackson, Mississippi: The Clarion Ledger/Jackson Daily News, 1980.

Robertson, Diane. *Jamaican Herbs*. Kingston, Jamaica: DeSola Pinto Associates, 1982.

Root, Waverly. *Food*. New York: Simon & Schuster, 1980.

Schneider, Elizabeth. *Uncommon Fruits and Vegetables: A Commonsense Guide*. New York: Harper & Row Publishers, 1986.

Scott, Natalie V. *Mandy's Favorite Louisiana Recipes*. Gretna, Louisiana: Pelican Publishing Co., 1929/1988.

Simonson, Thordis. *You May Plow Here: The Narrative of Sara Brooks*. New York & London: W. W. Norton & Co., 1986.

Spence, Wenton O. *Jamaican Cookery: Recipes from Old Grandmothers*. Kingston, Jamaica: Heritage Publishing, 1981.

Tannahill, Reay. *Food in History*. New York: Stern & Day, 1973.

Viola, Herman, and Margolis, Carolyn, eds. *Seeds of Change*. Washington, D.C.: Smithsonian Institute, 1991.

Wall, Allie Patricia, and Layne, Ron L. *Hog Heaven: A Guide to South Carolina Barbecue*. Lexington, South Carolina: The Sandpiper Store, 1979.

Walter, Eugene. *American Cooking: Southern Style*. New York: Time-Life Books, 1971.

Wilson, Charles Reagan, and Ferris, William, eds. *Encyclopedia of Southern Culture*. Volume I. North Carolina: University of North Carolina Press, 1989.

Wolfe, Linda. *The Cooking of the Caribbean Islands*. New York: Time-Life Books, 1970.

Recommended Reading

African:

Iron Pots and Wooden Spoons, Africa's Gifts to New World Cooking by Jessica B. Harris,
        Ballantine Books, New York, 1989

The Africa News Cookbook, African Cooking for Western Kitchens, Africa News Service, Inc.,
        edited by Tami Hultman, Penguin Books, New York, c. 1985

A Taste of Africa by Dorinda Hafner, Ten Speed Press, P.O. Box 7123, Berkeley, CA, c. 1993

A Good Soup Attracts Chairs: A First African Cookbook for American Kids by Fran Osseo-Asare,
        Pelican Publishing Company, Gretna, Louisiana, 1993.

Brazilian:

Tasting Brazil, Regional Recipes and Reminiscences by Jessica B. Harris, Macmillan Publishing
        Co., New York, 1992

Caribbean:

Sky Juice and Flying Fish, Traditional Caribbean Cooking by Jessica B. Harris, Simon & Schuster,
        New York, 1991

Jerk, Barbecue from Jamaica by Helen Willinsky, The Crossing Press, Freedom, California, 1990

Caribbean and African Cooking by Rosamund Grant, Interlink Books, New York, 1988 & 1993

Creole:

The Dooky Chase Cookbook by Leah Chase, Pelican Publishing Co., Louisiana, 1990

Chez Helene, House of Good Food Cookbook by Austin Leslie, De Simonin Publications, New
        Orleans, Louisiana, 1984

Soul/General African-American:

What's Cooking at Piney Woods, a fundraising cookbook published by the International Culinary
        Club at Piney Woods Country Life School, The Office of Special Projects, Highway 49
        South, Piney Woods, Mississippi 39148; $5.00 donation.

Family of the Spirit Cookbook, Recipes and Remembrances from African-American Kitchens by
        John Pinderhughes, Simon and Schuster, New York, 1990

Our Family Table, Recipes and Food Memories from African-American Life Models by Thelma
        Williams, copies from The Wimmer Companies, 800-727-1034, 1993

The Black Family Dinner Quilt Cookbook, Health Conscious Recipes and Food Memories by
        Dorothy Height & the National Council of Negro Women, Inc., The National Council of
        Negro Women, Inc, copies from The Wimmer Companies, 800-727-1034, 1993

The Black Family Reunion Cookbook, Recipes and Food Memories by The National Council of Negro Women, Fireside Book, Simon & Schuster, New York, 1991

Big Mamma's Old Black Pot Recipes by Ethel Dixon, Stoke Gabriel Enterprises, Alexandria, Louisiana, 1987

Vibration Cooking, or The Travel Notes of a Geechee Girl by Vertamae Smart-Grosvenor, Ballantine Books, New York, 1970

In Pursuit of Flavor by Edna Lewis, Alfred A. Knopf, New York, 1988

Soul Food, Classic Cuisine from The Deep South, Sheila Ferguson, Grove Press, New York, 1989

Sylvia's Soul Food: Recipes from Harlem's World Famous Restaurant by Sylvia Woods, Hearst Books, New York, 1992

Acknowledgments

This token of recognition shares the names of the wonderful cooks and other sources who contributed to this book. With boundless gratitude and love to you all. Yao Afantchao, Togo and Baltimore, Maryland. Alabama Bureau of Tourism. Demades and Maria Lourdes Araujo, Salvador, Bahia. Auburn Avenue Rib Shack, Atlanta, Georgia. Bahiatoursa, Salvador, Bahia. Amy Becker, Atlanta, Georgia. Alberta Beckwith, Florence, Alabama. Kevin Belton, New Orleans School of Cooking, Louisiana. Fanta, Bennachin Restaurant, Metarie, Louisiana and Gambia. Doris Bentley, Lafayette, Louisiana. Maria Emilia Bettencourt, Salvador, Bahia. Lee Bickford, Montego Bay, Jamaica. Alphonso Brown, Gullah Tours, Charleston, South Carolina. Lillie Brown, Middleton, California. Brad Brownson, Little River, California. Anthony Bundy, Rita's Olde French Quarter Restaurant, New Orleans, Louisiana. Katie and Brian Bussey, Houston, Texas. Maureen Callanan, Varig Airlines, New York. Joelene Campbell, Savannah, Georgia. Michael Cathey, Elgin, Texas. Handley Cellars, Philo, California. Leah Chase, Dooky Chase, New Orleans, Louisiana. Benny Wade Clewis, Rosharon, Texas. Vera Coachman, Walpax, Rio de Janeiro, Brazil. Helen Comeaux, Lafayette, Louisiana. Glenn R. Conrad, Center for Louisiana Studies, University of Southwestern Louisiana, Lafayette, Louisiana. Continental Airlines. Cora Lee Conway, Jackson, Mississippi. Lauro Costa, Sao Paolo, Brazil. Mellville Currie, Accompong, Jamaica. Nicia Maria Dantas, Salvador, Bahia. Judy Rhodes Davis, Jackson, Mississippi. Rosalyn Denis, Bridge House Hotel, Black River, Jamaica. Moussa Dieme, Senegal and Mendocino, California. Enid Donaldson, Kingston, Jamaica. Melonee Ebanks, Bridge House Hotel, Black River, Jamaica. Addie Echols, Arthur Bryant's, Kansas City, Missouri. E & L Barbecue, Jackson, Mississippi. Edith Ezigbo, African King, Atlanta, Georgia, and Nigeria. Leon Finney, Sr., Leon's Barbecue, Chicago, Illinois. Florence Alabama Chamber of Commerce. Evangeline Fogam, Cameroon and Alameda, California. Geneva Francais, African Brown Bag, Atlanta, Georgia. Georgia Department of Industry and Trade. Virginia Gilluly, Florence, Alabama. Erica Gillette, Washington D.C. and Mississippi. Wilbert Guillory, Opelousas, Louisiana. Edward and Paula Hamilton, Oakland, California. Louise Haney, Florence, Alabama. Fanny Marie Harris, Shreveport, Louisiana. Loretta Harrison, Loretta's Authentic Pralines, New Orleans. Bob and Irma Haughy, Richmond, California. Harold Henderson, Mendocino, California. Rebecca Henry, Opelousas, Louisiana. Merline Herbert, Creole Lunch House, Lafayette, Louisiana. Dot Hewitt, Dot's Place, Austin, Texas. Ed Hilliard, Jackson, Mississippi. Stanley Jackson, Kabby's, New Orleans, Louisiana. Kennell Jackson, Stanford, California. Olite Jacobs, Lafayette, Louisiana. Roupert Jeanty, Haiti and Mississippi. Margaret and Jim Jennings, Lafayette, Louisana. Mary Johnson, King's Tavern, Natchez, Mississippi. Mike Johnson, The Landing, Lafayette, Louisiana. Akberet Keleta, Eritrea and Santa Rosa, California. Lottie Kennedy, Savannah, Georgia. Rosemary Kennedy, Oakland, California. Doug Keyes, Doug's Bar-B-Que, Oakland, California. Karin Koser, Atlanta, Georgia. Michel Laguerre, African-American Studies, University of California, Berkeley. Gene Lee, Big Apple Inn, Jackson, Mississippi. Mike Lemons, Lem's Bar-B-Q, Chicago, Illinois. Cheri Lewis, Alabama Bureau of Tourism. Edna Lewis, Unionville, Virginia. Juanita Love, Monmouth, Natchez, Mississippi. Ceceline McIntyre, Mandeville Hotel,

Mandeville, Jamaica. Diane McIntyre-Pike, Astra Country Inn, Mandeville, Jamaica. Jean McWashington, Red Door Barbecue, Enterprise, Mississippi. Nardos Makonnen, Ethiopia and Mississippi. Stephen Martin, Jackson, Mississippi. Sam Mayes, Sam's Barbecue, Austin, Texas. Maaza Haile Michael, Eitrea and Sunnyvale, California. Mississippi Department of Tourism. Virginia Mitchell, Brazil and Philo, California. Anne Mohon, Natchez, Mississippi. Leannie Moore, Berkeley, California. Martha Murphy, Point Richmond, California. William Ndiaye, La Savane, San Francisco and Senegal. Valmor Neto, Bahia Brasil, San Francisco, California. Gerard Noel, La Belle Creole, Emeryville, California and Haiti. Bob and Joy Owens, Newport Beach, California. Roger Pacheco, Varig Airlines, SanFrancisco. Golden Park Best Western Hotel, Brazil. Tânia de Paixão, Feijoada de Biu, Bahia. Payne's BBQ, Memphis, Tennessee. Piney Woods International Culinary Club, Piney Woods Country School. Icilda Pinnock, Mammee Bay, Jamaica. Marsha Polk Townsend, RSVP Catering, Alemeda, California. Hecky Powell, Hecky's, Evanston, Illinois. Steven Pratt, Chicago, Illinois. Ron Preston, Oakland, California. Prince Neville, Prince Neville's, San Francisco, California. Paul Prudhomme, K-Paul's, New Orleans, Louisiana. Dona Conceição de Reis, Salvador, Bahia. Dye Rhodan, Hilton Head, South Carolina. T.J. Robinson, Gingerbread House, Oakland, California. San Francisco Professional Food Society. Yvonne Scott, King's Tavern, Natchez, Mississippi. Judy Shaper, San Francisco, California. Samuel Simons, Showcase Eatery, College Park, Georgia. Kelly Simon, San Francisco, California. Ora Smith, Panama and Colton, California. Lloyd Spence, Zulu's, Montego Bay, Jamaica. Ann and Jim Stirgis, Vicksburg, Mississippi. Freddie Strong, Powell's Place, San Francisco, California. Sweet Olive Tree Manor, Natchez, Mississippi. Rhoda Teplow, Mendocino, California. Carol Terrel, Arizona. Jesse Thomas, Thomas Barbecue, Houston, Texas. Linda Thompson, Dusty's, Atlanta, Georgia. Raymond Thoya, Kenya and Mendocino, California. Jamaica Tourist Board. J.L. Terrel, Berkeley, California. Icy Vincent, Geva's, San Francisco, California. Aissatoui Ayola Vernita, Ebony Museum of Art, Oakland, California. Rob Walsh, Austin, Texas. Arthur Wardsworth, Southshore Restaurant, Kenner, Louisiana. Raymond Washington, Catfish Hill, Dell Valley, Texas. Daniel Watkins, Piney Woods, Mississippi. Anita Wilder, Mendocino, California. Herocine Williams, Walnut Hills Restaurant, Vicksburg, Mississippi. Adelaide Wilson, Sierra Leone and Jackson, Mississippi. Rip Wilson, Soul Brother's Kitchen, Oakland, California. Garfield Wright, Jr., Maxwell's, Vicksburg, Mississippi. Benmett Johannes. And to everyone who shared books, names, and tested recipes.

With extra appreciation to Antonia Allegra, Jessica Harris, Vern Davis, Reuben and Sarah Greenberg, Nancy McLelland, and Milla Handley for invaluable assistance and support; to my agent Fred Hill and my editor Bill Le Blond; to Sharon Silva for her meticulous editing; to Shannon and Brendan who have been trying the recipes for years; and to Barry, for putting up with the mess in the kitchen and taking over as primary parent, recipe tester, and bottle washer for the whole year.

Index

Abarás, 77
Acarajés, 76–77
Achari, 246
Achiote. *See* Annatto
Ackee, Codfish and, 42–43
Alabama Hot Slaw, 116
All-Purpose Caribbean Spice Blend, 26
All-Purpose Seasoning Rub, 210
Annatto
 about, 42, 267
 Annatto Oil, 267
Arroz à Baiana, 82
Arroz con Coco, 82
Atakelte, 256
Avocados, 47

Bajan Fish Spice, 27
Bajia, 246
Baked Catfish, 129
Baked Chayote, 32
Baked Grits, 123
Baked Plantains, 29
Bakes, 59
Baking Powder Biscuits, 142–43
Baking Powder Dumplings, 137
Baloumbum, 248
Bammies, 59
Bananas
 about, 267
 Banana Coconut Bread, 60
 Banana Pudding, 155
 Boiled Green Bananas, 30
 Fried Bananas, 63
 Mashed Bananas, 254
 Steamed Banana Pudding, 265
Bananes pesées, 29
Barbecuing
 Barbecued Chicken, 223
 Barbecued Corn on the Cob, 233
 building the fire, 206–7
 Grilled Plantains, 234
 Jerked Chicken Drumettes, 230

 Jerked Fish, 231
 Jerked Pork, 229
 K.C.'s Barbecued Goat Marinade, 226
 Oven-Barbecued Ribs, 233
 ribs, 208
 sauces for, 209–22
 seafood, 232
 Skillet-Barbecued Shrimp, 232
 Smoked Turkey, 231
 Spicy Meat Sticks, 228
 Tennessee-Style Chopped Pork
  Shoulder, 225
 Texas Brisket, 224–25
Basic Corn Bread, 239
Basic Red Barbecue Sauce, 213
Beans
 about, 124, 267
 Bean Pudding, 251
 Benny Clewis's Gas-Free Beans, 125
 Black Bean Soup, 83
 Black-eyed Pea Fritters, 76–77
 Creamed Beans, 81
 Haitian Red Beans and Rice, 36
 Ham Hocks, Greens, and Black-eyed
  Peas, 126
 Hoppin' John, 179
 Meat and Black Bean Stew, 84–85
 Molasses Baked Beans, 236–37
 Pigeon Peas and Rice, 35
 Pot of Beans, 124–25
 Red Beans and Rice, 178
 soaking, 267
 Soul Brothers Beans, 125
 Southern Green Beans, 118
Beaten Biscuits, 143
Beef
 Black Bean Soup, 83
 Caribbean Meatballs, 55
 Creole Meat Loaf, 193
 Cuban Picadillo, 58–59
 Eggplant Dressing, 173
 Grilled Meat, 263
 Jamaican Meat Pastries, 56–57
 Meat and Black Bean Stew, 84–85

 Nigerian Stew, 258
 Oxtail or Short Rib Stew, 140
 Spicy Meat Sticks, 228
 Spicy Mixed Meat and Vegetable Stew,
  86–87
 Texas Brisket, 224–25
Beets, Pickled, 237
Benne Cookies, 156
Benny Clewis's Gas-Free Beans, 125
Benny's Hoecake, 141
Berberé, 247
Bird chiles, 53
Biscuits
 Baking Powder Biscuits, 142–43
 Beaten Biscuits, 143
 Sweet Potato Biscuits, 149
Black Bean Soup, 83
Black Cake, 66–67
Black-eyed peas
 Bean Pudding, 251
 Black-eyed Pea Fritters, 76–77
 Ham Hocks, Greens, and Black-eyed
  Peas, 126
 Hoppin' John, 179
 Soul Brothers Beans, 125
Boiled Green Bananas, 30
Bolinhos de Bacalhau, 92
Bolinhos de Estudante, 97
Brazilian Salad, 78
Bread
 Bakes, 59
 Baking Powder Biscuits, 142–43
 Banana Coconut Bread, 60
 Basic Corn Bread, 239
 Beaten Biscuits, 143
 Benny's Hoecake, 141
 Bread Pudding, 196
 Corny Corn Bread Muffins, 144
 Crackling Bread, 147
 Skillet-Baked Corn Bread, 194
 Spoon Bread, 195
 Sweet Potato Biscuits, 149
 Yeast-Risen Wheat Bread, 241
Breadfruit, 31

Bronze Barbecue Sauce, 215
Brown Sugar Cookies, 200
Buttermilk Fried Chicken, 134–35

Cabbage
  about, 115
  Alabama Hot Slaw, 116
  Cool Coleslaw, 234
  Ethiopian Cabbage, 256
  Smothered Cabbage, 115
Cakes
  Black Cake, 66–67
  Tea Cakes, 150–51
Callaloo, 34
Camarão à Baiana, 94
Candy
  Coconut Candy, 62
  Creamy Pralines, 197
  Goober Brittle, 151
  Groundnut Toffee, 264
Caramel flavoring, 52
Caramel Glue, 199
Caribbean Fried Chicken, 51
Caribbean Meatballs, 55
Caruru, 79
Cassava
  about, 64, 258, 267–68
  Cassava Chips, 33
  flour, 73
  Toasted Cassava Meal, 73
  Yam Balls, 250
  Yellow Farofa, 73
Cast-iron skillets, 268
Catfish
  about, 128
  Baked Catfish, 129
  Catfish Stew, 130–31
  Fried Catfish, 128
  Guillory Gumbo, 183
Chayotes
  Baked Chayote, 32
  Papaya-Chayote Hot Sauce, 24
  Stewed Squash, 169
Chicharrónes, 148

Chicken
  about, 268
  Barbecued Chicken, 223
  Buttermilk Fried Chicken, 134–35
  Caribbean Fried Chicken, 51
  Chicken and Dumplings, 136–37
  Chicken and Shrimp Gumbo, 180–81
  Chicken Peanut Stew, 262–63
  Chicken with Peanuts and Shrimp,
    88-89
  Curried Chicken, 53
  Fried Chicken, 134–35
  Grilled Chicken, 263
  Guillory Gumbo, 183
  Haitian Gumbo, 48–49
  Jamaican Meat Pastries, 56–57
  Jambalaya over Rice, 186–87
  Jerked Chicken Drumettes, 230
  Jollof Rice, 259
  Nigerian Stew, 258
  Pepperpot, 40–41
  Southern Fried Chicken, 134–35
  Spiced Chicken, 52
  stock, 269
  Traditional Jambalaya, 184–85
Chili Sauce, 221
Chitterlings, 133
Chow Chow, 240
Cobbler, Fruit, 158–59
Cocada, 62
Cocada Branca, 96
Cocoa tea, 67
Coconut
  about, 55, 270
  Arroz con Coco, 82
  Banana Coconut Bread, 60
  Coconut Candy, 62
  Coconut Mousse, 95
  milk from, 81, 270
  opening, 270
  Tiny Coconut Custards, 98
  White Coconut Compote, 96
Cod
  about, 92

Codfish and Ackee, 42–43
Codfish Croquettes, 92
Stamp and Go, 44–45
Coleslaw
  Alabama Hot Slaw, 116
  Cool Coleslaw, 234
Collard Greens, 119
Colombo, 53
Colombo de cochon, 54
Conch, 48
Congri, 35
Coo-coo, 38
Cookies
  Benne Cookies, 156
  Brown Sugar Cookies, 200
  Granny Brown's Gingerbread Cookies
    198-199
Cool Coleslaw, 234
Corn
  about, 270
  Barbecued Corn on the Cob, 233
  Corn Dressing, 174
  Corn Pudding, 120
  Corny Corn Bread Muffins, 144
  freezing, 270
  parched, 120
  Rebecca's Maque Chou, 175
  removing from cob, 174
Cornmeal
  Basic Corn Bread, 239
  Corn Bread Dressing, 121
  Corn Dumplings, 146
  Cornmeal Mush, 176
  Cornmeal with Okra, 38
  Corny Corn Bread Muffins, 144
  Crackling Bread, 147
  Skillet-Baked Corn Bread, 194
  Spoon Bread, 195
Couche couche, 176
Couscous de mais, 38
Couve, 78
Cozido, 86–87
Crab
  Callaloo, 34

Low Country Boil, 133
Okra Soup, 257
she-crab soup, 129
Stuffed Crab, 90
stuffing, 128
Crackling Bread, 147
Cracklings, 148
Crawfish
  about, 189
  Crawfish Boil, 189
  Rebecca's Crawfish Étouffée, 190
Creamed Beans, 81
Creamy Pralines, 197
Creamy Spiced Seafood and Peanuts,
  80-81
Creole Meat Loaf, 193
Creole Sauce, 167
Croquettes. See Fritters
Cuban Picadillo, 58-59
Curried Chicken, 53
Curried Fish, 53
Curried Goat, 53
Curried Pork and Vegetables, 54
Curry Blend, 28

Dendê oil, 270
Desserts
  Banana Pudding, 155
  Benne Cookies, 156
  Black Cake, 66-67
  Bread Pudding, 196
  Brown Sugar Cookies, 200
  Coconut Candy, 62
  Coconut Mousse, 95
  Creamy Pralines, 197
  Fried Bananas, 63
  Fried Pies, 154
  Fruit Cobbler, 158-59
  Gingerbread, 157
  Goober Brittle, 151
  Granny Brown's Gingerbread Cookies,
    198-199
  Groundnut Toffee, 264
  Homemade Ice Cream, 160-61

Lime Meringue Pie, 64
Pecan Pie, 201
Steamed Banana Pudding, 265
Sweet Milk Pudding, 99
Sweet Potato Pie, 153
Sweet Potato Pone, 65
Tea Cakes, 150-51
Tiny Coconut Custards, 98
Tropical Fruit Compote, 61
White Coconut Compote, 96
Dirty Rice, 188
Djon djon, 37
Dolce de Leite, 99
Dressings
  Corn Bread Dressing, 121
  Corn Dressing, 174
  Eggplant Dressing, 173
Dumplings
  Baking Powder Dumplings, 137
  Chicken and Dumplings, 136-37
  Corn Dumplings, 146
  Egg Dumplings, 138
  Old-Fashioned Dumplings, 137

East African Spice Mixture, 247
Efo, 258
Egg Dumplings, 138
Eggplant
  Eggplant Dressing, 173
  Fried Eggplant Fingers, 170
Empanadas, 56
Equipment, 16
Escabeche, 50
Escovitch, 50
Ethiopian Cabbage, 256

Farofa, 73
Farofa Amarela, 73
Feijoada Completa, 84-85
File powder, 180, 271
Fish
  about, 191
  Baked Catfish, 129
  Catfish Stew, 130-31

Codfish and Ackee, 42-43
Curried Fish, 53
dried, 78
Fish Stew, 260-61
Fish Stew in Coconut Milk, 93
Fried Catfish, 128
Garfish Boulettes with Herbed Tomato
  Sauce, 192
Grilled Fish, 263
Grilled Grouper, 91
Guillory Gumbo, 183
Jerked Fish, 231
Nigerian Stew, 258
Pickled Fish, 50
Redfish Creole, 191
St. Peter's Fish and Peppers, 132
Salmon Patties, 131
Stamp and Go, 44-45
Steamed Whole Fish with Aromatic
  Spices, 47
stock, 271
Flour, Seasoned, 107
Foutout, 250
Fried Bananas, 63
Fried Catfish, 128
Fried Chicken, 134-35
Fried Eggplant Fingers, 170
Fried Green Tomatoes, 117
Fried Okra, 112
Fried Pies, 154
Fried Plantains, 29
Frites de manioc, 33
Fritters
  about, 188
  Black-eyed Pea Fritters, 76-77
  Codfish Croquettes, 92
  Hush Puppies, 145
  Shrimp-Potato Fritters, 46-47
  Tapioca Fritters, 97
Frosting, Sugar, 199
Fruits. See also individual fruits
  Black Cake, 66-67
  Fried Pies, 154
  Fruit Cobbler, 158-59

Homemade Ice Cream, 160–61
Tropical Fruit Compote, 61
Fufu, 38, 249
Fufu Nyame, 250
Funchi, 34, 38

Game, 140
Gardens, 38, 108–9, 185
Garfish Boulettes with Herbed Tomato
  Sauce, 192
Gingerbread, 157
Gingerbread Cookies, Granny Brown's
  198–99
Glazed Ham, 139
Glazed Yams, 112
Goat
  about, 53, 226
  Curried Goat, 53
  K.C.'s Barbecued Goat Marinade, 226
Goober Brittle, 151
Granny Brown's Gingerbread Cookies,
  198-199
Gravy, 106
Green Beans, Southern, 118
Green Chile Relish, 212
Green Chile Sauce, 246
Green Gumbo, 181–82
Greens
  Callaloo, 34
  Collard Greens, 119
  Green Gumbo, 181–82
  Ham Hocks, Greens, and Black-eyed
    Peas, 126
  Nigerian Stew, 258
  Sautéed Greens, 78
  Spiced Greens, 255
Grilled Fish, Chicken, or Meat, 263
Grilled Grouper, 91
Grilled Plantains, 234
Grits, 122
Grits, Baked, 123
Groundnut Toffee, 264
Guava, 92
Guillory Gumbo, 183

Gumbo
  Chicken and Shrimp Gumbo, 180–81
  Green Gumbo, 181–82
  Guillory Gumbo, 183
  Haitian Gumbo, 48–49

Haitian Gumbo, 48–49
Haitian Red Beans and Rice, 36
Haitian Rice, 37
Ham
  about, 139, 272
  Glazed Ham, 139
  Ham Hocks, Greens, and Black-eyed
    Peas, 126
Hoecakes, 141
Homemade Ice Cream, 160–61
Hominy, 122
Hoppin' John, 179
Hot Sauce, 74
Hot Sauce with Lime, 75
Hush Puppies, 145

Ice Cream, Homemade, 160–61
Ingredients, 14–16
Injera, 250

Jamaican Meat Pastries, 56–57
Jamaican Meat Patty Filling, 57
Jambalaya, Traditional, 184–85
Jambalaya over Rice, 186–87
Jamma Jamma, 255
Jerked Chicken Drumettes, 230
Jerked Fish, 231
Jerked Pork, 229
Jerk Seasoning, 211
Jollof Rice, 259
Juneteenth celebrations, 143

K.C.'s Barbecued Goat Marinade, 226
K.C.'s Homemade Barbeque Sauce,
  218-19
Kelewele, 253
Kimanga, 250
Kinolo, 265

Lamb Peanut Stew, 262–63
Lentil Stew, 252
Leon's Basic Barbecue Sauce, 214
Limes
  Hot Sauce with Lime, 75
  Lime Meringue Pie, 64
Low Country Boil, 133

Mahogany Sauce, 216
Mangoes
  about, 25
  Mango Relish, 25
  peeling, 25
Manioc. *See* Cassava
Maque Chou, 175
Marinades. *See* Sauces, marinades,
  and relishes
Mashed Bananas, 254
Mashed Yams, 249
Matoke, 254
Mayonnaise, 168
Meat and Black Bean Stew, 84–85
Meatballs, Caribbean, 55
Meat Loaf, Creole, 193
Milk, sour, 147
Millet, 259
Molasses Baked Beans, 236–37
Môlho de Pimenta, 74
Môlho de Pimenta e Limão, 75
Moqueca de Peixe, 93
Moros y Cristianos, 35
Mousse de Coco, 95
Moyinmoyin, 251
Muffins, Corny Corn Bread, 144
Mushrooms
  Haitian Rice, 37

Nigerian Stew, 258

Okra
  about, 271
  Chicken and Shrimp Gumbo, 180–81
  cooking, 111
  Cornmeal with Okra, 38

freezing, 181
Fried Okra, 112
Green Gumbo, 181–82
Guillory Gumbo, 183
Okra Soup, 257
Okra-Tomato Pilau, 108
Stewed Okra, 111
Stewed Okra with Dried Shrimp, 79
Old-Fashioned Dumplings, 137
Original Clewis Barbecue Sauce, 221
Oven-Barbecued Ribs, 233
Oven Rice, 109
Oven-Roasted Peanuts, 43
Oxtail Stew, 140

Pain aux coco et banane, 60
Papayas
about, 24
Papaya-Chayote Hot Sauce, 24
Paprika, 106
Peanuts
about, 43, 127
Goober Brittle, 151
Groundnut Toffee, 264
Lamb or Chicken Peanut Stew, 262–63
Oven-Roasted Peanuts, 43
parched, 120
Senegalese Peanut Sauce, 248
Southern Goober Soup, 127
Pecans
Creamy Pralines, 197
Pecan Pie, 201
toasting, 197
Peixe Grelhado, 91
Pepperpot, 40–41
Peppers
about, 269
Chili Sauce, 221
Green Chile Sauce, 246
Pepper Vinegar Sauce, 105
Rebecca's Maque Chou, 175
Red Chile Sauce, 246
Red or Green Chile Relish, 212
St. Peter's Fish and Peppers, 132

Shrimp-Pepper Pilau, 108
Stuffed Bell Peppers, 172
Picadillo, Cuban, 58–59
Pickled Beets, 237
Pickled Fish, 50
Pies
Fried Pies, 154
Lime Meringue Pie, 64
Pecan Pie, 201
Pie Crust, 152
Sweet Potato Pie, 153
Pigeon Peas and Rice, 35
Pig's Ear Sandwiches, 227
Piri piri, 247
Pit cooking, 207
Plain Rice, 107
Plantains
about, 271
Baked Plantains, 29
Fried Plantains, 29
Grilled Plantains, 234
peeling, 271
Spicy Fried Plantains, 253
Poisson aux aromates, 47
Poisson grossel, 47
Poke salet, 108
Pone
about, 155
Sweet Potato Pone, 65
Pork. See also Sausage
about, 54, 186–87, 271–72
Caribbean Meatballs, 55
Cracklings, 148
Creole Meat Loaf, 193
Curried Pork and Vegetables, 54
Eggplant Dressing, 173
Glazed Ham, 139
Ham Hocks, Greens, and Black-eyed
Peas, 126
Jamaican Meat Pastries, 56–57
Jambalaya over Rice, 186–87
Jerked Pork, 229
Meat and Black Bean Stew, 84–85
Oven-Barbecued Ribs, 233

Pig's Ear Sandwiches, 227
Smothered Pork Chops, 138–39
Spicy Mixed Meat and Vegetable Stew,
86–87
Tennessee-Style Chopped Pork
Shoulder, 225
Traditional Jambalaya, 184–85
Potatoes. See also Sweet potatoes;
Yams
Potato Salad, 235
Shrimp-Potato Fritters, 46–47
Smothered Potatoes, 114
Pot of Beans, 124–25
Pralines, Creamy, 197
Puddings
Banana Pudding, 155
Bean Pudding, 251
Bread Pudding, 196
Corn Pudding, 120
Steamed Banana Pudding, 265
Sweet Milk Pudding, 99

Quindins de Yaya, 98

Rebecca's Crawfish Étouffée, 190
Rebecca's Maque Chou, 175
Red Beans and Rice, 178
Red Chile Relish, 212
Red Chile Sauce, 246
Redfish Creole, 191
Red Rice, 110
Red Yellow Sauce, 219
Relishes. See Sauces, marinades, and
relishes
Rémoulade Sauce, 168
Ribs
about, 272
barbecuing, 208
Oven-Barbecued Ribs, 233
Short Rib Stew, 140
Rice
about, 178, 272–73
Arroz con Coco, 82
Corn Dressing, 174

Dirty Rice, 188
Fish Stew, 260–61
Haitian Red Beans and Rice, 36
Haitian Rice, 37
Hoppin' John, 179
Jambalaya over Rice, 186–87
Jollof Rice, 259
Okra-Tomato Pilau, 108
Oven Rice, 109
Pigeon Peas and Rice, 35
Plain Rice, 107
Red Beans and Rice, 178
Red Rice, 110
Rice, Bahian Style, 82
Rice Pilau, 108
rinsing, 272
Shrimp-Pepper Pilau, 108
Southern Goober Soup, 127
Riz et pois, 36
Roux, 166
Run Down, Vegetable, 39

St. Peter's Fish and Peppers, 132
Salada de Bahia, 78
Salads. *See also* Coleslaw
  Brazilian Salad, 78
  Potato Salad, 235
Salmon Patties, 131
Sandwiches, Pig's Ear, 227
Sauces, marinades, and relishes
  for barbecue, 209–22
  Basic Red Barbecue Sauce, 213
  Bronze Barbecue Sauce, 215
  Chili Sauce, 221
  Creole Sauce, 167
  Green Chile Sauce, 246
  Hot Sauce, 74
  Hot Sauce with Lime, 75
  K.C.'s Barbecued Goat Marinade, 226
  K.C.'s Homemade Barbecue Sauce,
    218–19
  Leon's Basic Barbecue Sauce, 214
  Mahogany Sauce, 216
  Mango Relish, 25

Original Clewis Barbecue Sauce, 221
Papaya-Chayote Hot Sauce, 24
Pepper Vinegar Sauce, 105
piquante, 23
Red Chile Sauce, 246
Red or Green Chile Relish, 212
Red Yellow Sauce, 219
Rémoulade Sauce, 168
Senegalese Peanut Sauce, 248
Spicy Meat Sauce, 222
Tomato-Onion Relish, 212
Vinegar Marinade, 210
West Indian Hot Sauce, 23
Yellow Sauce, 217
Sausage
  Caribbean Meatballs, 55
  Guillory Gumbo, 183
  Haitian Gumbo, 48–49
  Jambalaya over Rice, 186–87
  Low Country Boil, 133
  Meat and Black Bean Stew, 84–85
  Spicy Meat Sauce, 222
  Spicy Mixed Meat and Vegetable Stew,
    86-87
  Traditional Jambalaya, 184–85
Sautéed Greens, 78
Seafood. *See also* individual seafood
  barbecuing, 232
  Creamy Spiced Seafood and Peanuts,
    80-81
  Fish Stew in Coconut Milk, 93
  Haitian Gumbo, 48–49
Seasoned Flour, 107
Seasonings. *See* Spice blends
Senegalese Peanut Sauce, 248
Shiro Wot, 252
Shortcakes, 142
Short Rib Stew, 140
Shrimp
  Chicken and Shrimp Gumbo, 180–81
  Chicken with Peanuts and Shrimp,
    88-89
  dried, 80
  Guillory Gumbo, 183

Jambalaya over Rice, 186–87
Low Country Boil, 133
Nigerian Stew, 258
Shrimp-Pepper Pilau, 108
Shrimp-Potato Fritters, 46–47
Skillet-Barbecued Shrimp, 232
Spicy Shrimp in Coconut Milk, 94
Stewed Okra with Dried Shrimp, 79
stock, 185
Traditional Jambalaya, 184–85
Siris Recheados, 90
Skillet-Baked Corn Bread, 194
Skillet-Barbecued Shrimp, 232
Slaw. *See* Coleslaw
Smoked Turkey, 231
Smothered Cabbage, 115
Smothered Pork Chops, 138–39
Smothered Potatoes, 114
Sofrito, 23
Sopa de Feijão, 83
Sorghum, 263
Soul Brothers Beans, 125
Soups
  Black Bean Soup, 83
  Chicken and Shrimp Gumbo, 180–81
  Green Gumbo, 181–82
  Guillory Gumbo, 183
  Haitian Gumbo, 48–49
  Okra Soup, 257
  Southern Goober Soup, 127
Southern Fried Chicken, 134–35
Southern Goober Soup, 127
Southern Green Beans, 118
Spice blends
  All-Purpose Caribbean Spice Blend, 26
  All-Purpose Seasoning Rub, 210
  Bajan Fish Spice, 27
  Curry Blend, 28
  East African Spice Mixture, 247
  Jerk Seasoning, 211
Spiced Chicken, 52
Spiced Greens, 255
Spicy Fried Plantains, 253
Spicy Meat Sauce, 222

Spicy Meat Sticks, 228
Spicy Mixed Meat and Vegetable Stew, 86-87
Spicy Shrimp in Coconut Milk, 94
Spoon Bread, 195
Squash
  Baked Chayote, 32
  Papaya-Chayote Hot Sauce, 24
  Stewed Squash, 169
Stamp and Go, 44–45
Steamed African Yams, 31
Steamed Banana Pudding, 265
Steamed Whole Fish with Aromatic Spices, 47
Stewed Okra, 111
Stewed Okra with Dried Shrimp, 79
Stewed Squash, 169
Stock
  chicken, 269
  fish, 271
  quick, 121
  shrimp, 185
Stuffed Bell Peppers, 172
Stuffed Crab, 90
Sugar, 113
Sugarcane, 62
Sugar Frosting, 199
Sweet Milk Pudding, 99
Sweet potatoes. *See also* Yams
  about, 273
  Sweet Potato Biscuits, 149
  Sweet Potato Pie, 153
  Sweet Potato Pone, 65
  Twice-Baked Sweet Potatoes, 113
  Yams Louisiane, 177
  yams vs., 112

Tablette, 62
Tapioca Fritters, 97
Tea Cakes, 150–51
Tennessee-Style Chopped Pork Shoulder, 225
Texas Brisket, 224–25
Tiebe Dienn, 260–61

Tiebe Yape, 261
Tiny Coconut Custards, 98
Toasted Cassava Meal, 73
Tomatoes
  about, 273
  Bronze Barbecue Sauce, 215
  Chili Sauce, 221
  Chow Chow, 240
  Creole Sauce, 167
  Fried Green Tomatoes, 117
  Garfish Boulettes with Herbed Tomato Sauce, 192
  Jollof Rice, 259
  K.C.'s Homemade Barbecue Sauce, 218-19
  Okra-Tomato Pilau, 108
  Original Clewis Barbecue Sauce, 221
  Rebecca's Maque Chou, 175
  Red Rice, 110
  skinning, 273
  Spicy Meat Sauce, 222
  Tomatoes à l'Espagnol, 171
  Tomato-Onion Relish, 212
  West Indian Hot Sauce, 23
Tostones, 29
Traditional Jambalaya, 184–85
Tropical Fruit Compote, 61
Turkey
  Jamaican Meat Pastries, 56–57
  Smoked Turkey, 231
Tutu, 81
Twice-Baked Sweet Potatoes, 113

Vatapá, 80–81
Vegetables. *See also* individual vegetables
  Chow Chow, 240
  cooking, 118
  Curried Pork and Vegetables, 54
  Pepperpot, 40–41
  Spicy Mixed Meat and Vegetable Stew, 86-87
  Vegetable Run Down, 39
Vinegar Marinade, 210

Watermelon
  about, 238
  Watermelon Rind Pickle, 238–39
West Indian Hot Sauce, 23
White Coconut Compote, 96
Wild game, 140

Xinxim de Galinha, 88–89

Yams. *See also* Sweet potatoes
  about, 248, 273
  Black Cake, 66–67
  Glazed Yams, 112
  Mashed Yams, 249
  Steamed African Yams, 31
  sweet potatoes vs., 112
  Yam Balls, 250
  Yams Louisiane, 177
Yassa, 263
Yeast-Risen Wheat Bread, 241
Yellow *Farofa,* 73
Yellow Sauce, 217
Yuca frita, 33

Table of Equivalents

The exact equivalents in the following tables have been rounded for convenience.

US/UK

oz	= ounce
lb	= pound
in	= inch
ft	= foot
tbl	= tablespoon
fl oz	= fluid ounce
qt	= quart

Metric

g	= gram
kg	= kilogram
mm	= millimeter
cm	= centimeter
ml	= milliliter
l	= liter

Weights

US/UK	Metric
1 oz	30 g
2 oz	60 g
3 oz	90 g
4 oz (¼ lb)	125 g
5 oz (⅓ lb)	155 g
6 oz	185 g
7 oz	220 g
8 oz (½ lb)	250 g
10 oz	315 g
12 oz (¾ lb)	375 g
14 oz	440 g
16 oz (1 lb)	500 g
1½ lb	750 g
2 lb	1 kg
3 lb	1.5 kg

Oven Temperatures

Fahrenheit	Celsius	Gas
250	120	½
275	140	1
300	150	2
325	160	3
350	180	4
375	190	5
400	200	6
425	220	7
450	230	8
475	240	9
500	260	10

Liquids

US	Metric	UK
2 tbl	30 ml	1 fl oz
¼ cup	60 ml	2 fl oz
⅓ cup	80 ml	3 fl oz
½ cup	125 ml	4 fl oz
⅔ cup	160 ml	5 fl oz
¾ cup	180 ml	6 fl oz
1 cup	250 ml	8 fl oz
1½ cups	375 ml	12 fl oz
2 cups	500 ml	16 fl oz
4 cups/1 qt	1 l	32 fl oz

Length Measures

⅛ in	3 mm
¼ in	6 mm
½ in	12 mm
1 in	2.5 cm
2 in	5 cm
3 in	7.5 cm
4 in	10 cm
5 in	13 cm
6 in	15 cm
7 in	18 cm
8 in	20 cm
9 in	23 cm
10 in	25 cm
11 in	28 cm
12 in/1 ft	30 cm

Equivalents for Common Used Ingredients

**All-Purpose (Plain) Flour/
Dried Bread Crumbs/Chopped Nuts**

¼ cup	1 oz	30 g
⅓ cup	1½ oz	45 g
½ cup	2 oz	60 g
¾ cup	3 oz	90 g
1 cup	4 oz	125 g
1½ cups	6 oz	185 g
2 cups	8 oz	250 g

Whole-Wheat (Wholemeal) Flour

3 tbl	1 oz	30 g
½ cup	2 oz	60 g
⅔ cup	3 oz	90 g
1 cup	4 oz	125 g
1¼ cups	5 oz	155 g
1⅔ cups	7 oz	210 g
1¾ cups	8 oz	250 g

Brown Sugar

¼ cup	1½ oz	45 g
½ cup	3 oz	90 g
¾ cup	4 oz	125 g
1 cup	5½ oz	170 g
1½ cups	8 oz	250 g
2 cups	10 oz	315 g

White Sugar

¼ cup	2 oz	60 g
⅓ cup	3 oz	90 g
½ cup	4 oz	125 g
¾ cup	6 oz	185 g
1 cup	8 oz	250 g
1½ cups	12 oz	375 g
2 cups	1 lb	500 g

Raisins/Currants/Semolina

¼ cup	1 oz	30 g
⅓ cup	2 oz	60 g
½ cup	3 oz	90 g
¾ cup	4 oz	125 g
1 cup	5 oz	155 g

Long-Grain Rice/Cornmeal

⅓ cup	2 oz	60 g
½ cup	2½ oz	75 g
¾ cup	4 oz	125 g
1 cup	5 oz	155 g
1½ cups	8 oz	250 g

Dried Beans

¼ cup	1½ oz	45 g
⅓ cup	2 oz	60 g
½ cup	3 oz	90 g
¾ cup	5 oz	155 g
1 cup	6 oz	185 g
1¼ cups	8 oz	250 g
1½ cups	12 oz	375 g

Rolled Oats

⅓ cup	1 oz	30 g
⅔ cup	2 oz	60 g
1 cup	3 oz	90 g
1½ cups	4 oz	125 g
2 cups	5 oz	155 g

Jam/Honey

2 tbl	2 oz	60 g
¼ cup	3 oz	90 g
½ cup	5 oz	155 g
¾ cup	8 oz	250 g
1 cup	11 oz	345 g

Grated Parmesan/Romano Cheese

¼ cup	1 oz	30 g
½ cup	2 oz	60 g
¾ cup	3 oz	90 g
1 cup	4 oz	125 g
1⅓ cups	5 oz	155 g
2 cups	7 oz	220 g